50 HIKES

ON MICHIGAN & WISCONSIN'S
NORTH COUNTRY TRAIL

50 HIKES

ON MICHIGAN & WISCONSIN'S
NORTH COUNTRY TRAIL

Thomas Funke

THE COUNTRYMAN PRESS

A division of W. W. Norton & Company

Independent Publishers Since 1923

Page 24: © Craig Sterken/Shutterstock.com; 33: © ehrlif/Shutterstock.com;
107: © Dean Pennala/Shutterstock.com; 141: © Ken Wolter/Shutterstock.com;
177: © John McCormick/Shutterstock.com

For information about permission to reproduce selections
from this book, write to Permissions, The Countryman Press,
500 Fifth Avenue, New York, NY 10110

For information about special discounts for bulk purchases, please contact
W. W. Norton Special Sales at specialsales@wwnorton.com or 800-233-4830

Manufacturing by Versa Press
Book design by Chris Welch

Library of Congress Cataloging-in-Publication Data

Names: Funke, Thomas, author.
Title: 50 hikes on Michigan & Wisconsin's North Country Trail / Thomas Funke.
Other titles: Fifty hikes on Michigan and Wisconsin's North Country Trail
Description: Woodstock, VT : The Countryman Press, [2016] | Includes
bibliographical references and index.
Identifiers: LCCN 2016002147 | ISBN 9781581572254 (pbk. : alk. paper)
Subjects: LCSH: North Country National Scenic Trail—Guidebooks. |
Hiking—North Country National Scenic Trail—Guidebooks. |
Hiking—Michigan—Guidebooks. | Hiking—Wisconsin—Guidebooks. |
Walking—Michigan—Guidebooks. | Walking—Wisconsin—Guidebooks. |
Trails—Michigan—Guidebooks. | Trails—Wisconsin—Guidebooks. |
Walking—North Country National Scenic Trail—Guidebooks. | Trails—North
Country National Scenic Trail—Guidebooks.
Classification: LCC GV199.42.N67 F85 2016 | DDC 796.510977—dc23
LC record available at http://lccn.loc.gov/2016002147

The Countryman Press
www.countrymanpress.com

A division of W. W. Norton & Company
500 Fifth Avenue, New York, NY 10110
www.wwnorton.com

1 2 3 4 5 6 7 8 9 0

I dedicate this book to my wife Susan,
and my son Nathaniel.
May he inherit my sense of adventure and
my wife continue to support my future projects.

Contents

Acknowledgments

This project would not have been possible without the support of the North Country Trail Association, its chapters, and its chapter volunteers. Most importantly, these volunteers are the heart and soul of the trail. Their hard work in identifying, creating, and maintaining over 1,000 miles of hiking trail is an incredible feat. Their on-the-ground knowledge is greatly appreciated in helping review the accuracy and general layout of the trail.

The North Country Trail Association allowed me to draw from previously published guides and resources, such as Wes Boyd's guide to the North Country Trail and Byron and Margaret Hutchins's guide. These resources allowed me to "fill in the gaps" for any features I may have missed, and also served as historical resources about the trail.

Land managers, who own the land over which the trail crosses, deserve a special mention as well. The North Country Trail's tread crosses national and state forests, national and state parks, county and city parks, land conservancies, and private lands. There are hundreds if not thousands of staff and volunteers working and volunteering for these various landowners to make sure the trail is useable as it crosses their property.

Credit for financial support for this project mostly goes to my wife, Susan, for allowing me the latitude to incur the expenses of travel, lodging, meals, purchasing maps, and employing photographers and artists.

I'd especially like to thank all the chapter members who took time to edit the manuscript. Particularly, Jim Stamm, Anne Billiard, Dennis Fay Harbor Springs Chapter; Duane Lawton, Jordan Valley 45 Degree Chapter; Arlen Matson, Ed Morse, Dick Naperala Grand Traverse Hiking Club; Joan Young, Spirit of the Woods Chapter; Charles Vannette, Western Michigan Chapter; Larry Pio, Chief Noonday Chapter; Mike Dundas Chief Baw Beese Chapter; Peter Nordgren, Bill Menke, Tim Mowbray, Mark Van Hornweder, Philip Anderson, John and Joan Pearson, Chuck Zosel, Marty Swank, Eric Nordgren, Brule–St. Croix Chapter; Mike Ducheck Heritage Chapter; Marty Swank, Chequamegon Chapter, Richard Swanson, Ni-Miikanaake Chapter; Doug Welker and Connie Julien, Peter Wolfe Chapter; Lorana Jinkerson, North Country Trail Hikers; Tim Haas, Ellen Haas, Ed Bowen, Karla Bowen, and Ken Rugaber Superior Shoreline Chapter; and Kay Kujawa, Hiawatha Shore to Shore Chapter.

I'm certain these chapter representatives circulated the manuscript to others for review; I'm in debt to them as well.

Bill Menke, Bruce Mathews, and Matt Rowbotham provided the North Country Trail Association's assistance and guidance.

In addition, Mark Weaver, superintendent of the North Country Trail, provided assistance as well.

Financial support provided by Bill Young, Heather Gorning, Deanna Legert, Sharon Kelly, Samuel Haraldson, Lynne Smith, Dove Day, Roxanne Jordan, and Paul Peterson.

Preface: The North Country Trail

I first discovered the North Country Trail while researching a cross-the-Upper-Peninsula backpacking trip in the mid-1990s. At first, it appeared to be a loose patchwork of trail across the Upper Peninsula. With a little Internet research (which was in its infancy way back when), I discovered that it was a trail between North Dakota and Vermont.

I was hooked. I decided to become a member of the nonprofit North Country Trail Association, and soon learned they are the supporting organization for the North Country National Scenic Trail (its full name), part of the national park system.

The longer sibling of the more famous Appalachian Trail, the North Country Trail runs east to west, while the other national scenic trails (Continental Divide, Pacific Crest, etc.) mostly run north to south.

It was the National Trails Act of 1968 that officially established the Appalachian and Pacific Crest Trails as National Scenic Trails. Both had been in existence for many years before. However, the North Country Trail wasn't even authorized to be a trail until 1980, when Congress passed legislation authorizing its creation.

A task force was assembled to study the daunting task of creating what was appearing to be a 4,000-mile-long hiking trail. The Bureau of Outdoor Recreation (to be later absorbed by the National Park Service) had a report written by none other than Tom Gilbert, who at the time was fresh out of college but would become the first superintendent of the North Country Trail.

Many proposals were considered in determining the authorized route for the trail. Some ideas came to fruition, others did not, and some are still on the back burner. One in particular is linking up with the Appalachian Trail, which still simmers as a future potentiality.

Another, a loop trail in the Upper Peninsula, has long been forgotten; others, like the Arrowhead in Minnesota, have come, gone, and then been reborn.

What ended up happening was that I identified existing long stretches of trails in national forest, national parks, state forests, and state parks. The Manistee Trail in Michigan, the Buckeye Trail in Ohio, the Finger Lakes Trail in New York, the Kekekabic and Border Route Trails in Minnesota—and the namesake, the North Country Trail in Wisconsin—were identified and have since been incorporated into the trail we now know.

The daunting task of connecting these trails continues today. Many segments of trail have been pieced together using rail trails, bike trails, local parks, and private landowners. Although there are still significant road walks to connect the trail, they are becoming fewer and shorter.

CURRENT CHAPTER AND HEADQUARTERS STRUCTURE

The organizational structure of the trail can be confusing to folks hearing about the trail for the first time. The North

THE SUN SETS OVER THE PORCUPINE MOUNTAINS AND LAKE SUPERIOR

Country National Scenic Trail is part of the national park system—which interestingly enough does not own an inch of the trail, nor does it build or maintain the trail. The role of the national park is to provide management, oversight, and funding for the trail. The National Park Service has identified a superintendent of the North Country Trail, but typically does not have staff. This is where the North Country Trail Association, a private not-for-profit organization, comes in as the on-the-ground support organization for the trail. The North Country Trail Association works to create and maintain the trail through staff—but most importantly, volunteers. It utilizes a chapter model; the chapters are the primary drivers of recruiting, training, and motivating volunteers to create and maintain the trail.

There are 3 chapters in Wisconsin and 12 in Michigan. Chapters are fiscally and organizationally part of the nonprofit association. Each, however, has its own leadership and works independently to create, maintain, and interpret the trail in its area. It is the dedicated volunteers who make up these chapters who contribute to the North Country Trail's success. Without them, there would be no trail.

Climate, Geology, and Wildlife

CLIMATE

Climate is what you expect, weather is what you get.

Over a stretch of 1,000 miles that experiences four seasons, you could see just about any kind of weather—with the exception of a hurricane! Winters can be long and linger into late May some years in northern Wisconsin and the Upper Peninsula. Summers can be steamy and hot, not only in the southern Lower Peninsula but even in Marquette as well. Winter can start before Halloween in the Upper Peninsula. Spring may not be seen at all in the southern Lower Peninsula, as the winter frequently lingers; spring weather may last a few weeks, skipping right over to summer by Memorial Day.

With an enormous amount of weather data available on the Internet, one should be able to plan a trip using historical weather information. A great resource is Weather Underground (www .wunderground.com), where you can give it a range of dates and it will give you a report of highs, lows, precipitation, and extreme weather events.

Extreme high temperatures rarely make it to 100 degrees, although the humidity can give a heat index of well over 100 degrees. Extreme lows can hit -40 degrees in the Upper Peninsula and Wisconsin, and as low as -20 degrees in the southern Lower Peninsula.

Severe weather is commonplace in the southern Lower Peninsula, which averages several tornadoes and numerous thunderstorms in the spring and summer months. It is always a good idea to carry a weather radio with you during the spring and summer months, or have access to this information via smartphone.

Snow can be expected, either in accumulation or frosting the ground, anytime between October 1st and May 30th in the northern part of Wisconsin, the Upper Peninsula, and the northern Lower Peninsula. In the southern Lower Peninsula, this range is from about November 1st to May 1st.

Maximum snow depth and total accumulation ranges wildly along the trail. The Wisconsin part of the trail can experience a total accumulation of 50 to 120 inches in a given season, increasing as you go west; the Upper Peninsula, 120 to 400 inches of snow, is most close to Lake Superior. Since the trail is 30 miles or less from the Lake Michigan shore most of the way toward Grand Rapids, lake effect snows can dump upward of 200 inches in places in the north, and around 100 inches as far south as Grand Rapids. As the trail turns inland heading toward Battle Creek down to the state line, total accumulations rarely reach over 100 inches.

Snow depth is a whole different matter. Areas along the Lake Superior shore can have natural snow depths (not drifts) exceeding 6 feet. Not inches, but feet! In the northern Lower Peninsula, several feet of snow can accumulate. South of Grand Rapids, rarely is there more than 2 feet, but it is not unheard of to have drifting of 6 feet or more.

A great resource for planning for snow is the National Weather Service's

National Snow Analyses page at www
.nohrsc.noaa.gov/nsa/.

GEOLOGY

As soon as you cross the Mackinac
Bridge, you have entered a different
geological world. The Lower Peninsula
and the Upper Peninsula and Wisconsin are as geologically different as they
are geographically different. The Lower
Peninsula sits in what is called the Michigan Basin. Starting from the center of the
peninsula, concentric rings make their
way outward in all directions. The rock
formations in the center of the rings are
a mere 60 million years old. Moving outward and northwestward, they become
billions of years old in the Keweenaw.

Precambrian volcanic activity 3 billion years ago created the Canadian
Shield, very dense igneous rocks that
are the substrate for the western Upper
Peninsula and parts of Wisconsin. The
eastern Upper Peninsula and Lower
Peninsula rocks are of sedimentary origin, created during the Cambrian and
Jurassic periods, making them 60 to 600
million years of age.

The Mackinac breccia is the first geological formation witnessed as you drive
north on I-75 just north of the Mackinac
Bridge. The rocks only get more diverse
and interesting as you head west.

The Precambrian Era consists of 90
percent of all known geological time. It
was during this time the Earth was cool-
ing and forming the UP geology we enjoy
today. This period started about 5 billion
years ago, and only at 600 million years
ago did a new era start—the Paleozoic.
All time after the start of the Paleozoic
is called the Cambrian.

The geology formed during the Precambrian has seen many changes over
time. Volcanic activity, earthquakes,

uplift, faults, and deformations have
occurred and can be witnessed today.
Most of Michigan's mineral resources,
primarily copper and iron, find their origin in these rocks.

The Paleozoic's Devonian, Silurian,
Ordovician, and Cambrian Periods
(345–600 million years before present)
are when sedimentary rocks formed bedrock under the Lower Peninsula and the
easternmost part of the Upper Peninsula.
A notable exception is the Jacobsville
Sandstone that lies in a band forming the
eastern part of the Keweenaw Peninsula
and runs southwest toward Ironwood
and into Wisconsin; this was created by
an ancient river dumping sediment into
a sea.

A "lost interval," as it is called, is the
time period between the late Mississip-
pian and the beginning of our current
epoch, the Pleistocene, where there is
no record of new bedrock being formed.
The Pleistocene is known commonly as
the Ice Age, and we are still in a time
of glaciers scouring parts of the Earth—
although not one mile thick and covering
the entire state as they were thirty thousand years ago!

You can thank Canada for today's soil
and for covering virtually all the bedrock in the Lower Peninsula, most in the
Upper Peninsula, and most of northern
Wisconsin. This glacial till is hundreds
of feet thick in places and is made from
all sizes of rocks, from microscopic silt to
giant boulders the size of houses.

In many places in the Upper Peninsula and northeastern Wisconsin, the
bedrock is exposed or found just inches
underfoot. The igneous rocks were very
resistant to scouring by glaciers and, in
many places, the topography was not
conducive to residual deposits of any
great depth.

The Lower Peninsula has very little

exposed bedrock; mostly, glacial till covers the underlying bedrock. Soils lie thick over the bedrock and are a result of glacial action. Again, thank Canada for the soils while hiking in the Lower Peninsula.

The Lower Peninsula is home to many glacial features you'll be hard-pressed to find in the Upper Peninsula and parts of Wisconsin. One particular feature, kettle and kame topography, is prevalent in many areas of the Lower Peninsula. Pay particular attention at Yankee Springs Recreation Area and the Ott Biological Preserve for kettles, kames, and even an esker.

After passing through Homer, the landscape becomes quite flat, especially in Hillsdale County as you approach the state line.

Even so, as you hike, the geology of the North Country Trail will influence every step you take. Learn the geological history of this region to enjoy your outings.

BIOMES AND COMMUNITIES

The trail through Wisconsin, the Upper Peninsula, and the northern Lower Peninsula runs through the Boreal Hardwood Transition biome, which experiences long, cold winters and shorter growing seasons, which influences the proliferation of more northern species of plants and animals. Some of these plants and animals can be found to the south in the transition zone between this biome and the one that composes most of the southern Lower Peninsula, the Prairie Hardwood Transition biome. As its name states, the Prairie Hardwood Transition biome is a mix of prairies, oak savannas, and mostly deciduous forests, whereas the Boreal Hardwood Transitional Forest biome is a mix of more northern species

of deciduous and coniferous evergreens like pine, spruce, cedar, and hemlock.

The determining factor is the yearly average temperature. North of the line marking 47 degrees as the annual average temperature is the northern transitional forest biome; south, the deciduous forest biome. Since the glaciers retreated, this line of demarcation has slowly moved north, bringing with it more southern species and pushing north the species of the northern transitional forest biome.

Bogs, tamarack, cedar swamps, and pine forests are far more common in the northern transitional forest biome. In the deciduous forest biome; ash and maple swamps, beech-maple and oak-hickory forests, oak savannas, and prairies dominate.

WILDLIFE

Each biome shares some species with all the others; other species are found in one biome but not the other. In northern Wisconsin and the Upper Peninsula, wolves are found across the area and moose are found concentrated in a couple of areas, just west of Marquette and around the Tahquamenon Falls State Park, near Paradise.

Bears are found across the North Country as well, being densest in eastern Wisconsin and the western Upper Peninsula. Bears are present in the northern Lower Peninsula and decrease in density until the Grand River; they have very low numbers between the Muskegon and Grand Rivers and are essentially nonexistent south of the Grand River.

The 47-degree average temperature isotherm runs between Muskegon and Bay City. North of this line are common loons, mink frogs, and porcupines. For the bird-watcher, many of our wood warblers live north of this line, and the change is noticeable when hiking through this transition. Red and jack pine thrive north of this line, along with cedars and balsam fir.

South of the transition zone, porcupines disappear and opossums become more common. Southern flying squirrels and many snake species are found in the southern Lower Peninsula. Again, southbound bird-watchers will notice more titmice, cardinals, and mourning doves and fewer bald eagles, loons, and merlins.

When hiking, I try to carry some sort of field guide—whether it is for birds, flowers, ferns, or trees—to make my hike more enjoyable while increasing my knowledge of the area's natural history.

Hiking Primer

An enjoyable hike starts with planning, even if it is a 20-minute day hike. Having a plan, sticking to it, and having a contingency has separated those who have had a good time (and survived) from those who were miserable from a lack of such—or worse.

By no means is this a comprehensive guide to hiking; it is a general introduction. There are countless volumes of information out there on the topics covered below.

DAY HIKES

Every outdoors person should carry with them a small daypack with their 10 essentials. It still astonishes me that 95 percent of the hikers I encounter do not have even a daypack. Most do not even carry water with them. It is amazing that we do not hear more stories about hapless hikers spending the night in the forest. Do not become a news story or a statistic. Develop a list of ten or more items that you always bring with you on an outdoor adventure. Mine are:

1. Map
2. Compass
3. Water
4. Extra food
5. Extra clothes (pullover, rain gear)
6. Signal maker (whistle)
7. Knife
8. Fire starter
9. First aid kit
10. Flashlight

Some other items I bring are rope, duct tape, a water filter, an emergency blanket, bug dope, toilet paper, a shovel, and sunscreen.

Notice I did not list a Global Positioning System (GPS) device or a cell phone. If you know how to use a map and compass, there is no need for GPS. Cell phone coverage is spotty at best in the UP and northern Wisconsin. Both require batteries, which can die on you. Both give the user a false sense of security. Spend time outdoors, experience nature, and learn the skills necessary to hike and you will never need these gadgets.

Lastly, always—and I mean always—leave your itinerary with someone. Let them know where you are going, your planned route (leave them a map!), and when you expect to be back. I always leave a time, if the person has not heard from me by then, to call the authorities—with phone numbers to call. Thankfully, in all the years and thousands and thousands of miles I have hiked, only once have I not met my deadline.

CLOTHING AND EQUIPMENT

A mantra I stick to is "there is no such thing as bad weather, only bad clothing choices." Even in the worst of weather, if properly dressed and outfitted, you can still enjoy your hike.

The first order of business is footwear. I've seen everything from bare feet and flip-flops on long-distance backpackers to four hundred dollar pairs of solid-leather, high-end backpacking boots on the blistered feet of day hikers. Footwear is an extremely important factor in the level of comfort of any hike, and the hiker's choice comes down to personal preference. I can tell you what I wear; however, it is best to talk to a qualified boot vendor or outfitter and share with them your goals and aspirations, along with your footwear preferences. There are pros and cons with any footwear. Heavy-duty backpacking boots need to be broken in, usually weeks or months in advance. After purchasing my last pair, I wore them everywhere—even to church.

Socks are equally important and are usually not considered. You want to find socks that wick away moisture and reduce the likelihood of blisters, which can occur with any type of footwear. Avoid cotton socks like the plague. I haven't worn cotton socks in years and for good reason—they are terrible on your feet if you are on them all the time. There are many good brands out there worth trying. You will find they are expensive; however, they last much longer then cheap cotton socks, are more comfortable, and are worth the additional cost. You should experiment with wearing a pair of liner socks—very thin, very tight-fitting socks that your regular socks go over. Liner socks, if fitted correctly, drastically reduce the chances of blisters.

The second order of business continues with the notion that cotton is not the best fabric to be wearing when exerting yourself. Cotton absorbs moisture and holds onto it, which is great if you are in a hot, dry desert. This is because when the moisture evaporates from the fabric, it cools you, just as sweat does when it evaporates from your skin.

For most of the year, this is not an ideal situation. Instead, you want to move the moisture away from your skin and evaporate from an outer layer, not from your skin. There are a variety of fabrics out there that accomplish this function, from nature's wool to synthetic fleece and nylon. I've heard of "wicking underwear," which is recommended when hiking in the winter. However, if you wear blue jeans over them, you are only trapping the moisture against your body.

Most of the year, you'll probably be wearing two or more layers. The lighter the layers, the more layers you can use to help regulate your temperature by taking them on and off as needed. Carrying an extra outer layer during the warmer months could come in handy if the weather suddenly becomes cooler or you find yourself along a lake with a stiff wind. I carry in my daypack two sets of weather gear in stuff sacks, one labeled RAIN and the other WINTER. I always carry an extra fleece with me as well when day hiking.

Again, there is a huge amount of information out there about what kinds of fabrics are available and how to wear them. Any outfitter or sporting goods store worth its salt will be able to get you outfitted properly.

WATER

I am constantly amazed at the high percentage of day hikers who venture off into the backcountry without any water whatsoever. Watching them come back dehydrated, miserable, and longing to get to their vehicle to drink the fluids left behind is amusing to me, but a preventable mistake.

The general rule in the Midwest is to bring 1 quart for every 2 miles you are going to hike. Some bring more, some bring less. I tend to bring more, along with a water filter. Michigan and Wisconsin are blessed with an abundance of water and water sources. You are never more than 7 miles from a stream, lake, wetland, or pond. The trail, however, can keep you away from these areas; mix in a dry year, and you can go several miles on the North Country Trail without encountering a water source.

FOOD AND COOKING

When day hiking, it is always a good idea to bring a snack with you. Trail mix, granola bars, jerky, and fruit (dried or fresh) are popular choices. Always have water with you to wash it down, as food digestion is a great consumer of your body's water.

When it comes to backcountry cooking, the choices are as varied as the number of people using the trail. Some prefer the prepackaged meals. Others dehydrate their own food. I use off-the-shelf food products and stick to my "one pot, three ingredient" rule—two of the ingredients are *usually* water and salt. My staples are macaroni and cheese (or some sort of pasta and a pasta packet mix) for dinner, tortillas and cheese (sometimes powdered hummus) for lunch, and hot oatmeal and mocha for breakfast. I'm pretty simple when it comes to cooking in the backcountry. My choice has the benefit of saving on space and weight, but I sacrifice variety.

In some areas of the North Country Trail traverses, you are prohibited from having open fires, even for cooking. In addition, one should check with the local natural resource authorities, usually the Department of Natural Resources or US Forest Service, for local fire danger information. Carrying a cook stove with a canister of fuel eliminates the problem of having to cook using an open fire.

HEALTH, SAFETY, AND HIKING HAZARDS

Blisters. Getting lost. Bears. Dodging vehicles. "Interesting" people on the trail. Catching a waterborne disease. There are many risks involved with hiking, especially for the long-distance backpacker. Spending more time on the trail increases the chance you'll have some sort of malady or encounter that threatens your health or safety.

Knowing where you are, where you are going, and telling someone where you are going and when you'll be back may be the smartest things you'll ever do when it comes to safeguarding yourself from hazards. Even day hikers should tell someone their plans and give them instructions what do if they have not been heard from by a certain time. Contacting the landowner may be your best, first option, then authorities. The day hiker's most common maladies that end them up in the local media are getting lost and having to spend the night in the woods or getting injured and requiring an evacuation. Telling someone where you are and when you'll be back may keep you from spending a lonely night in the woods.

Critical skills to learn before taking a long adventure would be:

- Signal making
- Keeping warm when wet
- Swift water crossings
- Fire starting
- Overnight survival
- Orienteering with map and compass
- Self-defense
- Foot care
- Weather prediction
- Bear and other wildlife avoidance, detection, and protection
- Sanitation

Many of these skills can be learned though community programs, local colleges, nature centers, and outfitting stores.

No activity is free from risk, especially when traveling on foot in remote areas. Even if you become hopelessly lost, you are never more than seven miles from a road in the UP. In addition, if you were careless and left your map at home, take a bearing (OK, you *did* bring a compass, right?) and you will come to a road in less than half a day.

Search and rescue teams take lost hiker reports very seriously, so if you are late and it is approaching nightfall, make a camp for the night. Water and heat are your two most important items—therefore, resist the urge to eat unless you have a readily available supply of potable water, as digestion uses water to turn food into energy. You can go three weeks without food; you can only last three days without water. If you left your itinerary with someone and you stuck to your plan, you will be found in less than a day. If you are somehow off track, pull out the signal maker. Three successive blows on a whistle is a distress signal. If more than a day passes, start a small campfire and throw green leaves and needles on it. Nothing gets more attention than a fire in the Upper Peninsula!

Next to getting lost, weather is your principal enemy. The time of year will depend on which weather events to be prepared for. Another common adage us Michiganders say is "if you don't like the weather, just wait 15 minutes and it will change." Fronts can and do move through quickly in all seasons.

Hypothermia is a real concern as the weather does change—starting out with an 80-degree day, then a front moving through and soaking you with rain, and finally the temperatures dropping into the mid-40s . . . all within three hours. Rain gear and a change of warm clothing stave off hypothermia and should be part of your daypack.

Summer brings thunderstorms and lightning, but the risk for tornadoes is very low. Using any trail during a thunderstorm is risky, especially if you are up in elevation. Always get a weather report before leaving and if you are caught in a storm, hunker down in a low area. In a forest, sit on top of your pack as far from tall trees as possible. In an open area, find a low spot and squat low to the ground—but do not lie on it. Do not resume until 30 minutes after you have heard your last roll of thunder.

Fall brings stable weather, but snow squalls can occur as early as late September. If you are caught in a squall, get out to the trailhead as soon as possible while staying on the trail. If you are lost or cannot make it any farther, hunker down for the night by creating a shelter out of natural materials. Your chances of survival are much higher snuggled in leaf litter than wandering around.

Winters are very cold but snowfall varies across the UP. Along Lake Superior, some communities get over 200 inches of snow a year. Along the northern shore of Lake Michigan, it is more moderate with less than 100 inches in a winter's season. You can snowshoe all of these trails in the winter months, so use winter preparedness techniques when venturing out.

Spring is snowbound until late April and early May. Spring brings the wildlife hazards of mosquitoes, black flies, and no-see-ums, even when there is still snow on the ground; bug spray or clothing will solve the problem. Ticks are present but not common throughout Michigan and Wisconsin, and their density is lowest in the UP. Stable or beach flies are a surprise to most non-Yoopers as they land on your legs—they look like an innocuous housefly, but they bite like a horsefly and are immune to DEET.

Many folks unfamiliar with wilderness are nervous about the presence of animals such as rattlesnakes, lynx, moose, bear, and wolves. You will probably never see a lynx or a wolf in your lifetime—and moose are extremely rare, except on Isle Royale. Since the black bear is aggressively hunted in Michigan, it is terrified of most humans and flees on sight. However, if you find yourself in the presence of a bear, especially a mother bear and her cubs, you need to take evasive action. The likelihood she would attack is extremely remote; however, she could bluff charge in your direction to convince you to leave the area. If the bear does not see you, move on without drawing attention. If they see you (they have poor eyesight, she is smelling you), wave your arms and make some noise, like "Nice bear! I'm leaving now!" Walk backward away from the bear and all should be well. The more time you spend in the UP, the greater the chance is you will see a bear.

There are no venomous snakes in the Upper Peninsula or northern Wisconsin, no matter what anyone tells you. However, they are present in the Lower Peninsula (but in very low numbers). Probably your greatest opportunity to see these snakes will be along the marshes in Barry County, although the author has lived in Barry County for over 12 years and has seen a grand total of three snakes. Rest assured, there is venom out there, but it's in the countless spiders trying their hardest to eat all those mosquitoes and flies. Poison ivy grows in just about every terrestrial habitat, while poison sumac is only found in swamps. Learn how to identify these plants and how to treat yourself if contaminated with their oil. Poison oak does not grow in Michigan.

Forest fires occur nearly every year in the Upper Peninsula and northern Wisconsin, although they tend to be very small and are put out quickly. The Sleeper Lakes Fire of 2007 burnt over 18,000 acres and the Duck Lake Fire burnt over 20,000 acres in 2012 (both just west of Tahquamenon Falls State Park, including several miles of the North Country Trail), reminding everyone that fire is a real and present danger. Thankfully, no one was hurt and very little property was destroyed. Always check with the local US Forest Service or Michigan Department of Natural Resources office for an update on fire danger before embarking on any hike in fire-prone habitats.

SHELTERS AND CAMPSITES

Of all the pleasures of hiking, walking into camp at the end of your day's hike is probably the most rewarding. Road walks aside, there are plenty of camping opportunities in Michigan and Wisconsin. From modern campgrounds to throwing your gear into the bush and practicing Leave No Trace, you have many options on the North Country Trail.

In this book, I've listed as many of the campsites as I could find. Some campsites are just places where enough people have camped in the past that the area "looks" like a campground, and this is usually because there is a water access nearby. I call these places "bivouacs" in the book, as these are not separate campsites per se, but just a beat-down area to pitch a tent or two.

In your state and national forests, the general rule is you can camp anywhere you wish, though in Wisconsin, it is encouraged to camp in designated sites or obtain a permit. Michigan state forests require a free permit, which you fill out and leave at the campsite. This way forest staff can track usage. Campsites are to be set up more than 100 feet from the trail and 200 feet from water. Michigan state game areas allow dispersed camping by permit, but only during the fall and winter hunting seasons. County forests and game areas in Wisconsin also allow dispersed camping by permit.

With few exceptions, you must use designated campsites in state and national parks in both Wisconsin and Michigan. There is the occasional three-sided shelter on the North Country Trail; these are available on a first-come, first-served basis.

IF SOMETHING GOES WRONG

In this day and age of cell phones, it is just a good idea to carry one and make sure the battery is charged, despite their not making it to my "Essentials" list. Leave it off while hiking and enjoy your surroundings. Turn it on at the end of your hike or in case you have a problem. For most of the trail, there will be some coverage. Today's phones can find your position using the GPS in the phone to pinpoint your location.

If you have no phone or no signal, your choices are to find a road or signal for help. You are rarely more than a few miles from a road, albeit a lightly traveled one, in Wisconsin and Michigan. Once you get into the Lower Peninsula, you are rarely more than 1 mile from a road. Figure out where you are on the map as best as possible, take a bearing, and bushwhack to a road. I've done it

before; it works only if you know how to use a map and compass.

If you are injured and are not ambulatory or if you are with someone who cannot move, then you can signal for help. If you told someone your itinerary, use your whistle and make three long blasts, which is the standard call for "we need help." Repeat regularly—at least once every five minutes, more often if you can. Remember, if someone is looking for you and they know you have a whistle, you are making their job to find you easier.

If for some reason you are in a remote area with no roads and you've exhausted all your options, there is a guaranteed way to get the attention of authorities. Let me preface this method with the warning that you should only do this in a life-or-death situation. Start a fire, a big, rip-roaring bonfire. Nothing gets the attention of folks living in northern Wisconsin and the Upper Peninsula of Michigan like seeing a plume of smoke billowing up from within a national or state forest. You'll need to make smoke; do so by throwing green leaves on a hot fire, which creates white, billowing smoke. Be judicious—we don't want to start a real forest fire—which is entirely possible—as you'll be sending hot embers up into the sky. You can make a lot of smoke and still have a small, controllable fire.

LEAVE NO TRACE

Every long-distance backpacker has a story about how they had to throw their gear into the bushes and create a camp for the night. There are significant gaps between official and designated campsites on the trail, so the through-hiker's being familiar with and utilizing Leave No Trace is a must. However, I'm always surprised that a large percentage of backpackers and even more day hikers have never heard of these seven easy rules of the trail. The basic premise is leaving the backcountry the way you found it. Here they are:

1. Plan ahead and prepare
2. Travel and camp on durable surfaces
3. Dispose of waste properly
4 Leave what you find
5. Minimize campfire impacts
6. Respect wildlife
7. Be considerate of other visitors

Pretty simple, actually. When camping, leave the campsite as you found it.

PETS

Pets are commonplace in American families. Dogs are frequently seen traveling with their masters on vacations and cats are traveling more and more every year. Our pets are great travel companions in our vehicles, in our campgrounds, and on the trail. However, there are times when pets are prohibited for various reasons on a trail or there is a compelling reason not to bring them with you.

Bears, moose, and wolves are the wild residents of the North Woods. A dog can be seen as a threat to these animals. Being in their natural habitat, you never know if that particular bear, wolf, or moose is going to charge, run away, or attack you or your best friend. Although these incidents are rare, they do happen. Many dogs are killed each year by wolves.

Some landowners, especially the nature conservancies, prohibit pets, as they can disrupt wildlife. Keep in mind, too, that your pet could pick up some nasty disease if it encounters the waste of any wild animal, especially other carnivores.

In general, pets are allowed on most segments of the North Country Trail. Keep in mind that in some places pets are illegal and the law is enforced, such as in the Pictured Rocks National Lakeshore. In other places, it is just not a good idea to take your dog into the woods as there is a greater possibility you could encounter one of those wild animals. I would discourage bringing pets into the backcountry, especially on overnight trips, in bear and wolf country. Enjoy your pets responsibly.

How to Use This Book

REGIONS

I broke the book into four regions: Wisconsin, Upper Peninsula, northern Lower Peninsula, and southern Lower Peninsula. Wisconsin and the Upper Peninsula regions are easy to demarcate. Michigan's Lower Peninsula has two biomes, separated by what is known as the transition zone, which runs from Muskegon to Bay City. The transition zone starts at the southernmost part of the Manistee National Forest and is complete by Rockford. Therefore, for the purposes of this book I chose to start the Rogue River and White Pine Trail in the southern Lower Peninsula.

If I had to pick one trail in each region on which to take someone who has never hiked the North Country Trail, to give them a feel for this wonderful trail, I'd hike the Brule Bog Boardwalk and Portage Trail segments in Wisconsin, to give the feel of what it looked like before Europeans came and changed everything. Next stop would be Trap Hills in the Upper Peninsula for the rugged terrain, remoteness, and great views. In the northern Lower Peninsula, my favorite segment is south of Nichols Lake in the Manistee National Forest. Finally, I would spend an afternoon during early April taking in the wildflowers of the Lost Nations State Game Area.

TEXT

I've provided an overall narrative description of each hike. The narrative primarily covers the basic feel of the hike, along with other pertinent information about the difficulty, history, and other features worth noting like overlooks and waterfalls.

The second part of each chapter describes the trail in a point-to-point fashion, with mileages between each point. The text for each segment gives the hiker a feel for the trail, landmarks, and basic amenities.

MAPS

You cannot use the excuse that a map does not exist for your journey into Michigan's outdoors. However, when I hiked across the Upper Peninsula in 1998, the quality and volume of maps was less than desirable. I bought a DeLorme Atlas and laminated the pages that were pertinent to my hike. I also acquired various national forest, state forest, and state park maps. Remember, the Internet was in its infancy and I was relying on calling various resource professionals and having them mail me maps. Using US Geological Survey (USGS) 7.5 quadrangles was considered, but their large size and lack of trail placement on the maps made them impractical to use.

I did purchase the Hutchins's guide to the North Country Trail, which featured very basic, hand-drawn maps that showed the relationship of the trail to roads and land ownership. The narrative was very basic—a few paragraphs would describe hikes of 10 miles or more. They were helpful, though, as I traced the route of the trail as best I could onto the DeLorme maps so I could at least know the relationship of the trail to nearby roads.

Today, with the advent of GPS, the Internet, ArcGIS, smart phones, tablets, and nearly 100 percent cell phone coverage, today's average person can find his or her way across the landscape without ever using a compass and a map. However, when the batteries die or the cell phone coverage is nonexistent, it is best to know how to use a paper map and compass.

In this book, the maps were created using data provided by the North Country Trail and superimposed on USGS 7.5 quadrangles, then formatted to fit on the pages of this book. These maps are good for basic navigation. There are other paper options as well. The North Country Trail produces durable, water-resistant trail maps that are good for planning and navigation. I own a set for all of Wisconsin and Michigan; they are great to bring on hikes, as they are small enough to carry, durable, and have all the pertinent information for a good hiking experience. I strongly recommend purchasing these maps to supplement this book, as these maps will be updated more regularly. You'll have to wait for the next edition of this book for an update.

On the North Country Trail website, you can find an excellent online mapping tool that superimposes the trail onto the map of your choice. The three maps that are best for planning are aerial photographs, topographical, and street maps. This mapping tool is available as an application, ArcGIS, through Google Play, and the App Store on your Mac.

For those preferring paper maps, the USGS has created a series of 7.5-minute wide maps that cover the entire state of Michigan. Some trails are marked on these maps; most are not. Learn how to use a compass with these maps and it will only make your hikes more enjoyable. Nothing is more satisfying than thinking you are hopelessly lost, triangulating your position, locating yourself on the map, recognizing the landscape, then reconnoitering yourself back on track.

All segments of the North Country Trail have maps available from the headquarters. Most chapters have produced maps of their segment of trails. Many of the public land agencies (National Park Service, State Forests, Michigan DNR, etc.) have maps as well. Most of the trails in this guide have a local map. Nearly every trail less than 2 miles in length has its own map that will probably suffice. The longer the route, the more remote the area, and the less used the trail, the more you will want to bring a USGS 7.5 quadrangle with you. These are free and found online at www.usgs.gov.

ERRORS AND OMISSIONS

With any hiking guidebook, especially one that covers over 1,000 miles, expect that information will change over time. The North Country Trail is in a constant state of change. Trail segments are closed, rerouted, abandoned, created, and moved. Campsites and shelters are opened, closed, and even moved. I expect the reader to understand that between the time I sent the manuscript to the publisher—even after being meticulously examined by North Country Trail chapter volunteers familiar with their trail sections—and when it was published, there have been changes. In fact, expect changes, especially over time.

The North Country Trail Association tracks changes in trail conditions, but relies on you, the user, to report conditions. Before embarking on a hike, whether it be a day hike or a multiweek adventure, it is always a good idea to check with the local chapter and the North Country Trail website.

FOR MORE INFORMATION

For more information about each trail section, visit the author's website at www.tomfunke.com. You can directly ask the author questions, provide feedback on trail conditions, and find more information about each trail segment, especially local eateries, outfitting, hardware, grocery stores, and more.

Hikes at a Glance

Hike Number	County	Distance in miles	Views	Waterfalls
1	Emmet	23.1		
2	Emmet and Charlevoix	23.4	✓	
3	Emmet	16.4		
4	Emmet	26.6		
5	Emmet and Antrim	31.5	✓	
6	Antrim and Kalkaska	37.0	✓	
7	Kalkaska	22.1		
8	Kalkaska and Grand Traverse	17.4		
9	Grand Traverse	18.2		
10	Wexford	17.9	✓	
11	Wexford	37.7	✓	
12	Manistee and Mason	11.8	✓	
13	Lake	13.5		
14	Lake	27.7		
15	Newaygo	12.1		
16	Newaygo	44.6		
17	Kent	22.3		
18	Kent	32.5		
19	Kent	23.0	✓	
20	Barry	38.7	✓	
21	Kalamazoo and Calhoun	38.2	✓	
22	Calhoun	33.2	✓	
23	Hillsdale	41.7		
24	Douglas	48.4	✓	✓
25	Douglas	20.3	✓	
26	Douglas	18.1	✓	
27	Bayfield	11.4	✓	
28	Ashland	20.7		

Family Friendly	Camping	Pets	Basic Services
L, 3	2	3	F, G, PO, RR
3	2	3	Full
2	2	3	F
2	2	3	Full
1	2	3	
2	2	3	PO, G
2	2	2	Full
2	2	2	
2	2	1	F, PO
1	2	1	F, G, PO
1	2	1	F, G, PO
1	2	1	
2	2	1	
2	2	1	
3	2	2	
3	2	2	
3	2	3	Full
3	2	3	Full
3	0	3	Full
3	2	3	F, G, PO, RR
3	0	3	Full
3	0	3	Full
2	2	3	Full
3	2	3	RR
2	2	1	F, G, PO, RR
2	2	1	
2	2	1	
1	2	1	F, G, PO, RR

FAMILY FRIENDLY: L (makes a loop with other trails); 3 (easy to find, hike, and follow); 2 (challenging in places to find, hike, and follow); 1 (difficult/unsafe places for children); 0 (not recommended

PETS: 0 (illegal); 1 (prohibited); 2 (allowed but not recommended); 3 (allowed); 4 (pet friendly))

CAMPING: 0 (no camping); 1 (backcountry camping only); 2 (designated campsites/trail shelter)

BASIC SERVICES: F (food); G (groceries); PO (post office); M (medical); RR (restrooms); Full (all services)

Hike Number	County	Distance in miles	Views	Waterfalls
29	Ashland	28.4	✓	
30	Ashland	27.5	✓	✓
31	Ashland, Iron, Gogebic	36.2	✓	✓
32	Gogebic and Ontonagon	27.4	✓	✓
33	Ontonagon	8.6	✓	✓
34	Ontonagon	12.9.		
35	Ontonagon	20.1	✓	
36	Ontonagon	25.7	✓	✓
37	Ontonagon and Houghton	13.6	✓	✓
38	Houghton and Baraga	31.3		✓
39	Baraga and Marquette	16.2	✓	
40	Marquette	24.1	✓	✓
41	Marquette	26.7	✓	✓
42	Marquette and Alger	22.9		✓
43	Alger	30.0		✓
44	Alger and Luce	27.2	✓	
45	Luce	21.2	✓	✓
46	Chippewa	22.5	✓	
47	Chippewa	19.8		
48	Chippewa and Mackinac	22.3		
49	Mackinac	22.7		
50	Mackinac and Emmet	5.0	✓	

Family Friendly	Camping	Pets	Basic Services
1	2	1	F, G, PO, RR
3	2	3	RR
1	2	1	Full
1	2	1	RR
0	1	1	
1	1	1	
0	1	1	
0	2	1	
1	Y	1	
1	Y	1	
1	2	1	
0	1	1	
3	2	2	Full
2	2	2	F, G, M,
2	2	1	Full
2	2	2	F, G, PO, RR
2	2	2	F, RR
2	2	2	RR
2	2	2	RR
2	2	3	RR, G
3	2	3	Full
3	0	0	RR

FAMILY FRIENDLY: L (makes a loop with other trails); 3 (easy to find, hike, and follow); 2 (challenging in places to find, hike, and follow); 1 (difficult/unsafe places for children); 0 (not recommended)

CAMPING: 0 (no camping); 1 (backcountry camping only); 2 (designated campsites/trail shelter)

PETS: 0 (illegal); 1 (prohibited); 2 (allowed but not recommended); 3 (allowed); 4 (pet friendly)

BASIC SERVICES: F (food); G (groceries); PO (post office); M (medical); RR (restrooms); Full (all services)

I.

NORTHERN LOWER PENINSULA

1

Wilderness
State Park

START: Mackinaw City

END: CR 66/Levering Road

APPROXIMATE HIKING TIME: 8–12 hours

LENGTH OF SECTION: 23.1 miles

Welcome to the Lower Peninsula! Mackinaw City is a full-service tourist town. Rated as the most popular tourist destination in Michigan by AAA, don't be surprised if you ramble into town and experience a sea of humanity. The resident population is under 1,000, but probably triples or more in size in the summer months—not only with tourists, but seasonal workers as well.

Jean Nicolet was the first European to travel through the area in 1633. His maps and records of the area allowed the French to send Father Jacques Marquette to set up a mission, which he did in 1671 before then moving it across the straits to St. Ignace. At the time, there was a Native American presence of Ojibwe, Odawa, and Potawatomi. There wasn't a permanent settlement at the Straits of Mackinaw at the time, but Native Americans who were out on hunting and fishing forays visited this area. This area was a vital crossroad for trading routes. These routes led to Montreal via Lake Nipissing and Detroit via Lake Huron.

Through various wars over the years the French, English, and Americans (Revolutionary, French and Indian, Pontiac's Rebellion, War of 1812) claimed the area as theirs. The history of the area is interpreted at Fort Michilimackinac and is definitely worth a visit.

The village of Mackinaw City was finally platted and "settled" in 1857. They had the vision to set aside the northern shore for a future replica Fort Michilimackinac and lighthouse. Both have come to fruition. The town's primary industry for years has been tourism, even before the completion of the Mackinac Bridge.

The hike is a short one on city sidewalks until you walk under an overpass just south of the Mackinac Bridge onto a

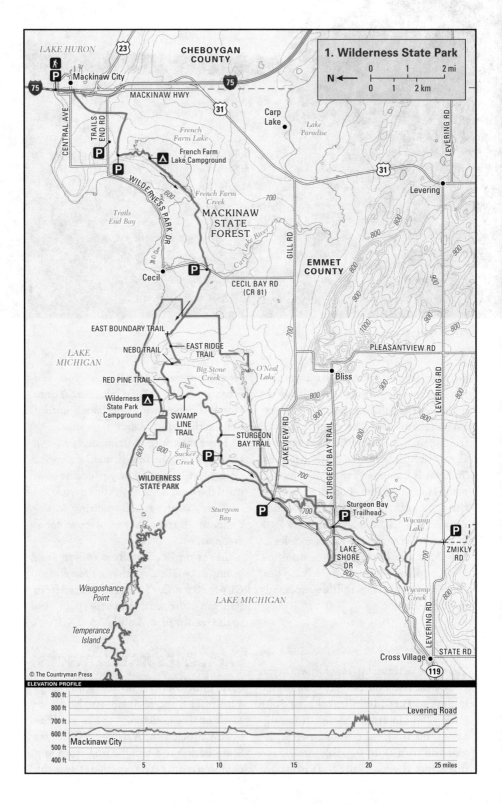

1. Wilderness State Park

LAKE HURON

CHEBOYGAN COUNTY

Mackinaw City

MACKINAW HWY

Central Ave

TRAILS END RD

Carp Lake

Lake Paradise

Levering

French Farm Lake

French Farm Lake Campground

WILDERNESS PARK DR

French Farm Creek

MACKINAW STATE FOREST

Trails End Bay

Carp Lake River

Cecil

GILL RD

CECIL BAY RD (CR 81)

EMMET COUNTY

LEVERING RD

EAST BOUNDARY TRAIL

NEBO TRAIL

EAST RIDGE TRAIL

LAKE MICHIGAN

RED PINE TRAIL

Big Stone Creek

O'Neal Lake

PLEASANTVIEW RD

Wilderness State Park Campground

SWAMP LINE TRAIL

STURGEON BAY TRAIL

Bliss

LAKEVIEW RD

STURGEON BAY TRAIL

LEVERING RD

WILDERNESS STATE PARK

Big Sucker Creek

Sturgeon Bay

Sturgeon Bay Trailhead

Wycamp Lake

ZMIKLY RD

LAKE SHORE DR

Waugoshance Point

LAKE MICHIGAN

Wycamp Creek

Temperance Island

LEVERING RD

Cross Village

STATE RD

© The Countryman Press

119

ELEVATION PROFILE

900 ft					
800 ft					Levering Road
700 ft					
600 ft					
500 ft					
400 ft	Mackinaw City				
	5	10	15	20	25 miles

Thomas Funke

FRENCH FARM LAKE LOOKING NORTH

paved trail on an abandoned rail grade to the southern city limits. You'll leave the multiuse trail, and hike past the 800-acre French Farm Lake. The name is derived from agricultural activities that supplied Fort Michilimackinac with produce. Today it is managed for wildlife as part of the Mackinaw State Forest. Hike along the edge of the lake, then into Wilderness State Park. Wilderness State Park is 10,000 acres in size with 26 miles of Lake Michigan beach and 250 campsites. It is a popular camping and hiking destination, flush with wildlife—especially migrating birds.

HOW TO FIND

Your hike will start in Mackinaw City at Old Mackinac Point Lighthouse, which is part of Fort Michilimackinac State Park. Coming from the north (southbound on I-75), take the Jamet Street exit and turn right (north) onto Louvigny Street; the road will bend to the right (east), change name to Huron Street, and cross under I-75. Turn left (north) onto North Nicolet Street and take it until it ends at the lighthouse.

From the south (northbound on I-75), take the Jamet Road exit, turn left (north) onto North Nicolet Street and take it until the road ends at the lighthouse.

There is street-side parking in the residential areas, but subject to local ordinances.

Levering Road is the southern endpoint. Take US 31 south from Mackinaw City for 8.7 miles (or north 6 miles from Pellston), turn west, and drive 9.4 miles to the trailhead at Zmikly Road.

FACILITIES AND SERVICES

Mackinaw City has all services except a hospital. Central Avenue is the downtown business district; the post office is on East Central Avenue. Wilderness State Park has a small camp store and camping is only at designated sites in the state park. In the Mackinaw State Forest, camping is allowed off trail.

THE HIKE

It is important to note that the Mackinac Bridge is closed to pedestrian traffic. As the Mackinac Bridge is part of the North Country Trail, and is only available for pedestrians one day a year (Labor Day), you'll need to start at Old Mackinac Point Lighthouse (0.0 mile) and walk North Nicolet Street to the south to where the old railroad grade starts. Turn right (west) onto the grade and pass underneath I-75 (0.5 mile) for a short distance to Trails End Road (1.7 miles). The trail turns to cinder after crossing the road.

At the 2.2-miles mark, leave the rail grade, turning right (west) at a trail intersection. Hike westward while enjoying the scenery of a second-growth forest. Pass an intersection with a spur trail coming from your north, then (about 0.2 mile later) come to an intersection with a gravel road at a parking lot.

At the small parking lot and trail kiosk at the northern tip of French Farm Lake (2.7 miles), turn left (south) and hike the trail as it parallels and occasionally uses the road leading into the campground. Hike south through the rustic French Farm Lake campground, which has nine campsites in a wooded lakeside setting, where you will retrieve your water. Your next campsite will be in 8.8 miles.

The trail continues to weave to the east and west sides of the campground road in several locations. The camp road ends and your hike continues to parallel the lake, then bends to a westerly direction through the state forest, which is heavily wooded. French Farm Creek is at the southern edge of the lake and is a reliable water source. Just before County

Route 81 (CR 81) (7.9 miles), cross Carp Lake River on a footbridge.

Turn left (south) on CR 81, a paved road. Walk the road for 100 feet or so and cross into the woods to your right (west). Just over 1.0 mile to the north of this road crossing is a small grocery store with a phone in unincorporated Cecil.

Hike east and enter Wilderness State Park at the 9.5-mile mark. At last report, there is a sign demarking the boundary between the state park and the state forest, which overlooks a small pond. You'll cross East Boundary Trail, then merge with East Ridge Trail heading west. Turn right (north) onto Nebo Trail, then left (west) onto Red Pine Trail. The Red Pine and the North Country Trail (NCT) will leave the woods and will be on the south side of a pond.

At the 9.9-mile mark, come to the intersection with the East Ridge Trail. Continue to the left on a wide, well-used trail through mature forest.

At the 10.8-mile mark is the Nebo Trail. Bear north (right), and at the 11.3-mile mark it merges with the Red Pine Trail, which is a well-worn path headed in a westerly direction through mature forest.

At the 12.5-mile mark, follow a pond around to its south, then take an old road north, the Pondside Trail, north to the campground in the state park.

The Wilderness State Park modern campground has 250 campsites and cabins for rent. The setting is an open one on the Lake Michigan shore; it is 8.4 miles until your next camping opportunity.

Pondside Trail changes names to Swamp Line Trail south of a service gate, and heads south into swampier land. Be on the lookout for bear tracks in the mud! Enjoy the mature forest and large hemlock and white pine trees lining the trail in places.

At the 14.3-mile mark you come to an

intersection with Sturgeon Bay Trail and South Boundary Trail. The Swamp Line Trail ends and changes names to Sturgeon Bay Trail as it bends back to the north and the NCT heads southwest—where the tread can be hard to find, be sure to follow those blazes. If you get lost, bear due west to Lake Michigan, no more than 0.5 mile away.

At 16.3 miles, the trail enters a parking area at Lakeview Road. Take in the view; this is the first time where the trail meets up with Lake Michigan. Cross the road and wind through wooded dunes. Look for abundant blueberries in late summer for a tasty treat.

The Sturgeon Bay Trailhead (18.6 miles) is your next reference point, which has a small parking area alongside the road. The trail goes in a southwesterly direction and levels out as it hugs the shore of Wycamp Lake, which is the site of an abandoned state forest campground and is still used as a bivouac by backpackers. This location breaks up a long hike between Wilderness State Park to the north and the next camping opportunity 10.3 miles away to the south.

Continue south, and come to CR 66/Levering Road Trailhead at the 23.1-mile mark.

Little Traverse Wheelway

START: Waller Road, Charlevoix Township

END: Hoyt Street Community Park, Harbor Springs

APPROXIMATE HIKING TIME: 8–12 hours

LENGTH OF SECTION: 23.4 miles

The Little Traverse Wheelway is a multiuse, nonmotorized, mostly paved trail that stretches between Charlevoix and Harbor Springs, running through Petoskey. "The Bike Path," as it is called locally, is a popular trail mostly with locals and summer residents, but it is becoming more popular with tourists. Its shining feature is that it is in close proximity to Lake Michigan for most of its length, offering great views and vistas of the lake. The trail runs mostly through developed areas, so opportunities abound for shopping, eating, lodging, and sightseeing.

This trail is yet another of the many abandoned railways that have been converted to multiuse trails. However, this is one of the longer rail trails that does not allow motorized vehicles. The trail has been an ongoing project for over 10 years—paving the trail, moving the trail off road shoulders and away from highways, and developing facilities and connecting trails.

HOW TO FIND

The southern trailhead is in Charlevoix, at the intersection of US 31 and Waller Road. Charlevoix is west of Petoskey via US 31.

The northern terminus is in Harbor Springs at the ball fields near Lake Street and Hoyt Street on the east side of town. Drive north on MI 119 from Petoskey, past the airport, and look for the recreational complex on the north side of the road.

FACILITIES AND SERVICES

This trail corridor runs through many developed areas and passes by all services. Business directories can be found with the chambers of commerce of

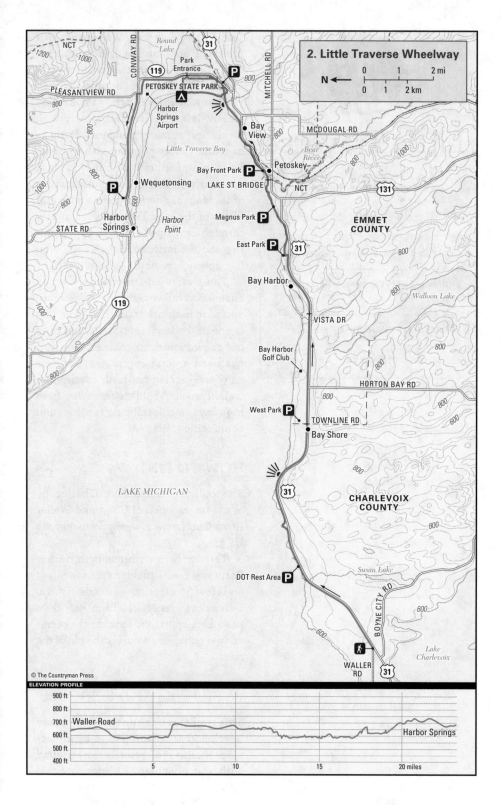

2. Little Traverse Wheelway

N ←
0 · · · 1 · · · 2 mi
0 · · 1 · · 2 km

NCT

1200 · 1000

Round Lake

Park Entrance

CONWAY RD

31

119

PETOSKEY STATE PARK

PLEASANTVIEW RD

Harbor Springs Airport

800

Little Traverse Bay

MITCHELL RD

800

Bay View

MCDOUGAL RD

Bear River

800

1000

Bay Front Park

Petoskey

LAKE ST BRIDGE

NCT

131

Wequetonsing

1000

600

800

P

Harbor Springs

State Rd

Harbor Point

Magnus Park

East Park

31

EMMET COUNTY

800

Bay Harbor

Walloon Lake

VISTA DR

800

Bay Harbor Golf Club

800

HORTON BAY RD

800

600

West Park

800

TOWNLINE RD

Bay Shore

LAKE MICHIGAN

31

CHARLEVOIX COUNTY

800

800

DOT Rest Area

Susan Lake

600

BOYNE CITY RD

600

WALLER RD

Lake Charlevoix

31

© The Countryman Press

ELEVATION PROFILE

900 ft
800 ft
700 ft — Waller Road
600 ft
500 ft
400 ft

5 · · · 10 · · · 15 · · · Harbor Springs · · · 20 miles

Harbor Springs, Petoskey, and Charlevoix. There is even an airport in Harbor Springs.

THE HIKE

Although there is a spur trail that starts in Charlevoix and comes in from the west, the official trail starts when it comes into contact with US 31 at Waller Road. This segment includes 3.0 miles of asphalt and over 0.5 mile of boardwalk through a wetland. The trail closely follows US 31 and Lake Michigan most of the way to Petoskey.

At the 3.0-mile mark, a Michigan Department of Transportation rest area and park has parking, bathrooms, and a picnic area. Take a break and ramble down to the Lake Michigan shore. From here, the path weaves into the woods and back to US 31, coming in close proximity to Lake Michigan.

Your first developed overlook at the 5.5-mile mark is managed by the Michigan Department of Transportation, which offers an overlook of Lake Michigan and Little Traverse Bay.

Enter the community of Bay Shore at 7.3 miles, cross Townline Road, and continue east along US 31 through residential areas, including a golf course on the north side of the highway.

Bay Harbor is another small community at 11.3 miles, where you cross the Bay Harbor main entrance at Vista Drive. Enter Bay Harbor through West Park, which has parking and amenities located several hundred yards north of the trail on Townline Road. This segment consists of 5.0 miles of asphalt trail in close proximity to US 31. There are some sweeping views of Lake Michigan and the nearby business district called the Village at Bay Harbor. There is street and lot parking at both West and nearby East Parks, as well as in the Village district with its many shopping opportunities.

The East Park entrance, at the 12.3-mile mark, is the start of a 1.3-mile segment allowing users to hike along the railroad grade above Little Traverse Bay without using the busy US 31 shoulder. This area was a past industrial site whose contamination issues have been cleaned up to the point where there are no problems with travel through the park. This segment runs 10–50 feet or more above the bay and is widely regarded as the most scenic on the entire Wheelway.

Magnus Municipal Park, at the 13.5-mile mark, has parking and modern camping. This segment of trail runs west of Ingalls Avenue through a new section of parkland and across the Bear River to the bay side of Petoskey City Hall. This section has also seen the erection of two Little Traverse Wheelway arches like the one further east along the wheelway. Check out the metal sculpture of a big-wheel bicycle in the new park.

Enter Petoskey proper, pass the intersection of US 31 and US 131, and enter Petoskey Bay Front Park at the 14.5-mile mark. This scenic 2.5-mile segment runs through Bay Front Park and utilizes a short stretch of sidewalk before reaching Bay View. Bay Front Park is a recreational park located along the shore of Lake Michigan. Parking, playgrounds, bathrooms, a marina, and picnic areas are all within a short walking distance of downtown Petoskey.

The Little Traverse History Museum has wonderful exhibits depicting Petoskey's place in history. The museum is a must-stop for those interested in the history of the Little Traverse region, including the role played by the original Little Traverse Wheelway. The bicycle arrived here along with the railroad and the new

Dove Day

SUNSET OVER CROOKED LAKE

wave of settlers who came for economic and religious reasons.

The trail goes to the lakeside of the history museum from the parking area in the rear. Use the nonmotorized bridge to cross over the Bear River. It is at this point that the North Country Trail (NCT) joins from the south, and follows the Little Traverse Wheelway until MI 119.

This segment also goes through the community of Bay View along a pinkish-colored sidewalk. Petoskey's neighboring summer community grew up along with the city in the 19th and early 20th centuries. Today it continues to display its majestic homes and their interesting architecture and landscaping.

Tannery Creek (17.0 miles) has an overlook—a good place to stop and view the bay. It is a popular picnic area not only for tourists, but locals on their lunch break as well. Opposite the overlook on the rearside of D & W Fresh Market is a beautiful mural by artist Terry Dickinson depicting transportation scenes along the Wheelway corridor at various times in history. Just past the mural, a side path takes you to the campground in Petoskey State Park. The trail then continues 1.0 mile through a young oak and white pine forest to MI 119 (17.6 miles).

The Little Traverse Wheelway splits at this point when the North Country Trail/Northwestern State Trail crosses over MI 119 and heads northeast. Little Traverse Wheelway follows along MI 119 toward the entrance of Petoskey State Park (18.6 miles).

Use the park entrance road to access this small, albeit 303-acre, state park. Its modern campground and opportunity to find the coveted Petoskey stone, Michigan's state rock, draw in hundreds of thousands of visitors—mostly in the summer months.

You'll pass by three nature preserves owned by the Little Traverse Conservancy: Menonaqua, Huffy, and Kuebler Trippe. You'll pass by the end of the runway to the Harbor Springs airport. The path will bend to the west into the airport, pass the terminal, and then bend north to cross MI 119, following the highway west. From this point until Harbor Springs you either follow the shoulder of MI 119 or a nearby separate trail.

Enter Harbor Springs (23.4 miles) and just past Bluff Walk Road, which goes south, the trail will split away from MI 119 to the northwest as it enters Harbor Springs proper. Like Charlevoix and Petoskey, Harbor Springs is a wonderful travelers' destination with beautiful views and a multitude of things to do.

Mackinaw State Forest– Pellston Area

START: CR 66/Levering Road Trailhead

END: Brutus Road Trailhead

APPROXIMATE HIKING TIME: 6–10 hours

LENGTH OF SECTION: 16.4 miles

Enter the 700,000-plus acres of the Mackinaw State Forest, which is found in parts of eight counties. The state forest is mostly second growth, having been logged over during the lumber boom of the late 19th and early 20th centuries. By 1910, the area was devoid of its majestic white and red pine. In 1918, elk were reintroduced to the forest, but they do not live in the area you will be hiking. Today the second growth forest is managed for multiple uses. Tree species run the spectrum from the aforementioned pine to maple, aspen, spruce, cedar, and fir.

Probably the most noticeable feature (or lack thereof) is the absence of water. There are no reliable sources of surface water, and the only potable water is at the bar at Larks Lake. For thru-hikers, the next potable water going north is at Wycamp Lake, and going south it is at Conway.

HOW TO FIND

Levering Road is the northern trailhead. Take US 31 south from Mackinaw City for 8.7 miles (or north 6 miles from Pellston), turn west, and drive 9.4 miles to the trailhead at Zmikly Road.

The Brutus Road Trailhead is north of Harbor Springs. Take Pleasantview Road from MI 119, which intersects with the state highway on the north side of the municipal airport. Drive 4.9 miles north, then turn east (right) onto Brutus Road for another 1.5 miles to the trailhead.

Another access is on South Larks Lake Road. Continue past Brutus Road 0.75 mile on Pleasantview Road, turn left on Stutsmanville Road, and after another 0.75 mile turn north on Larks Lake Road and travel 1.7 miles to another trailhead.

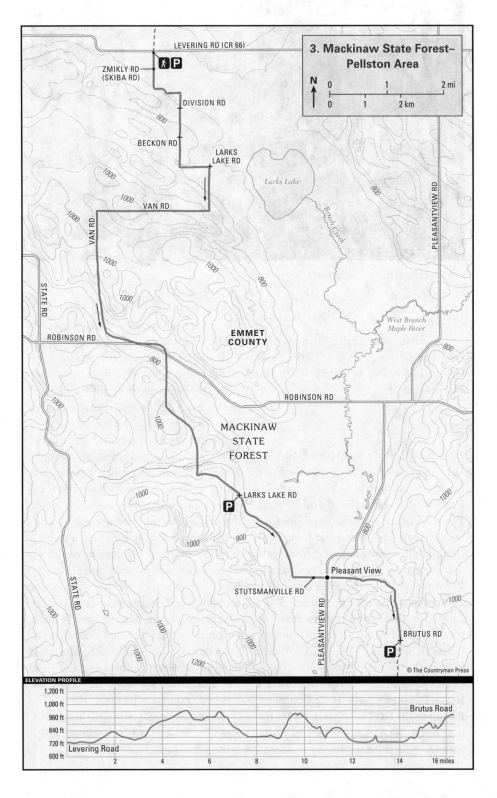

3. Mackinaw State Forest–Pellston Area

LEVERING RD (CR 66)

ZMIKLY RD
(SKIBA RD)

DIVISION RD

BECKON RD

LARKS
LAKE RD

Larks Lake

VAN RD

VAN RD

Brush Creek

ROBINSON RD

EMMET
COUNTY

West Branch
Maple River

ROBINSON RD

MACKINAW
STATE
FOREST

LARKS LAKE RD

Pleasant View

STUTSMANVILLE RD

PLEASANTVIEW RD

PLEASANTVIEW RD

BRUTUS RD

STATE RD

STATE RD

800

1000

1000

1000

1000

1000

800

1000

1000

800

800

800

1000

1000

1000

800

1000

1000

800

1200

1000

© The Countryman Press

N

0   1   2 mi

0   1   2 km

ELEVATION PROFILE

1,200 ft
1,080 ft
960 ft
840 ft
720 ft
600 ft

Brutus Road

Levering Road

2   4   6   8   10   12   14   16 miles

NORTH COUNTRY TRAIL EMBLEMS DENOTE CERTIFIED TRAIL

FACILITIES AND SERVICES

At 1 mile to the east of the Van and Larks Lake Road there is a bar at Larks Lake. Off-trail camping is permitted in the national forest.

THE HIKE

From the County Route 61 (CR 66)/ Levering Road Trailhead, hike south on Zmikly Road South (also known as Skiba Road) and cross Division and Beckon. The road bends left (east) and goes 0.5 mile to Larks Lake Road and then turns right (south); continue your road walk 0.5 mile until you turn right (west) onto Van Road. Van Road turns left (south) at its intersection with Rugged Road and continues south 0.75 mile, where the road becomes a trail after the intersection with Blackberry Trail and Johnson Hill Road.

At the 6.3-mile mark, you'll find a North Country Trail (NCT) Trailhead. Although the NCT is uncertified for the next few miles, it is useable. You'll hike through sparse second growth forest, mostly open canopy. You'll climb and then descend to your next road crossing (Robinson Road) at the 8.7-mile mark. This section starts out flat, then climbs to the top of a hill, descends to a small creek, then travels up slightly and hugs the contour until your next road crossing at Larks Lake Road (11.8 miles).

Larks Lake Road is gravel with a parking area at the trail and road intersection. The trail hugs the edge of a wet meadow being invaded by small trees. Several short boardwalks help keep your feet dry on this flat segment of trail.

At Stutsmanville Road (13.6 miles), turn left (east) to hike the paved road. There is a water pump available at the township hall, at the corner with Pleasantview Road. Hike 0.5 mile east past Pleasantview, and Stutsmanville Road becomes gravel. Continue on Stutsmanville Road for 0.5 mile. Look for the trailhead on the right (south) side of the road. The trail crosses a creek 1.0 mile after leaving Stutsmanville Road.

At the 16.4-mile mark is the Brutus Road Trailhead; look for parking on the south side of the road.

Petoskey

START: Brutus Road Trailhead	
END: Harmon Road	
APPROXIMATE HIKING TIME: 10–15 hours	
LENGTH OF SECTION: 26.6 miles	

Petoskey is a vibrant tourist town. The town's name is derived from an Odawa word meaning "where the light shines through the clouds." The area was named after the community's founder, Chief Ignatius Petosega, as was the Petoskey stone. Petosega's father was a French Canadian fur trader and his mother was Odawa.

As with the other tourist towns in northern Michigan, the population swells in the summertime. Just over 6,000 people call Petoskey home. The lakeshore, shops, trails, and other natural amenities of the area draw many more thousands during the summer months. The 303-acre Petoskey State Park, just north of the trail on MI 119, is a popular destination for campers and day users in search of the popular Petoskey stone, Michigan's state rock. The park has been mostly picked clean of these desirable rocks, but they can be found on other less-used beaches in the area.

The lightly used trail ends at the north end of Conway at Kipp Road; a short road walk then leads to a multiuse trail, the Northwestern State Trail. Thankfully, the area has seen tremendous trail development—albeit multiuse, mostly paved trails. You will use parts of three paved rail trails, the Northwestern State Trail, the Little Traverse Wheelway, and the Petoskey Bear River Recreation Area Trail. You'll cut through the campus of North Central Michigan College onto their nature trails, then exit the campus and utilize a mix of road walks and lightly used trails. The trail will take you through the lakeside park district, then bisect the downtown shopping district via the Bear River Trail, paralleling the river of the same name.

Enjoy all types of trail on this section! Old railroad grades, paved bike trails, sidewalks, well-groomed ski trails, roads

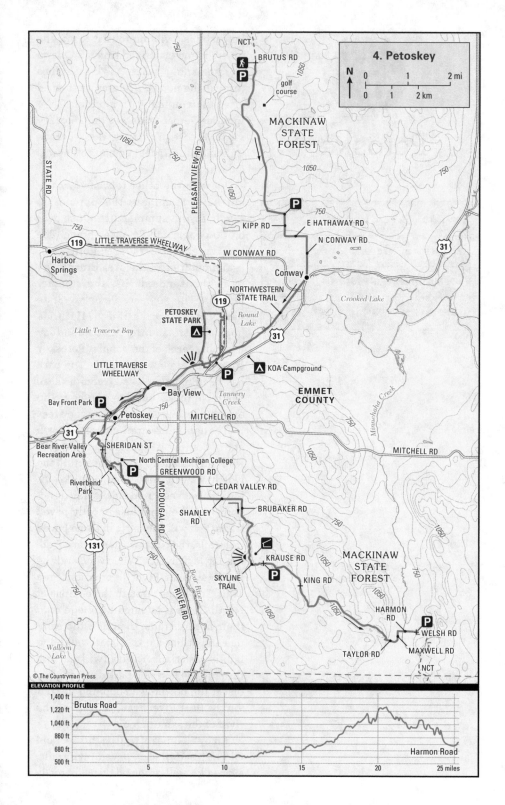

4. Petoskey

N

| 0 | | 1 | | 2 mi |
| 0 | 1 | | 2 km | |

NCT
BRUTUS RD
golf course

MACKINAW STATE FOREST

1050

750

750

1050

STATE RD

PLEASANTVIEW RD

KIPP RD
E HATHAWAY RD
N CONWAY RD
W CONWAY RD

119
Harbor Springs

LITTLE TRAVERSE WHEELWAY

750

Conway
Crooked Lake

31

NORTHWESTERN STATE TRAIL

Round Lake

PETOSKEY STATE PARK

119

Little Traverse Bay

31

KOA Campground

LITTLE TRAVERSE WHEELWAY

EMMET COUNTY

Bay View

Tannery Creek

Minnehaha Creek

Bay Front Park

750

Petoskey

MITCHELL RD

750

31

SHERIDAN ST

MITCHELL RD

Bear River Valley Recreation Area

North Central Michigan College
GREENWOOD RD

1050

MCDOUGAL RD

CEDAR VALLEY RD

Riverbend Park

SHANLEY RD

BRUBAKER RD

131

750

KRAUSE RD
SKYLINE TRAIL

MACKINAW STATE FOREST

1050

KING RD

RIVER RD

1050

HARMON RD
WELSH RD

Walloon Lake

750

750

TAYLOR RD

MAXWELL RD

1050

NCT

© The Countryman Press

ELEVATION PROFILE

1,400 ft					
1,220 ft	Brutus Road				
1,040 ft					
860 ft					
680 ft					
500 ft				Harmon Road	
	5	10	15	20	25 miles

both paved and unpaved, and well-worn and lightly used trail. You'll pass through Petoskey, a cosmopolitan tourist town, only to leave civilization behind as the trail takes you through a network of private and public lands. It continues to be a hilly hike.

HOW TO FIND

The Brutus Road Trailhead is north of Harbor Springs. Take Pleasantview Road from MI 119, which intersects with the state highway on the north side of the municipal airport. Drive 4.9 miles north, then turn east (right) onto Brutus Road for another 1.5 miles to the trailhead.

Harmon Road is southeast of Petoskey. From the intersection of US 31 & US 131, take US 131 south 5.75 miles to Bear River Road, turn east (left), drive 5.3 miles until the road forks, and take the left fork (Maxwell Road). The first intersection on the east (right) is Harmon Road (1.5 miles); turn east (right) and continue to Welsh Road in about 0.7 mile.

FACILITIES AND SERVICES

Petoskey is a full-service town; all services are on or within 0.5 mile of the trail. There are two post offices, one at 318 State Street in Petoskey and one at 3459 US 31 N in Conway. Petoskey State Park has a modern campground. McLaren Northern Michigan Hospital is located just off US 31, about 0.5 mile west of where the trail goes under US 31.

Long-distance hikers need to load up on supplies in Petoskey as there are no services between here and Boyne Falls, which is 3.0 miles from the trail & 26.0 trail miles away from Petoskey. Boyne Falls has few services but it does have

a post office. Another small town, Alba (60.0 trail miles to the south and 1.0 mile from the trail) also has few services available, but it does have a post office as well. Your next full-service town is Kalkaska, 90.0 trail miles away.

THE HIKE

South of Brutus Road, be aware there has been recent logging activity. This trail segment is very hilly; you'll be climbing up, leveling out, and then experiencing an abrupt downhill. For entertainment purposes, look to the east and see a golf course through the trees while keeping your eyes open for errant golf balls on the trail.

At the 4.7-mile mark, the trail ends at Kipp Road. Turn right and hike Kipp Road south, turn left (east) on East Hathaway Road, then right (south) on North Conway Road. This will be the end of your quiet, natural hiking until you pass through Petoskey. You'll hear the roar of heavy traffic in the near distance, which is US 31.

At the 6.6-mile mark you come to an intersection with US 31 and a trailhead for the Northwestern State Trail, which the North Country Trail will use into Petoskey. Turn right (southwest) onto this paved and popular multiuse trail. The shared trail parallels the busy US 31 through town. Most services are found along US 31; an alternative is to walk along the mix of sidewalks. Many services are at this intersection, including the Conway post office, which is on the northwest corner of US 31 and West Conway Road.

At the 8.9-mile mark, pass Shaw Road and there is a KOA down the street about ¼ mile away. Continue hiking through the commercial district as you head toward Petoskey.

The paved trail continues to parallel US 31, although behind a residential area along some wetlands and lakes. At the 9.3-mile mark is the MI 119 and US 31 intersection. The Little Traverse Wheelway, Northwestern Michigan Trail, and North Country Trail intersect at this point. Restaurants, a drug store, and other shopping are close by. Petoskey State Park is just 1.0 mile to the north on the Little Traverse Wheelway, and there are more services close to Petoskey State Park, including banks, groceries, and a brewery. Petoskey State Park has a modern campground on the shore of Lake Michigan with 180 campsites. Southbound, all three trails share the same trail corridor into Petoskey. The trail continues to be paved in close proximity to US 31. Before entering Bay Front Park, the trail goes behind a commercial district. Bay Front Park is a well-developed park with bathrooms, a playground, and picnic facilities.

At the 12.6-mile mark, just before the Bear River Bridge, turn left (south) onto the paved Bear River Trail. Hike past Petoskey City Hall, and cross West Lake Street into the Bear River Valley Recreation Area. Follow the east bank of the river under the US 31 Bridge. Cross to the west bank, eventually reaching Sheridan Street. The trail is uphill and parallels Bear River, which has been converted into a kayak course.

The trail, although in a residential area, keeps you along a natural corridor. Cross Sheridan Street (13.7 miles), a busy cross street, and continue south to Riverbend Park, crossing the railroad tracks.

At Standish Avenue (14.3 miles), at the entrance to Riverbend Park, turn left (north) onto Standish Avenue, cross Bear River again, and travel on sidewalks for a few hundred feet before the trail crosses Standish Avenue and goes up a steep hill between two commercial buildings.

At the top of the hill is an entrance drive into a parking lot for North Central Michigan College (14.5 miles). Follow the edge of the parking lot to the trailhead for the North Central Michigan College natural area. The trail enters woods, follows the Bear River in a southeasterly direction, passes through an open area, and then hairpins to the northeast back through the same open area into the woods. The trail then turns right (east), leaves the woods, and follows a fencerow on private property.

Leave North Central Michigan College at the 16.6-mile mark. The property boundary is noticeable as you leave the woods, hike a mowed trail, and bear east to the intersection of McDougal and Greenwood Roads (16.7 miles).

The maintained trail ends and you'll cross McDougal Road and walk Greenwood Road east 1.0 mile, turn right (south) on Cedar Valley Road for 0.5 mile, left (east) on Shanley Road for 1.0 mile, then south on Brubaker Road.

Where Brubaker Road bends left (easterly) at the 20.1-mile mark, the trail will cut right into the 865 Acre City of Petoskey Forest Preserve or 1.3 miles before it crosses Krause Road. Also called Skyline Trail, it is quite hilly and heavily forested. After 1.0 mile, you will pass three side trails. The first goes right to a viewing platform from which you can see Petoskey with Little Traverse Bay on Lake Michigan in the distance; for westbound long-distance hikers, this will be your first view of Lake Michigan (and for eastbound, your last view). The second trail heads left up the hill to the Skyline Camp, which has a trail shelter.

The North Country Trail will traverse

private property in a southeasterly direction as it crosses King Road and then Taylor Road, and the trail will then parallel the north side of Taylor Road until the trail comes down the side of a hill and dumps you onto Taylor Road, where you will turn left (east) and hike 0.1 mile to the intersection of Taylor and Maxwell Road. Turn left (north) for 0.2 mile until you reach the next intersection at Harmon Road, turn right (east) for 0.3 mile until you reach Welsh Road (26.6 miles), Harmon jogs south, then east, and the trail enters the woods to the right, 0.1 mile past Welsh Road. Southwest of the intersection (on private land at the first farm) is a flowing well accessible with permission from the owner.

Mackinaw State Forest-North

START: Harmon Road–North Country Trail intersection
END: MI 32/Warner Creek Pathway parking
APPROXIMATE HIKING TIME: 12–18 hours
LENGTH OF SECTION: 31.5 miles

The Mackinaw State Forest is quite hilly on this stretch of trail. In general, you'll walk the contours along the sides of hills and through valleys. The trail designers really took the time to minimize your effort and maximize the views, as there will be several.

Between Welsh and Springvale Roads, you'll hike along the ridge and your views will be to the west. After crossing Springvale Road, you go right back up and snake around the hills, keeping mostly to the contour, until crossing Thumb Lake Road. You'll road walk to Kuzmik Road, you'll slowly gain elevation as you walk the Kuzmik itself, and then take the trail into the woods. Between here and Giem Road, there are many ups and downs over a short stretch until a road walk before US 131. The trail between US 131 and MI 32 continues its hilly nature.

HOW TO FIND

Harmon Road is southeast of Petoskey. From the intersection with US 31, take US 131 south 5.75 miles to Bear River Road, turn east (left), drive 5.3 miles until the road forks, and take the left fork (Maxwell Road). The first intersection on the east (right) with Harmon Road is 1.5 miles farther; turn east (right) and follow Harmon until it ends at Welsh Road in about 0.7 mile. The trailhead is about 0.2 mile east from the Welsh and Harmon Road intersection. The Warner Creek Pathway Trailhead is off MI 32, just 1.5 miles west of the intersection with US 131. The intersection is between the communities of Boyne Falls and Mancelona.

FACILITIES AND SERVICES

Boyne Falls is 3.0 miles west from the intersection of Thumb Lake Road (CR

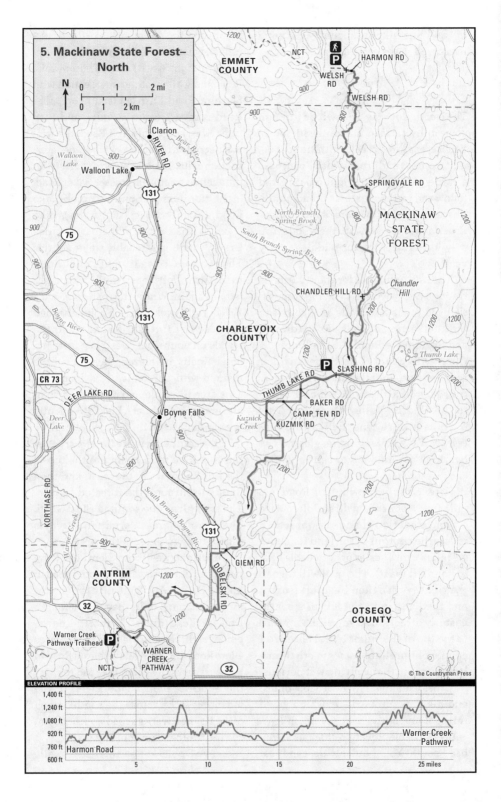

5. Mackinaw State Forest–North

N

0   1   2 mi

0   1   2 km

EMMET COUNTY

NCT

HARMON RD

WELSH RD

WELSH RD

SPRINGVALE RD

MACKINAW STATE FOREST

Clarion

RIVER RD

Bear River

Walloon Lake

Walloon Lake

131

75

North Branch Spring Brook

South Branch Spring Brook

Chandler Hill

CHANDLER HILL RD

Chandler Hill

CHARLEVOIX COUNTY

131

Boyne River

75

CR 73

DEER LAKE RD

Deer Lake

Boyne Falls

Kuznick Creek

SLASHING RD

Thumb Lake

THUMB LAKE RD

BAKER RD

CAMP TEN RD

KUZMIK RD

KORTHASE RD

Warner Creek

South Branch Boyne River

131

GIEM RD

DOBELSKI RD

ANTRIM COUNTY

32

OTSEGO COUNTY

Warner Creek Pathway Trailhead

NCT

WARNER CREEK PATHWAY

32

© The Countryman Press

ELEVATION PROFILE

1,400 ft
1,240 ft
1,080 ft
920 ft
760 ft
600 ft

Harmon Road

5   10   15   20   25 miles

Warner Creek Pathway

48) and Kuzmik. Backcountry camping is allowed in the state forest.

THE HIKE

The North Country Trail winds through some hilly terrain as you head south. You'll cross three creeks within about 0.5 mile, come to and cross Welsh Road, pass a cattle gate on your right (south), and follow the trail as it starts going uphill. There are the headwaters of Minnehaha Creek about 100 feet into the woods. You may have to search for puddles in dry years.

The trail undulates for about 2.0 miles through heavy woods, utilizing some little-used roads and trails as it comes to the intersection of Welsh Road (gravel) and Springvale Road. At the Emmet & Charlevoix county line, there is a hiker register box. Shortly thereafter, a spur trail goes off to the right, which is a loop to the Cherry Valley Overlook. This 0.9 mile hike rejoins the North Country Trail 0.3 miles farther down. The overlook can make a decent bivouac, sans water."

After crossing Springvale Road (5.6 miles) in a southerly direction, notice a slight elevation change upward, then follow the contour of the land for about 2.5 miles with a series of noticeable hills to your left (east). The trail will turn to the right (west), then bear left (south) and then a turn to the left in a south-easterly direction as you climb upward to the top of Chandler Hill. There are a couple of unreliable streams that may have water in them during wet periods.

Cross Chandler Hill Road (10.4 miles) and hike up onto a ridge, which you'll travel along for the next several miles—with noticeable elevation changes as you head south. You'll quickly descend just before coming to Thumb Lake Road (13.7 miles), where there is a small creek.

Turn right (west) onto Thumb Lake Road and walk past the intersection with Slashing Road. Turn left (south) on Baker Road (gravel), walk 0.5 mile, and turn right (west) on Camp Ten Road; the trail will become a quiet road walk at the intersection with Kuzmik Road. There is an unreliable stream that crosses Baker Road.

At the intersection of Thumb Lake Road/Kuzmik Road (16.2 miles), hike Kuzmik Road south and cross Kuznick Creek, which is a reliable water source. The road walk heads uphill and south, then turns left (east) and then right (south) again. Where the road comes to a Y, veer right (west). At this point, the road has become a rutted affair and enters the woods on your right (west) just after the bend. Roads are blazed; the trail start is marked with Carsonite posts. Be aware: This area is frequented by off-road vehicles and snowmobilers. Blazes frequently are vandalized on this stretch of trail.

Hike southerly, leave the two track at the 19.2-mile mark, climb to the top of the hill for views to the west, and then undulate through the forested terrain. The trail turns due south to Giem Road. There are several intermittent streams that may have water in this area.

Turn right (west) onto Giem Road (24.3 miles), an unimproved road you'll need to hike to US 131. At US 131, turn left (south) for less than 0.5 mile, then veer left onto Dobleski Road (gravel). Future trail development will reroute the trail so it crosses Giem Road and parallels Dobleski Road to the west, possibly using the road to cross the South Branch Boyne River. In the meantime, hike across the south branch of the Boyne River as a road walk until you see the trailhead on your right.

Leave Dobleski Road at the 26.5-mile

mark, hike 0.1 mile through the woods, up and over US 131, and into a hilly woods for a short distance. The trail climbs to the ridges and stays high with a couple of dips before reaching MI 32 at the 31.5-mile mark.

After crossing MI 32 to the south side of the highway, the North Country Trail soon joins the Warner Creek Pathway Loop Trail, which it follows west to the parking lot on the south side of MI 32, about 0.8 mile to the west.

Mackinaw State Forest– South

START: Warner Creek Pathway parking

END: Pickerel Lake State Forest Campground spur trail intersection

APPROXIMATE HIKING TIME: 12–18 hours

LENGTH OF SECTION: 37.0 miles

The North Country Trail utilizes parts of the Warner Creek and Jordan River Pathways, which are very popular two-day-and-one-night backpacking destinations. The Jordan River Valley is an 18,000-acre area that holds the Jordan River, Michigan's first waterway to be designated as a wild and scenic river. The area is popular with weekend backpackers, as there is a loop trail of which the North Country Trail uses the northwest part.

A landmark on the non-NCT loop is known as Deadman's Hill and is named for Stanley Graczyk, a young lumberjack. On May 20, 1910, he was to marry his childhood sweetheart. "Big Sam," as he was known, went to work that morning and was driving a team of horses pulling a "big wheel" loaded with timber. The cart went out of control going down the hill, running him over. Sadly, he never made it to the altar. It has been known as Deadman's Hill ever since. This is an alternate access point for the trail and a spectacular overlook, with a great view over the Jordan River Valley.

The trail winds along the trout-filled Jordan River along high ridges and down steep valleys. There are a few gut-wrenching climbs and steep descents before you slowly climb out of the valley between Pinney Bridge Road and Cascade Road, where you will pass the only point on the 4,600-mile-long trail where it crosses the 45th parallel. After Landslide Lookout, the trail will level out for the next 15.0 miles.

It is a flat and rather waterless road walk on blazed roads (Harvey, Corey, and Doerr Roads) until the Five Lakes Area. Although you are in the Mackinaw State Forest, this area is relatively open, with many open fields and open savanna until crossing Starvation Lake Road, where it becomes more forested.

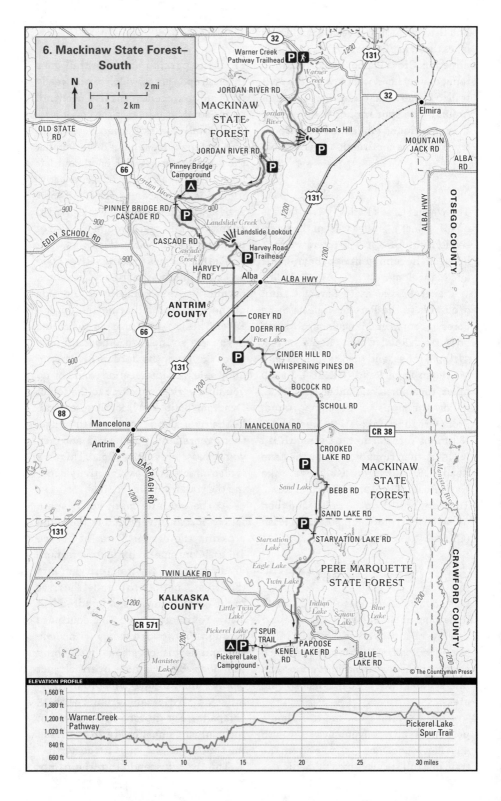

6. Mackinaw State Forest–
South

N

0   1   2 mi

0   1   2 km

Warner Creek
Pathway Trailhead

32

131

1200

OLD STATE
RD

JORDAN RIVER RD

MACKINAW
STATE
FOREST

Warner
Creek

32

Elmira

66

Jordan River

Jordan
River

Deadman's Hill

JORDAN RIVER RD

Pinney Bridge
Campground

PINNEY BRIDGE RD/
CASCADE RD

900

900

900

131

MOUNTAIN
JACK RD

ALBA
RD

ALBA HWY

OTSEGO COUNTY

EDDY SCHOOL RD

Landslide Creek

Landslide Lookout

CASCADE RD

Cascade
Creek

900

Harvey Road
Trailhead

HARVEY
RD

Alba

ALBA HWY

ANTRIM
COUNTY

COREY RD

DOERR RD

66

Five Lakes

CINDER HILL RD

WHISPERING PINES DR

BOCOCK RD

131

1200

SCHOLL RD

88

Mancelona

Antrim

MANCELONA RD

CR 38

MACKINAW
STATE
FOREST

Manistee River

DARRAGH RD

1200

CROOKED
LAKE RD

Sand Lake

BEBB RD

SAND LAKE RD

131

Starvation
Lake

STARVATION LAKE RD

Eagle Lake

PERE MARQUETTE
STATE FOREST

CRAWFORD COUNTY

TWIN LAKE RD

Twin Lake

Indian
Lake

Squaw
Lake

Blue
Lake

1200

KALKASKA
COUNTY

1200

Little Twin
Lake

CR 571

Pickerel Lake

SPUR
TRAIL

Pickerel Lake
Campground

KENEL
RD

PAPOOSE
LAKE RD

BLUE
LAKE RD

Manistee
Lake

1200

© The Countryman Press

ELEVATION PROFILE

1,560 ft
1,380 ft
1,200 ft
1,020 ft
840 ft
660 ft

Warner Creek
Pathway

Pickerel Lake
Spur Trail

5   10   15   20   25   30 miles

You'll wind along several ponds and lakes through hilly terrain in a southerly direction. Cross Papoose Lake Road and immediately head west toward the spur trail to Pickerel Lake State Forest Campground. The spur trail goes 0.1 mile to the campground while the North Country Trail turns south at this intersection.

HOW TO FIND

The Warner Creek Pathway Trailhead is off MI 32 just 1.5 miles west of the intersection with US 131. The intersection is between the communities of Boyne Falls and Mancelona.

Pickerel Lake State Forest Campground is in the Pere Marquette State Forest. From from Mancelona, go south on Darragh Road (County Route 571 [CR 571]) 9.0 miles, and turn east (left) onto Manistee Lake Road (CR 612). In 4.0 miles, turn north on Sunset Trail Road. Follow the signs to the campground. From Grayling, take MI 72 west about 18.0 miles, turn north onto Darragh Road (CR 571), then right onto Manistee Lake Road (CR 612). From Kalkaska, take Nash Road (CR 612) to Darragh Road. Turn left (north), go 2.0 miles, and then go east (right) onto Manistee Lake Road (CR 612).

FACILITIES AND SERVICES

Backcountry camping is allowed in state forests but not in the Warner Creek/Jordan River Pathway areas (between MI 32 and Alba Road). There is a convenience store 1.0 mile west of the Starvation Road intersection, and Five Lakes has a picnic area.

Alba, 1.0 mile from the trail, has a post office and a convenience store with an ATM. Mancelona, 5.0 miles from the trail, has full services except medical.

THE HIKE

From the parking area, the trail goes through open areas, which can be weedy if not mowed recently. The well-used trail bends south as it follows the creek.

The trail crosses Warner Creek (a reliable water source) and O'Brien Pond at the 2.1-mile mark, which is on your left (east). This area has a lot of beaver activity and is quite scenic because of their activity. The local chapter works hard to keep the trail open through the use of puncheons and "beaver deceivers."

The trail comes to Jordan River Road at the 2.0-mile mark and uses it for about 0.5 mile before crossing to the other side of the road and following the Jordan River. This is a great place to go fishing, if you are so inclined. About 1.0 mile from the road, the Jordan River Trail Loop side trail intersection would bring you up a very steep climb to the top of Deadman's Hill. You'll continue to parallel the river along the base of the ridge, then over relatively flat terrain, and then you'll cross Jordan River Road. This area is also affected by beaver activity flooding the trail from time to time.

At the 6.0-mile mark you'll again follow Jordan River Road to the right, crossing the Jordan River at "Three Tubes." Continue hiking for several hundred yards until the trail turns left into the forest. Continue to parallel the river to the south from several hundred feet away. Your very scenic hike continues through the wooded valley with some ups and downs, occasionally touching the river. Enjoy a nice overlook just before Pinney Bridge Campground (10.6 miles), a rustic campground with 15 campsites. For the long-distance hiker, the nearest campsites are 26.7 miles to the south and 35.4 miles to the north.

The trail descends into the campground, and then follows the campground access road south to the Pinney Bridge Road and Cascade Road intersection (10.7 miles). Turn left onto Pinney Bridge Road and head south, which will take you on a climb up and out of the Jordan River Valley to the highlands and woods. Negotiate around the beginnings of a valley at an opening in the woods, then head southeast toward Cascade Road. You'll pass a sign noting the crossing of the 45th parallel: NORTH COUNTRY NATIONAL SCENIC TRAIL—4,600 MILES ONLY ONE 45 DEGREE N CROSSING.

At 12.5 miles, cross the gravel Cascade Road, and immediately cross Cascade Creek. Continue hiking along the ridge defining the Jordan River Valley, then negotiate around the source of Landslide Creek to Landslide Lookout. At this point the Michigan Department of Natural Resources Jordan River Pathway continues east along the valley lip, and the North Country Trail turns south on the Landslide Lookout access path, heading to the parking lot at the end of Harvey Road and a trailhead.

At 14.6 miles is the Harvey Road Trailhead. There are many hikers that will say that you've just finished one of the most beautiful hikes in the Lower Peninsula. From here, the topography and landscape change to a relatively flat, open landscape that starts out as a road walk through open farm country. But first, you'll hike into the woods on an old railroad grade for several hundred feet until you come out onto Harvey Road, turn right onto the road, and walk south.

Harvey Road crosses Alba Highway at the 16.1-mile mark. To the east 1.0 mile is unincorporated Alba. Keep hiking south; the road is blazed and flat to US 131 (17.0 miles), where Harvey Road changes names to Corey Road. The hik-

Thomas Funke

ROAD WALKS ARE NECESSARY TO CONNECT CERTIFIED SEGMENTS OF TRAIL SOUTH OF THE JORDAN RIVER VALLEY

ing continues to be flat through open farm country.

At 18.1 miles, turn left (east) on Doerr Road, which ends at Five Lakes (18.7 miles), a former picnic area with a high level of off-road vehicle use, which can make the trail hard to find in places. The area used to be a reliable water source and campground, but due to vandalism it has been closed—although you may still find remnant facilities. Take the trail around the south end of Five Lakes. The terrain is quite open and sandy.

At 19.4 miles, turn right (south) on

Cinder Hill Road. You'll follow the road for a short distance, then head southeast on a trail with a noticeable but gradual climb to the southeast. Cross Whispering Pines Drive (20.4 miles), and enter a small parcel of the Mackinaw State Forest as the trail levels out.

Cross Bocock Road (21.7 miles), and then you'll skirt the end of Scholl Road where it enters a wooded subdivision on your left (east). You are leaving the Mackinaw State Forest and—once you cross into Kalkaska County—entering the Pere Marquette State Forest. Walk under a power line and reenter the Mackinaw until you reach CR 38 in less than 0.5 mile (at the 24.2-mile mark).

Cross CR 38/Mancelona Road and note that the town of Mancelona is 4.0 miles to the west and has most services. Reenter the Mackinaw State Forest and head south on an old road, and cross Crooked Lake Road at the 24.6-mile mark.

Hike 0.3 mile past the road, crossing through open country, then 0.25 mile through a pine plantation on your east. Continue south on an old road until Sand Lake, and you'll start using

BEAVER POND NEAR DEADMAN'S HILL

Rob Burg

trail while negotiating around the small lake's beach in a clockwise direction. Be aware and keep your eyes open for where the North Country Trail splits from the beach walk. This may make a good bivouac campsite.

Cross Bebb Road (27.2 miles) and the trail will parallel Sand Lake Road. The trail crosses over Sand Lake Road in about 1.0 mile, to the right (west) side of the road through some pine plantations.

Cross Starvation Lake Road (31.2 miles), where there is roadside parking. For the next 4.5 miles, the trail will undulate up and down the rolling topography, cross several lightly used gravel roads, and pass several small lakes— coming into contact with Eagle Lake in 1.5 miles. You'll hear in the background the workings of numerous oil rigs.

The trail comes down to Eagle Lake (32.7 miles), which may make for a decent bivouac, then continues south through the second growth woodland. The trail climbs to the top of a hill, levels out, then descends to a gravel road. Use the gravel road to hike west 0.1 mile and back into the woods.

Cross Twin Lake Road (34.2 miles) and hike due south, cross Papoose Lake Road in 1.5 miles, turn right (due west), cross Kenel Road in 0.1 mile, and continue to head west up and down over small hills.

The Pickerel Lake Trail Spur is at the 37.0-mile mark, which is a marked intersection with the North Country Trail. Turn right (west), and Pickerel Lake State Forest Campground is 0.25 mile from the intersection and has 13 campsites.

Boardman River Headwaters

START: Spur trail to Pickerel Lake State Forest Campground

END: Guernsey Lake State Forest Campground

APPROXIMATE HIKING TIME: 10–14 hours

LENGTH OF SECTION: 22.1 miles

The North Country Trail can be a multiple-use trail. Usually, it means hikers are sharing with bicycles and other mechanized forms of travel—occasionally with horses. Up until recent years, the North Country Trail used the Shore to Shore Trail, a horse trail, in making its way to the Cadillac area. Thankfully, the local Grand Traverse Hiking Club has gone above and beyond, creating new trails in the state forest and allowing for a truly great hiking experience. The trail is well used and blazed and only shares the horse trail in a few places and only for short stretches.

After leaving Pickerel Lake, the trail is a nice tread for 1.3 miles before it comes out onto Manistee Lake Road for 7.3 miles of road walking. The road walk is blazed and intersects with the Shore to Shore Trail after the road changes names to State Road. Just before where State Road is crossed by a natural gas right-of-way, look for a gravel road (Foreman Drive NE) which parallels the right-of-way. Where Foreman Drive NE takes a slight bend to the left (south), the Shore to Shore Trail heads in an easterly direction through open country.

A recent major reroute of the trail by the Grand Traverse Hiking Club has taken most of the trail from this point to Guernsey Lake off the horse trail. Through the Kalkaska area, the North Country Trail enters Kalkaska in a lakeside neighborhood setting, then snakes its way through the woods into Kalkaska—to the main crossroads on the north end of the business district. Follow the blue blazes through surface streets to the west side of town, through the fairgrounds, then into the Pere Marquette State Forest.

The village of Kalkaska was settled in 1873 in anticipation of the arrival of the railroad. The assumption was cor-

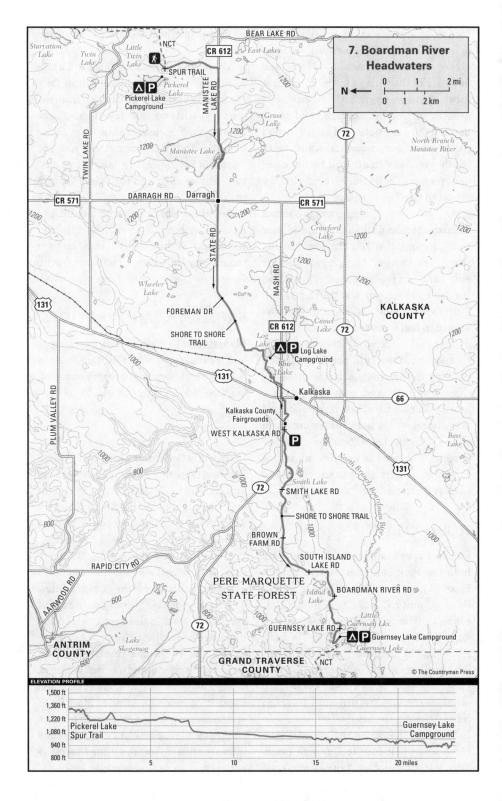

Starvation Lake

Twin Lake

Little Twin Lake

NCT

BEAR LAKE RD

CR 612

East Lakes

SPUR TRAIL

Pickerel Lake

Pickerel Lake Campground

MANISTEE LAKE RD

1200

Grass Lake

72

North Branch Manistee River

1200

TWIN LAKE RD

1200

Manistee Lake

CR 571

DARRAGH RD

Darragh

CR 571

1200

1200

Crawford Lake

1200

1200

STATE RD

Wheeler Lake

NASH RD

1200

1200

1200

131

FOREMAN DR

CR 612

Camel Lake

72

1200

KALKASKA COUNTY

SHORE TO SHORE TRAIL

Log Lake

Log Lake Campground

1000

131

Blue Lake

Kalkaska

66

Bass Lake

Kalkaska County Fairgrounds

WEST KALKASKA RD

P

131

1000

North Branch Boardman River

800

72

Smith Lake

SMITH LAKE RD

800

SHORE TO SHORE TRAIL

1000

BROWN FARM RD

1000

RAPID CITY RD

600

PLUM VALLEY RD

SOUTH ISLAND LAKE RD

PERE MARQUETTE STATE FOREST

Island Lake

BOARDMAN RIVER RD

AARWOOD RD

600

1000

Little Guernsey Lks.

72

Lake Skegemog

GUERNSEY LAKE RD

Guernsey Lake Campground

ANTRIM COUNTY

600

Guernsey Lake

GRAND TRAVERSE COUNTY

NCT

© The Countryman Press

7. Boardman River Headwaters

N ←

0   1   2 mi

0   1   2 km

ELEVATION PROFILE

1,500 ft
1,360 ft
1,220 ft
1,080 ft
940 ft
800 ft

Pickerel Lake Spur Trail

Guernsey Lake Campground

5   10   15   20 miles

rect, and the area was logged and lumber processed at the local sawmill. A massive fire in the summer of 1908 burnt the majority of the village to the ground. A local photographer, E. L. Beebe, was present with camera in hand and documented the destruction. He then turned the photos into postcards, which were wildly popular and are still found today and treated as collector's items. History repeated itself in 1910 and 1925.

In 1916, Ernest Hemingway visited and fished in the Kalkaska area, and later forever memorialized the town in his story "The Battler." Hemingway reportedly fished in the area, and a historical marker has been put in at the Rugg Pond Dam to document the one night he was known to fish from the pond.

The trail will wind its way mostly through new second growth and open country to the west, at times utilizing the horse trail and gravel roads but mostly on new trail. You'll pass several lakes in relatively flat country until you reach Guernsey Lake State Forest Campground. The area is lacking in mature forest—instead, it features an abundance of mixed oak and jack pine savannah.

HOW TO FIND

Pickerel Lake State Forest Campground is in the Pere Marquette State Forest. From Mancelona, go south on Darragh Road (County Route 571 [CR 571]) 9.0 miles, and turn east (left) onto Manistee Lake Road (CR 612). In 4.0 miles, turn right (north) on Sunset Trail Road. Follow the signs to the campground. From Grayling, take MI 72 west about 18.0 miles, turn right (north) onto Darragh Road (CR 571), then right onto Manistee Lake Road (CR 612). From Kalkaska, take Nash Road (CR 612) to Darragh Road. Turn left (north), go 2.0 miles, and then go east (right) onto Manistee Lake Road CR 612.

Guernsey Lake State Forest Campground is west of Cadillac in the Pere Marquette State Forest. Coming from the north, south, and east, take Island Lake Road from Kalkaska to the west about 8.0 miles to the campground. From the west and Traverse City, take MI 72 east to Williamsburg and turn right (south) to travel on Williamsburg Road for 3.5 miles, then left (east) onto Sand Lake Road (which changes names to Island Lake Road at the county line). Just past the county line, turn right (south) onto Guernsey Lake Road to the campground.

FACILITIES AND SERVICES

Manistee Lake has a convenience store and restaurant, while Kalkaska is a full-service town. Backcountry camping is allowed in the state forest.

THE HIKE

From the intersection of the spur trail to Pickerel Lake State Forest Campground and the North Country Trail, turn right and hike south on the North Country Trail in a maturing, mixed forest on a rather flat plain.

At Manistee Lake Road (1.8 miles), turn right (west) as your hike becomes a blazed road walk for the next 4.2 miles. There is a wide right-of-way on the south side of the road to the next intersection if you are so inclined. As you pass Manistee Lake, there is a small store with groceries, a phone, and outdoor vending.

At the 6.0-mile mark, cross Darragh Road; it changes its name to State Road and becomes gravel. On your left (south), you'll see a large amount of natural gas infrastructure. You are hiking in an area with major storage reservoirs for Mich-

OPEN SAVANNAHS CONSISTING OF JACK PINE ARE COMMONPLACE IN THE KALKASKA AREA

Thomas Funke

igan's natural gas supply. Just before a four-way intersection, look for a trailhead to the Shore to Shore Trail. It is immediately past Farrar Creek, which is an unreliable water source.

Turn left on Foreman Drive NE (9.0 miles), which is a gated and now closed to public vehicle use road. Hike 0.5 mile until it connects with the Shore to Shore Trail in 0.5 mile.

Welcome to the longest horseback trail in Michigan. This rutted, sandy affair has trail markers bearing horses and horseshoes as well as North Country Trail markers. You'll walk through open country, turn left (south) on a two track at the 9.6-mile mark, and leave the horse trail while merging with West Log Lake Road NE (9.9 miles) in a residential neighborhood. Log Lake Campground, a Kalkaska County park (11.8 miles) with

modern facilities and 60 campsites, is on your left—just before your next turn to the right (west) into the woods in 0.1 mile on an unnamed side street. Hike this narrow, gravel road into the woods. Stay left at the next intersection, then bear left on Shady Lane NE at the 12.0-mile mark. The narrow gravel road becomes a wide road walk through a residential neighborhood as you hike south to the next road.

At the 12.3-mile mark, turn right (west) onto Nash Road (CR 612) and immediately cross some active railroad tracks. Hike west into the commercial district of Kalkaska. Most services are located at the intersection of US 131 and CR 612.

Turn left (south) at US 131 (12.7 miles) and, one block south, turn right (west) onto Norway Street. Another block west, turn right (west) onto Arbor Street. Turn left (south) on South Birch Street, and continue your hike through residential neighborhoods.

Turn right (west) onto Courthouse Drive NW and enter the government campus for Kalkaska County. At the 13.4-mile mark, the trail enters (and cuts through the middle of) the Kalkaska County Fairgrounds.

Cross West Kalkaska Road (13.8 miles) and make a short jog to the left (south) and turn right (west) into the Pere Marquette State Forest. You'll parallel MI 72 in close proximity as you head west through open country. The trail comes to an escarpment at the top of a depression that holds Smith Lake (15.0 miles). Bear left (southwest) and hike south of the lake until it comes to the Shore to Shore Trail (15.7 miles).

Use the Shore to Shore Trail, the horseback trail, and hike east through open country. Cross Smith Lake Road (16.0 miles) and continue hiking through young, mixed, second growth forest. Cross Brown Farm Road (17.6 miles) and hike westerly through mixed and open forest and open fields; the trail then bends left (south).

The North Country Trail merges with a little-used gravel road, South Island Lake Road (19.1 miles). Island Lake is to your northwest. However, it is a very shallow lake with a marl bottom—in dry years, you'll sink in the marl if you try to access the water. In 0.1 mile, you'll cross South Island Lake Road again. Continue south to where the North Country Trail and the Shore to Shore Trail split at the 20.1-mile mark

The Shore to Shore Trail goes left (south), and the North Country Trail bears right (west), crossing Boardman River Road NW in a few hundred feet. Your hike winds in a westerly direction through a mix of open fields, savannahs of mixed oak and pine, pine forests, and oak forests. Crisscross an old road, Mustang Road, in several places before coming out to Guernsey Lake Road.

At the 21.5-mile mark, cross Guernsey Lake Road, which is a wide gravel road at this point. The access drive to Guernsey Lake State Forest Campground is 0.1 mile to the south, and it leads to a rustic campground with 38 campsites. From the campground, there is a spur trail from the day use parking lot that goes northwest and reconnects with the North Country Trail. Terrain continues to be a heterogeneous mix of forests and fields.

Hike to the spur trail to Guernsey Lake State Forest Campground, which is 0.3 mile to the service road and another 0.2 mile up the service road to the campground.

8

Boardman River

START: Guernsey Lake State Forest Campground

END: Mayfield Road

APPROXIMATE HIKING TIME: 8–10 hours

LENGTH OF SECTION: 17.4 miles

Until recent years, the North Country Trail utilized the Shore to Shore Trail, a horseback riding trail. The Grand Traverse Hiking Club has created many miles of new trail to create a premier hiking experience.

Hikers leaving Guernsey Lake will hike west to Scheck's Place State Forest Campground through rolling topography and varied habitats. The Pere Marquette State Forest is mostly young mixed hardwood and pine forest that weaves its way around several small lakes in this stretch.

After Scheck's Place, cross the Boardman River and head southwest into the Manistee River watershed. South of the Boardman is a varying landscape showing different types and stages of forestry. At Mayfield Road, the trail turns due south toward the Fife Lake area. After Cedar Creek Road, the trail has to snake around some swampy areas. After crossing MI 186, head east toward Fife Lake, then south through rolling terrain and areas where you'll again see varying stages of forest growth.

Continue south, and use the isthmus to pass between two of the Headquarters Lake using a maintained road, then parallel one of the lakes. At the southern end of the lake, you'll begin a 70.0-mile hike that parallels the Fife Lake Outlet and then the Manistee River. Fife Lake runs southwest, and the trail is in near proximity to it for most of your trek until it empties into the Manistee River. The trail will use the Number Four Road and then come back to a valley with Fife Lake's outlet into the Manistee; the Manistee is also cradled by a deep and steep river valley as it winds across US 131 to the Old US 131 Campground. The habitats continue to be a mix of open country and forest.

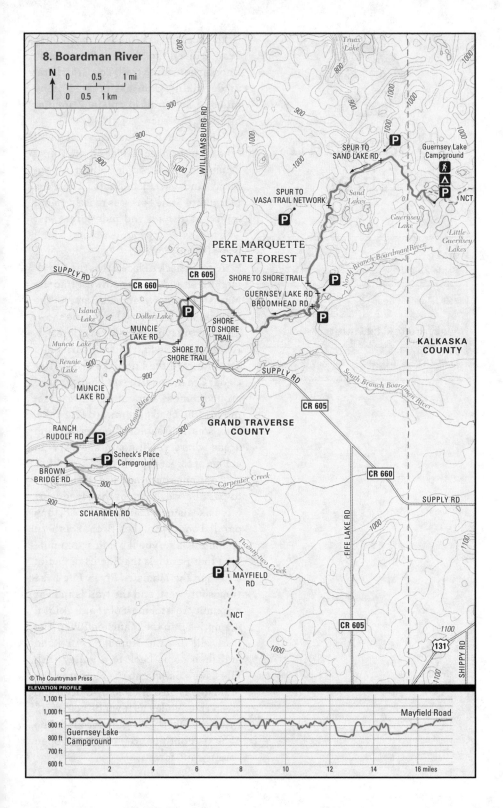

8. Boardman River

N
0   0.5   1 mi
0   0.5   1 km

Truax Lake

Guernsey Lake Campground

NCT

SPUR TO SAND LAKE RD

Sand Lakes

Guernsey Lake

Little Guernsey Lakes

SPUR TO VASA TRAIL NETWORK

PERE MARQUETTE STATE FOREST

WILLIAMSBURG RD

SUPPLY RD

CR 660

CR 605

SHORE TO SHORE TRAIL

North Branch Boardman River

GUERNSEY LAKE RD
BROOMHEAD RD

KALKASKA COUNTY

Island Lake

Dollar Lake

MUNCIE LAKE RD

SHORE TO SHORE TRAIL

Muncie Lake

SHORE TO SHORE TRAIL

Rennie Lake

MUNCIE LAKE RD

SUPPLY RD

South Branch Boardman River

CR 605

Boardman River

GRAND TRAVERSE COUNTY

RANCH RUDOLF RD

Scheck's Place Campground

BROWN BRIDGE RD

Carpenter Creek

CR 660

SUPPLY RD

SCHARMEN RD

FIFE LAKE RD

Twenty-two Creek

MAYFIELD RD

NCT

CR 605

131

SHIPPY RD

© The Countryman Press

ELEVATION PROFILE

1,100 ft
1,000 ft
900 ft
800 ft Guernsey Lake
700 ft Campground
600 ft

Mayfield Road

2   4   6   8   10   12   14   16 miles

HOW TO FIND

Guernsey Lake State Forest Campground is west of Cadillac in the Pere Marquette State Forest. Coming from the north, south, and east, take Island Lake Road from Kalkaska to the west about 8.0 miles to the campground. From the west and Traverse City, take MI 72 west to Williamsburg, turn left (south) on Williamsburg Road, travel for 3.5 miles, then turn east (left) onto Sand Lake Road, which changes names to Island Lake Road at the county line. Just past the county line, turn south (right) onto Guernsey Lake Road to the campground.

At Mayfield Road, there isn't a parking lot, only roadside parking. From Kingsley and MI 113, take County Route 611 (CR 611) north to Mayfield Road, turn right (east), and drive 6.0 miles until you see the signs marking where the trail crosses the road.

FACILITIES AND SERVICES

Backcountry camping is allowed in state forest.

THE HIKE

From the intersection of the spur trail to Guernsey Lake State Forest Campground and the North Country Trail, turn left and hike east and cross an outlet creek from the lake. Hike southwest and then bend northwest through rolling terrain with an open canopy of hardwoods and pines before merging with a forest road.

At the 1.2-mile mark you'll come to an intersection with a spur trail to Sand Lake Road to the north. The trail bends to the southwest and passes a small, unnamed lake at 1.6 miles and another at 2.4 miles. Both may make good biv-ouac camping sites. The trail bends left (southerly) after the second lake.

At the 2.8-mile mark is another intersection with a trail to the Vasa Trail Network, which is 4.0 miles to the west; a parking lot allows access to both the Vasa and North Country Trail 0.7 mile to the west on North Broomhead Road. At this point, you are hiking in a southerly direction.

Descend to Sand Lake (3.0 miles) and continue south through young forest. Walk in the lake basin up and over a ridge and back into a depression in the forest. Cross the Shore to Shore Trail (4.4 miles), then cross Guernsey Lake Road 0.2 mile to the south; 0.5 mile later, cross North Broomhead Road. The trail will descend to the Boardman River.

At the 5.2-mile mark, you'll begin to parallel the North Branch Boardman River. Cross Broomhead Road (with parking) and then a power line as you continue to follow the north branch of the Boardman River through second growth and open forest. The trail will follow the escarpment at times and descend into the river valley in a southwesterly direction.

At the 6.5-mile mark, the trail peels away from the north branch of the Boardman River, turns to the northwest, and moves through open hardwood and pine forest. Going up and over a few hills leads to a steeper climb to the Shore to Shore Trail (7.2 miles).

After crossing the horse trail, the habitat changes to mostly open pine savannah and small openings in the young forest. Just before crossing CR 605 at the 8.0-mile mark, the habitat becomes mostly open fields with scattered trees.

Cross the paved CR 605 back into open habitats, then cross the paved CR 660 (with parking) and head downhill to Dollar Lake (8.5 miles), which may make a good bivouac. Head south, up out of the depression holding the lake, level out, then head down into a bowl-like depression as you hike in a southerly direction. The trail will bend right (westerly) and cross the horse trail twice before reaching Muncie Lake Road. Habitats are very open, mostly open fields with scattered young trees.

Cross Muncie Lake Road (9.5 miles) and hike west across mostly level ground, turn south over mostly rolling and open terrain, and then southwesterly as you cross Muncie Lake Road for a second time at the 2.0-mile mark past your first crossing. The trail parallels the road and crosses Muncie Lake Road again for a third time at the 12.0-mile mark.

Within a few hundred feet you'll come to a parking lot accessed by Ranch Rudolf Road, which you'll cross in 0.2 mile. Hike west, and you'll come to a two track in the woods in 0.2 mile. Hike this southeast and it will cross Brown Bridge Road and become the entrance to Scheck's Place State Forest Campground, a rustic state forest campground with 30 campsites on the Boardman River. To reconnect with the North Country Trail, take the Shore to Shore Trail west 0.5 mile (or backtrack, although taking the horse trail is considerably shorter).

Cross the Boardman River on Brown Bridge Road at the 13.0-mile mark. Leave the road walk to your left and hike east along the south bank of the river; at 0.4 mile, the trail climbs up and over a steep hill in a southerly direction. The hill is more forested than the slopes on either side. Hike another 0.5 mile, cross the Shore to Shore Trail, and come out to a gravel road and utility right-of-way.

Cross the utility right-of-way (14.2 miles), hike 0.2 mile south, turn east, and cross the Shore to Shore Trail in a few hundred feet. The habitat becomes more forested, albeit with young pines and oaks. The trail will turn south in another 0.2 mile after crossing the horse trail.

Cross the gravelly Scharmen Road, bending easterly through the open, young forest, and descend downhill—bending east, climbing back up in elevation, and crossing Scharman Road again. Climb slightly, then descend into a valley. This may make an excellent bivouac.

At the 15.4-mile mark, hike along and parallel Twenty-two Creek through a maturing forest growing in the stream valley for 0.3 mile, then climb up out of the valley to more level ground and younger, open forest. The trail goes south for 0.3 mile, turns slightly south of east, crosses an intermittent stream in about 1.0 mile, then turns south toward Mayfield Road, which is reached at the 17.6-mile mark.

9

Fife Lake and Manistee River

START: Mayfield Road

END: Old US-131 State Forest Campground

APPROXIMATE HIKING TIME: 6–9 hours

LENGTH OF SECTION: 18.2 miles

For this hike, you'll be entering the Pere Marquette State Forest and the Manistee River watershed. The Pere Marquette's namesake should be a familiar one by now for the long-distance hiker, having been named after Father Jacques Marquette. At over 235,000 acres in size, it covers parts of 13 counties.

Your hike brings you to the outskirts of Fife Lake, a small village founded in 1872. The village began as a lumbering town, fueled by the operation of the Grand Rapids and Indiana Railroad. Most of the buildings are still the original ones built soon after the town was founded. The population grew to three hundred in 1877, and by 1885 the number of residents had grown to one thousand. The village was mainly meeting the needs of the many nearby lumbering camps. After the lumber boom, as with most towns, the population declined, but it has since rebounded some due to second homes and tourism in the area.

Hike south, through the state forest, and follow a tributary of the Manistee River that flows south out of Fife Lake, through the Headquarters Lakes, and on to the Manistee River. The name *Manistee* is thought to be an Odawa word. There is some debate about its meaning, but it may be from *ministigweyaa*, or "river with islands at its mouth."

Europeans would have been smart to name it the Grayling River, as it was once known for its world-class grayling fishery. This fishery thrived until the logging boom, when the river was used as a highway to move logs. To move logs, loggers frequently slid them down the banks, and the river was severely degraded. The grayling have since disappeared from the river.

This large river was ideal for the

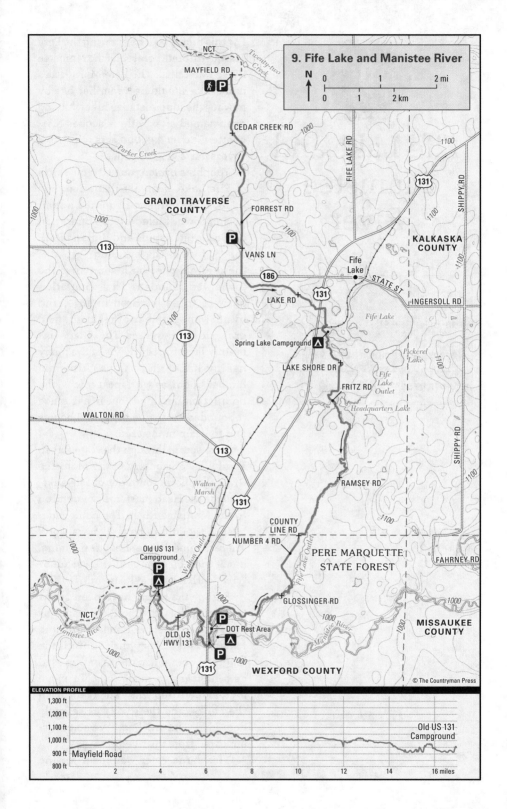

9. Fife Lake and Manistee River

N

| 0 | | 1 | | 2 mi |
| 0 | 1 | | 2 km | |

NCT

MAYFIELD RD

CEDAR CREEK RD

Twenty-two Creek

Parker Creek

1000

1100

FIFE LAKE RD

1100

131

SHIPPY RD

**GRAND TRAVERSE
COUNTY**

FORREST RD

**KALKASKA
COUNTY**

1000

P

VANS LN

113

186

Fife
Lake

STATE ST

INGERSOLL RD

131

1100

LAKE RD

Fife Lake

113

1100

Spring Lake Campground

LAKE SHORE DR

*Fife
Lake
Outlet*

*Pickerel
Lake*

1100

FRITZ RD

Headquarters Lake

WALTON RD

113

RAMSEY RD

1100

SHIPPY RD

1100

*Walton
Marsh*

COUNTY
LINE RD

NUMBER 4 RD

Fife Lake Outlet

**PERE MARQUETTE
STATE FOREST**

FAHRNEY RD

1000

131

Old US 131
Campground

P

Walton Outlet

1000

1000

1000

NCT

GLOSSINGER RD

Manistee River

**MISSAUKEE
COUNTY**

Manistee River

DOT Rest Area

OLD US
HWY 131

P

P

1000

131

WEXFORD COUNTY

© The Countryman Press

ELEVATION PROFILE

1,300 ft								
1,200 ft								
1,100 ft								
1,000 ft								Old US 131 Campground
900 ft	Mayfield Road							
800 ft								
	2	4	6	8	10	12	14	16 miles

movement of lumber downstream to sawmills. The Manistee is wide, has relatively stable flows, and there are few places where logs get jammed up. White pine logs, some exceeding 5 feet in diameter, were floated downriver to Manistee to be processed. The boom lasted from about 1890 to 1910.

Today, the Manistee is considered one of the best trout fisheries in the United States, which is surprising once you know the history. You'll end this segment's hike at the Old US 131 State Forest Campground. Take some time to do some fishing, and to write a thank-you card to the volunteers of the local chapter for creating such a great hiking experience.

HOW TO FIND

At Mayfield Road, there is no parking lot—only roadside parking. From Kingsley and MI 113, take County Route 611 (CR 611) north to Mayfield Road, turn east (right), and drive 6.0 miles while keeping your eyes open for the signs marking where the trail crosses the road.

The southern end of this segment is at Old US 131 State Forest Campground. Located off of US 131 between Manton and Fife Lake and at the county line between Grand Traverse and Wexford, take East County Line Road to the west a few hundred feet, then jog south onto Old US 131. The campground entrance is on the west side of the road in 1.6 miles.

FACILITIES AND SERVICES

Off trail camping is allowed in the state forest. Fife Lake has a convenience store, restaurants, a motel, and banks with ATMs.

THE HIKE

Cross the gravel Mayfield Road, then cross an intermittent stream in 0.2 mile and head mostly south. You will pass an oil pumping station on your right, and then the trail will merge with a little-used road as it continues south through open forest to the next road, Cedar Creek Road, at the 1.1-mile mark.

Continue in a southerly direction and enter a swampy area where the trail meanders a bit to utilize some ridges and hills in order to keep your feet dry. Wind through this more forested area for 1.0 mile and the trail comes out onto the seasonal Forest Road, which makes a straight shot to the south and crosses the paved Vans Lane (2.9 miles).

Vans Lane is a paved road; on the south side of the road there are two parking spots. Hike due south through a short stretch of private land to MI 189 at the 3.4-mile mark. The Shore to Shore Trail crosses the North Country Trail at this intersection.

Share the southeasterly horse trail for 0.3 mile; the trails will split, and you'll continue east and then southeast. The terrain is slightly rolling and the forest is more mature with nearly complete canopy coverage. Cross an old road in 0.4 mile, another in 0.3 mile, and another in 0.2 mile, finally coming out of the forest to Lake Road in another 0.1 mile at the 4.7-mile mark.

Cross Lake Road and continue southeast over rolling, forested terrain to the outskirts of Fife Lake. Cross the busy US 131 and head onto Fourth Street (5.2 miles). In 0.1 mile, turn right (south) onto the trail, up a long hill and onto an old road. Descend downhill and cross over a permanent water hole via a substantial bridge in the ravine. In 0.6 mile, cross a set of railroad tracks and immediately come to the entry drive to the Spring Lake State Forest Campground, a rustic campground with 32 campsites.

The trail continues downhill to the lake using the boat launch access road; at the lake it continues into the woods. From here to Ramsey Road, the forest is a patchwork defined by firebreaks, and each square mile section of forest is a different composition and age. Hike up and out of the bowl holding Spring Lake and over rolling topography to Lake Shore Drive at the 6.9-mile mark.

Upon crossing Lake Shore Drive, the trail negotiates around a depression in a clockwise direction to the east, then heads due south on a firebreak. In about 0.5 mile, the trail turns westerly, then southwesterly to Fritz Road.

Use Fritz Road (8.7 miles) to cross a channel connecting two of the Headquarters Lakes, which leaves the road to the left (east) in 0.3 mile. Follow the shore of the undeveloped lake, which may make a good bivouac. Hike along the lake for about 1.7 miles until you come to an outlet at the southern point of the lake.

Leave the Headquarters Lakes area (10.7 miles), and welcome to the Manistee River watershed. For long-distance hikers, you'll be in this wild and scenic area for several days as you exit the Pere Marquette and enter the Manistee National Forest. The trail follows the more forested Fife Lake outlet south, losing elevation slightly. If you find water anywhere along this stream, it could make a good bivouac.

At the 12.0-mile mark cross Ramsey Road, and continue to follow the Fife Lake outlet. There is the occasional large tree but you'll notice that conservation forestry practices come close to both sides of the creek.

The trail will turn to the right, parallel East County Line Road (13.4 miles) for about 0.1 mile, then cross to the south. You will immediately come to a fork in the road, and on your right will be West Road; hike it for 0.1 mile southwest and turn right onto Number 4 Road in order to avoid private land to the east. Number 4 Road traverses in a southwesterly direction through open forest and open fields.

At the 14.1-mile mark, the road walk ends and you leave Number 4 Road and hike into and along a pine plantation to the southeast, move through a mostly open field, and then travel back into the forested stream valley to the Fife Lake outlet (14.6 miles).

The trail merges and begins to parallel the outlet stream, winding through the forest in a mostly southwest direction. Pass by the terminus of Glossinger Road in 0.9 mile; in 1.7 miles, the trail will climb up out of the valley.

At the 16.0-mile mark, you'll see the Number 4 Road about 0.1 mile away to your north. To your south is the Manistee River; the Fife Lake outlet has finally emptied into this large river, which has carved a valley in the sandy soils. Hiking along the Manistee will be a test of your directional awareness—you'll wind in pretty much every direction as you follow the river valley through the forest.

Enter a Michigan Department of Transportation rest area (16.5 miles) and hike on the sidewalk past the boat launch and follow the river to the east. The rest area is closed in the winter months.

At the 17.0-mile mark you'll find a parking area for the US 131 trailhead and crossing. The parking lot for hikers is near the boat launch. The highway is on your right; cross the highway (to the west side) under the US 131 bridge, turn north, and in 0.8 mile cross an intermittent stream before heading west, winding through the woods.

At the 18.2-mile mark, cross the old highway (Old US 131, which is still in use) and follow the trail into the campground. The trail continues westerly between the canoe camper area and the main campground. The Old US 131 State Forest Campground, a rustic camping space with 25 sites, is on the shore of the Manistee River.

Manistee River–Wexford County East

This will be a very memorable stretch of trail. For the majority of this hike, you will be overlooking the Manistee River. Be prepared for many climbs, and it will seem there are more ascents than descents. There will be several views where you are several hundred feet above the river with, in every direction, not a sign of humans. It is hard to believe that such an area exists in the Lower Peninsula.

Although not a roadless area, the hike will definitely give you that feel. From the Old US 131 State Forest Campground, it is a 6.0-mile hike before you have to negotiate around some private land—and then you'll have another 7.0 miles before crossing MI 37. A mix of road walks and trails for the remaining part of your hike will bring you back to civilization.

HOW TO FIND

The eastern end of this segment is at Old US 131 State Forest Campground. Located off of US 131 between Manton and Fife Lake (at the county line between Grand Traverse and Wexford), take East County Line Road to the west a few hundred feet and then jog south onto Old US 131. The campground entrance is on the west side of the road in 1.6 miles.

The west end of the segment is at the terminus of Number 19 Road at the Manistee River. From Buckley at the intersection of Number 4 Road and Number 17 Road, take Number 4 Road east 1.0 mile, turn south on Number 19 Road, and drive almost 2.0 miles to the end.

FACILITIES AND SERVICES

This is a very rustic stretch, so there is nothing of note.

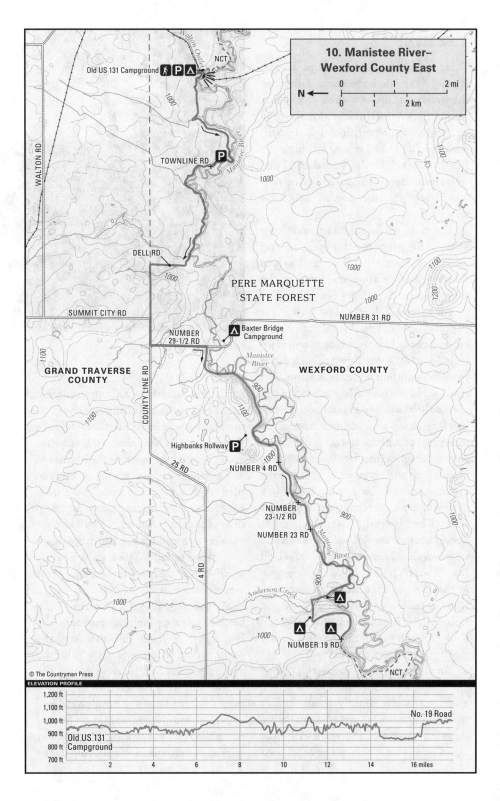

10. Manistee River–
Wexford County East

0   1   2 mi

N ◄——

0   1   2 km

Old US 131 Campground

NCT

Walton Outlet

WALTON RD

1000

Manistee River

TOWNLINE RD

1000

DELL RD

1000

SUMMIT CITY RD

PERE MARQUETTE
STATE FOREST

NUMBER 31 RD

1000

1100

1200

1100

NUMBER
29-1/2 RD

Baxter Bridge
Campground

Manistee River

900

GRAND TRAVERSE
COUNTY

WEXFORD COUNTY

COUNTY LINE RD

1100

1100

1100

Highbanks Rollway

NUMBER 4 RD

1000

25 RD

NUMBER
23-1/2 RD

NUMBER 23 RD

900

1000

4 RD

Manistee River

1000

Anderson Creek

900

1000

NUMBER 19 RD

NCT

© The Countryman Press

ELEVATION PROFILE

1,200 ft									
1,100 ft								No. 19 Road	
1,000 ft									
900 ft									
800 ft	Old US 131								
700 ft	Campground								
	2	4	6	8	10	12	14	16 miles	

THE HIKE

This segment may be blazed orange as it is part of the Fife Lake Route. Hike into the woods and cross Walton Outlet in a small valley. A trail intersection will give you the choice of turning right (north) onto the Fife Lake Loop or left onto the North Country Trail. Choose left, head westerly, and you are afforded an incredible view of the river as you walk high on a bluff.

The trail will undulate up and down slopes. Be prepared for climbs and descents! The trail will come down to the river before Townline Road at the 2.8-mile mark.

Your hike will skirt the Manistee River as you wind your way through heavy forest dominated by beech, maple, and hemlock. At 0.7 mile you'll switchback down to an intermittent stream crossing. The trail will follow just below the top of the river valley with good views of the river. You'll negotiate a ravine, and in about 2.0 miles cross another intermittent stream where it empties into the Manistee River. Hike along the river another 0.3 mile, cross another tributary, and follow a valley along an intermittent stream as the trail bends north. The trail will cross a couple of gas line right-of-ways and end up on an abandoned road (formerly Dell Road), which takes you north to a gate at the County Line Road intersection (the 6.2-mile mark). Turn left (west) on County Line Road, which will be a road walk through farmland that is scantily marked with connector blazes.

Turn left (south) on Number 29.5 Road (7.7 miles), walk downhill, cross a creek, and then climb slightly uphill before descending to the Manistee River. Before crossing the river, the trail will start again on the west side of the road. Bax-

THE MANISTEE RIVER

Rob Fahndrich

ter Bridge State Forest Campground, a rustic campground with 25 campsites on the Manistee River, is another 0.25 mile to the south on Number 29.5 Road after you cross the bridge across the Manistee.

Leaving the road at the 9.9-mile mark, turn right to enter the woods on a well-used tread, which immediately climbs up to another bluff. Again, you will experience many scrambles up and drops down over steep terrain. The area is heavily wooded but you are afforded many fine views of the river.

At the 12.3-mile mark is the Highbanks Rollway, which has parking. The Highbanks Rollway dates back to the early 1900s, when logs were piled up along the banks of the river during the winter and then released to roll down into the river once spring thaw had occurred and the logs could be floated down the river to the mills. The rollway region was also used extensively by the local Native Americans as a hunting and fishing area. The trail continues with its repertoire of climbs and descents through the woods as it negotiates the many ravines and the numerous hills created by the river as it winds through the sandy landscape. In the process, you will cross two little-used roads, Number 4 and Number 23.5 Roads.

About 0.5 mile past Number 23.5 Road, cross the remnants of Number 23 Road (14.8 miles), continue on westward along the bluff, then descend down to the river. The trail will peel away to the north and use the Anderson Creek drainage to climb in elevation. Look for a backcountry campsite at Anderson Creek at the 16.4-mile mark.

Anderson Creek is a mostly reliable stream. Hike north, turn left (west), descend to cross Anderson Creek, hike up out of the valley, turn south, and hike the bluff and follow it through the woods. You'll pass by the end of Number 19 Road (17.9 miles), which ends at the Manistee River and is a popular spot for partiers. This may be a good place for a bivouac, especially if you can find a spot several hundred feet away from the end of the road.

Manistee and Mason Counties

START: Number 19 Road

END: Marilla Trailhead Spur/Eddington Creek

APPROXIMATE HIKING TIME: 6–8 hours

LENGTH OF SECTION: 15.2 miles

This segment of the trail continues to impress, with the sweeping views of the Manistee River, the deep forests, and the solitude offered by the trail. The trail ends at the north end of the Hodenpyl Dam.

Hodenpyl Dam Pond was created in 1924–25 when the eponymous dam (originally called "County Line Dam") was constructed. Hodenpyl Dam Pond is approximately 4.5 miles long and, at full pool, it has a surface area of 2,025 acres and creates a normal head of 71 feet. The impoundment has become a destination for anglers, as it has an excellent fishery—both stocked by the Michigan Department of Natural Resources and native.

This last segment, from Number 17 Road to the Marilla Trailhead Spur Trail, is newly created, more direct to the Manistee National Forest, and reduces the amount of road walking. It brings you within 1.0 mile of Mesick, a small community with most services. The trail crosses MI 115 and bisects the Hodenpyl Dam Pond in the East–West direction past a few backcountry campsites. The Manistee River Trail, a loop trail around the river in between Hodenpyl and Tippy Dams, is a very popular hiking trail. This segment will end where the Marilla Trail Spur and the North Country Trail/Manistee River intersect at Eddington Creek.

HOW TO FIND

The northeast end of the segment is at the terminus of Number 19 Road at the Manistee River. From Buckley at the intersection of Number 4 Road and Number 17 Road, take Number 4 Road east 1.0 mile, turn south on Number 19 Road, and drive almost 2.0 miles to the end.

Marilla Trailhead (the west/south end) is off MI 115 near Mesick. MI 115

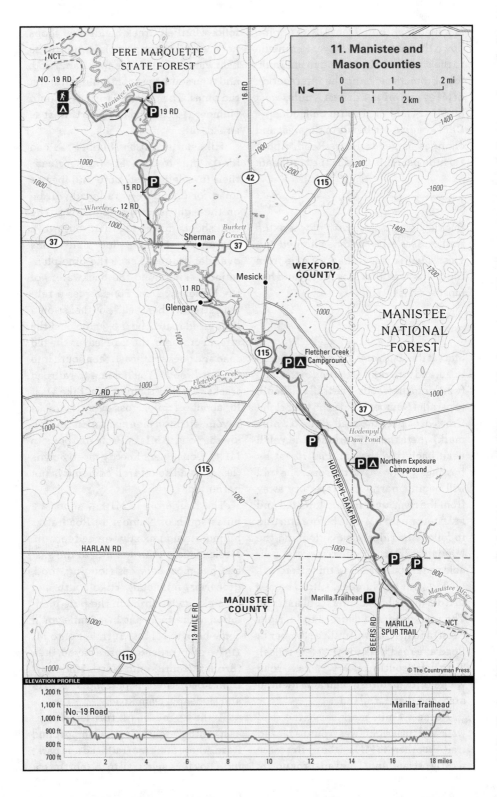

NCT

PERE MARQUETTE
STATE FOREST

NO. 19 RD

16 RD

1400

Manistee River

P

P 19 RD

1000

1000

1000

1000

1200

1200

115

1600

1400

P

15 RD

42

12 RD

Wheeler Creek

1000

Burkett
Creek

Sherman

37

37

1200

WEXFORD
COUNTY

Mesick

MANISTEE
NATIONAL
FOREST

11 RD

Glengary

1000

1000

115

Fletcher Creek
Campground

P △

Fletcher Creek

7 RD

1000

1000

Hodenpyl
Dam Pond

37

P

1000

1000

115

P △ Northern Exposure
Campground

HODENPYL DAM RD

HARLAN RD

1000

1000

P

P

800

Manistee River

1000

MANISTEE
COUNTY

Marilla Trailhead P

13 MILE RD

BEERS RD

MARILLA
SPUR TRAIL

NCT

1000

115

© The Countryman Press

ELEVATION PROFILE

No. 19 Road

Marilla Trailhead

1,200 ft
1,100 ft
1,000 ft
900 ft
800 ft
700 ft

2   4   6   8   10   12   14   16   18 miles

is a diagonal route from US 127 going down the center of the Lower Peninsula to the shore of Lake Michigan at Frankfort. From Mesick and the intersection of MI 37 and MI 115, drive 1.5 miles west on MI 115 and turn south on Hodenpyl Dam Road, which bends to the west and changes names to Beers Road. About 1.0 mile past this bend is the trailhead.

FACILITIES AND SERVICES

Buckley is 2.5 miles north of where the trail crosses MI 37 and has limited services. Mesick is less than 1.0 mile from the trail where it crosses MI 115 and has most services.

THE HIKE

Start at the south of the end of Number 19 Road, and turn right at the end of the road (west) into the woods. The trail will begin to parallel Number 19 Road on your right. Cross back over the road at the 0.7 mile mark, where there is parking, and you'll head back into the national forest by turning right (west) off the road. The trail will begin a northwest trajectory away from the river, over mostly forested and level terrain for 0.4 mile before starting to follow the ridgeline overlooking the Manistee River. There are several reliable water sources along this stretch.

At 2.9 miles, Number 15 Road comes in from the right and intersects the trail. The road bends 90 degrees to its right (west) and the trail will utilize Number 12 Road as a road walk to MI 37 (3.3 miles). Turn left (south) on MI 37 as a road walk—through forest, then a residential area, and then farmland.

At the 4.7-mile mark, leave the road walk and turn right (west) onto a blazed trail. From here to MI 115, the trail crosses mostly private land. The trail turns north, follows Burkett Creek, bends west, loops northwest through pine plantation to the backwaters of the Hodenpyl Dam Pond, and then southwest continuing through the pines. The trail will turn right onto Number 11 Road and head northwest as a road walk.

Hike northwest on Number 11 Road for 0.4 mile to Glengary (no services), then turn left (west) onto Number 14 Road for 0.1 mile—a trailhead will be on the right (south) side of road. The trail shoots due south, then southwest, continuing through pine plantations over flat ground. Leave the pine plantations, skirt along the backwaters of the Hodenpyl Dam Pond, cross a reliable stream, then head southeast on a little-used road. About 0.3 mile past the stream crossing, the trail leaves the old road and goes southeast, then south into the hardwoods. You'll come to railroad tracks, parallel them as you hike west for about 0.1 mile, cross over the tracks to your left into a pine plantation, and follow the pond to MI 115. From this point to MI 37, Consumers Energy mostly owns the land and so off-trail camping is not permitted.

The trail crosses MI 115 about 2.2 miles south of Number 14 Road after hiking through mostly wooded terrain. Mesick is less than 1.0 mile to the east and has most services (lodging, food, groceries, financial). Hike south and loop clockwise through the pine plantation to the pond, and in 0.8 mile you'll come back to MI 115. Turn left onto MI 115 (west) in order to cross a bayou, then turn left (south) onto North Hodenpyl Dam Road. There is parking at MI 115 and Hodenpyl Dam Road.

At the 9.5-mile mark, turn left (southeast) onto Fletcher Creek Campground Road, where there is a trailhead and parking. Look for a spur trail to the northwest leading to Fletcher Creek Campground, a rustic campground. About 0.4 mile further is a backcountry site on the shores of the pond. Hike southwest along the shore of Hodenpyl Dam Pond. The trail continues through woods along the pond, and comes to the intersection of (and a trailhead at) Manistee River Road and North Hodenpyl Dam Road.

Hike along the pond's edge and cut west through open woods and a small park, which parallels Manistee River Road and the water's edge. At the 11.8-mile mark, enter the private Northern Exposure Campground, RV, and Recreation Park, which has parking and four campsites designated for backpackers.

The trail leaves the mature forests of Northern Exposure and becomes young, open forest as it follows the boundary between forest and a wet area. The trail crosses a reliable stream, and continues along the heavily wooded shoreline of the pond.

After another 3.2 miles of hiking along the pond, you will come out to Hodenpyl Road. Turn left and walk west, cross into Manistee County, and turn right to stay

A HIKER TREADS ALONG ON THE NORTH COUNTRY TRAIL

Rob Burg

on Hodenpyl Dam Road—look for the trailhead on your left. If you miss the trailhead, the road changes names to Beers Road. In 0.1 mile, the North Country Trail leaves the road and goes south, where there is a parking lot. This is also the trailhead for the Manistee River Trail. The trail follows the contour and slightly climbs up the ridge of a valley cradling a small stream. Along the way, you'll pass another trail intersection for the Manistee River Trail, which goes south.

Another 1.3 miles, and you'll find yourself at the intersection of the Manistee River Trail and Marilla Spur Trail. The trail spur goes north to the Marilla Trailhead on Beers Road for 1.3 miles to a parking lot.

Manistee National Forest–Little Manistee River

START: High Bridge Road access/Manistee River Bridge

END: Spur trail to Bear Track Campground

APPROXIMATE HIKING TIME: 5–7 hours

LENGTH OF SECTION: 11.8 miles

The one thing you will notice about hiking in the Manistee National Forest is that the trail takes you through mostly closed-canopy, mature forests. This is a departure from most of your hike so far from the Mackinaw Bridge, where you've experienced all kinds of habitat—open fields, open canopy forest, and pine plantations. Enjoy your forested hike through the national forest as, when you leave it south of here, you'll be back to mostly open habitats dominated by human activities.

Your hike in this section stays the course up near a bluff, although lower, but does not come into contact with the Manistee. The trail comes out of the Manistee at Chicago Avenue, where you'll need to take a road walk. In the past, there were landowners in the area who were unfriendly and known to harass hikers and remove trail markers. Although there haven't been any problems in recent years, it may be a good idea to be aware of this situation on Chicago, Michigan, and Huff Roads.

Cross the Pine River using Huff Road, then reconnect with the North Country Trail to get to the popular Udell Trailhead. South of MI 55, mountain bikes are permitted. Although hikers have the right-of-way and bikes should yield, be aware of your surroundings as this stretch of trail probably sees more mountain bike activity than hiking. The trail will undulate through the national forest, cross the Little Manistee River at Nine Mile Bridge, and bend east through the forest and Dead Horse Marsh to Tyndal Road and then the spur trail at Bear Track Campground.

HOW TO FIND

High Bridge/Manistee River Bridge, in the Manistee National Forest, is just

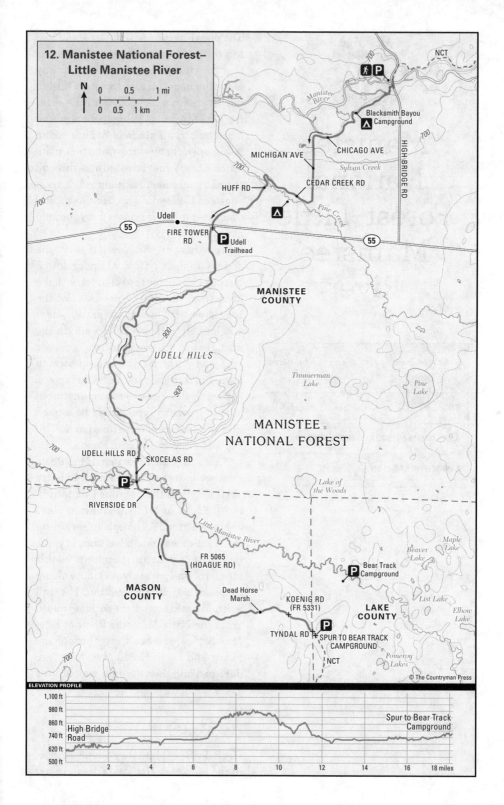

12. Manistee National Forest–Little Manistee River

N

0   0.5   1 mi
0 0.5 1 km

NCT

Manistee River

Blacksmith Bayou Campground

CHICAGO AVE

MICHIGAN AVE

Sylvan Creek

HIGH BRIDGE RD

700

HUFF RD

CEDAR CREEK RD

Pine Creek

Udell

55

FIRE TOWER RD

Udell Trailhead

55

MANISTEE COUNTY

900

UDELL HILLS

900

MANISTEE NATIONAL FOREST

Timmerman Lake

Pine Lake

700

UDELL HILLS RD

SKOCELAS RD

RIVERSIDE DR

Lake of the Woods

Little Manistee River

Maple Lake

Beaver Lake

FR 5065 (HOAGUE RD)

Bear Track Campground

MASON COUNTY

Dead Horse Marsh

KOENIG RD (FR 5331)

LAKE COUNTY

List Lake

Elbow Lake

TYNDAL RD

SPUR TO BEAR TRACK CAMPGROUND

NCT

Pomeroy Lakes

© The Countryman Press

ELEVATION PROFILE

1,100 ft
980 ft
860 ft
740 ft
620 ft
500 ft

High Bridge Road

Spur to Bear Track Campground

2   4   6   8   10   12   14   16   18 miles

north of MI 55 on High Bridge Road. High Bridge Road can be accessed 15.0 miles to the west at Manistee, or 9.5 miles from the east at the MI 37 and MI 55 intersection. Turn north on High Bridge Road and, 3.0 miles north, cross the Manistee River and find trailhead parking.

Bear Track Campground is accessed from the north at MI 55 by taking Udell Hills Road south to Campbell Road, crossing the Pere Marquette River (where there is a trailhead and parking), and immediately turning east (left) onto Riverside Drive. Take Riverside Drive about 4.0 miles to the entrance of Bear Track Campground. From the south and west (from US 31 between Scottville and Manistee) take Freesoil Road east through Freesoil; 8.0 miles from Freesoil, turn north on Tyndal, then right (east) onto E Koenig Road to the campground access drive.

FACILITIES AND SERVICES

Potable water is available at Udell Trailhead and Bear Track Campground; off-trail camping is allowed in the national forest.

THE HIKE

At the High Bridge Road access, there is parking and a pit toilet—note there is a required user fee for accessing the trail at this point. At High Bridge Road, turn right (south) to cross the Manistee to the south. Leave the Manistee River behind as you reenter the woods just beyond the guardrail and hike southwest away from the river through low, forested habitats. A small primitive campsite on a backwater of the river, Blacksmith Bayou Campground, offers a bivouac camping opportunity. After the bivouac site, hike up via a relatively short but steep climb

out of the river valley and turn right (west) onto Chicago Avenue.

Chicago Avenue (1.7 miles) is a gravel road, which you'll walk 0.4 mile west; then turn left (south) on Michigan Avenue, cross Sylvan Creek, and turn right (west) onto lightly used Cedar Creek Road.

You'll turn left (south) onto Huff Road, descend to cross Pine Creek, and then ascend. At the 4.7-mile mark, the trail enters woods at the southwest intersection of Huff and Pine Creek Roads. You'll leave the private land and road walks behind for a while as you are back on a long stretch of trail making its way south through the Manistee National Forest.

At MI 55 and the 5.9-mile mark is the Udell Trailhead—which boasts a large parking lot, pit toilet, and water pump. Again, there is a user fee to access the trail at this point. Your hike seems uneventful as you cross over MI 55 and snake southward through the mature forest.

At the 6.8-mile mark, you'll skirt along the west side of a large hill, then climb to the top for a magnificent view to the west. The trail will bend southeast and cross several forest roads, while ascending and descending several times through a forested landscape, before reaching Udell Hills Road. Note that this area is part of the Big M Cross-Country Ski Trails and associated mountain bike trails.

Cross the paved Udell Hills Road (5.8 miles), which you'll use briefly, then cross Madison Road to its east side—where it immediately merges with and changes its name to Skocelas Road, and heads south. As a road walk, you'll pass Nine Mile Bridge Road (6.1 miles) and the Manistee River, which at this point is a popular fishing spot. The North Country Trail turns left (east) onto Riverside Drive for a very short road walk.

Thomas Funke

PERE MARQUETTE RIVER

The trail turns right (south) as it reenters the Manistee National Forest and winds in a southeasterly direction. You'll enter some swamps, jack pine barrens, and red pine–dominated forests over relatively flat terrain. Pass through a large opening with regrowth, a result of straight-line winds.

After crossing Forest Road 5065 (FR 5065)/East Hoague Road at the 8.8-mile mark, you'll cross several Forest Service roads and reach the 600-foot-long board-walk through Dead Horse Marsh, continuing southeast. You'll cross FR 5331/Koenig Road (11.3 miles) and clip the southwest of the intersection of Koenig Road and Tyndal Road on benched trail above a valley.

At Tyndal Road (11.8 miles), there is parking for two cars. There is a spur trail on the east side of Tyndal Road that takes you 1.1 miles to Bear Track Campground (which is rustic, with 16 sites and 4 group sites).

13

Manistee National Forest–Lake County

START: Bear Track Campground Trail Spur	
END: McCarthy Lake	
APPROXIMATE HIKING TIME: 7–12 hours	
LENGTH OF SECTION: 13.5 miles	

The Manistee National Forest was created in 1938, and combined with the Huron National Forest in 1945 to be administered as one national forest. Comprising nearly 1 million acres, the Huron-Manistee National Forests contain a significant stretch of the North Country Trail, which is called the Manistee Trail locally.

Covering parts of nine counties, the Manistee's several big-name rivers and many small ones make for an excellent fishery. The North Country Trail comes into contact with many of these, including the Manistee and Pere Marquette Rivers. Lakes dot the heavily forested landscape; natural water is relatively abundant throughout the national forest.

The nearly 500,000 acres comprising the Manistee National Forest unit were cleared of their majestic forests in the late 1800s and early 1900s. Forest fires, drought, and failed agricultural practices took their toll on the land. Today you will be hard-pressed to see any signs of these past activities, as the forest has rebounded nicely over time.

Being just north of Grand Rapids, the area has become quite the recreational destination. One point to note is that several segments of the North Country Trail in the Manistee are open to mountain bikes. Although this was a contentious decision at the time, things have settled down and both user groups tend to get along. However, just be aware of their presence.

The trail winds through the forest over mostly rolling to flat terrain. Just north of 8 Mile Road expect swampy footing (with interesting botany); you'll see the same again after you leave 5 Mile Road. Cross through a lowland swampy area, using the Vince Smith Bridge to cross the Big Sable River, before a couple

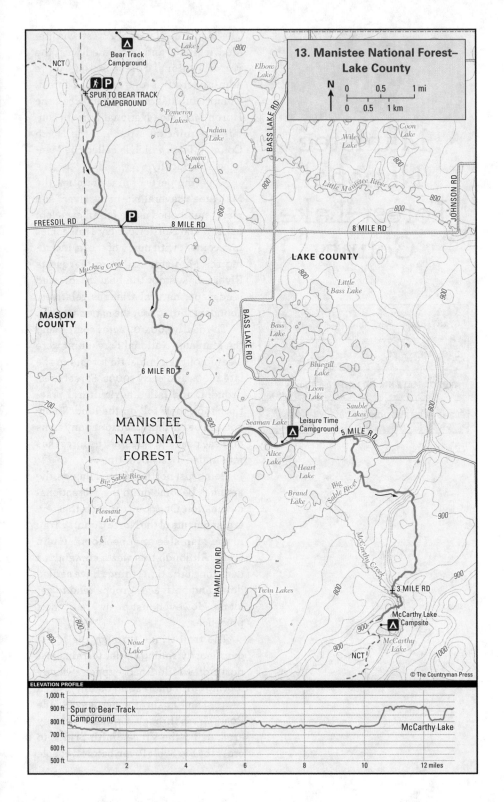

13. Manistee National Forest– Lake County

List Lake

Elbow Lake

800

N
| 0 | 0.5 | 1 mi |
| 0 | 0.5 | 1 km |

Bear Track Campground

NCT

SPUR TO BEAR TRACK CAMPGROUND

P

Pomeroy Lakes

Indian Lake

Squaw Lake

BASS LAKE RD

800

Wile Lake

Coon Lake

800

Little Manistee River

800

JOHNSON RD

FREESOIL RD

P

8 MILE RD

8 MILE RD

800

Muckwa Creek

LAKE COUNTY

Little Bass Lake

800

MASON COUNTY

BASS LAKE RD

Bass Lake

900

6 MILE RD

800

Bluegill Lake

Loon Lake

MANISTEE NATIONAL FOREST

800

700

Seaman Lake

Leisure Time Campground

5 MILE RD

Sauble Lakes

Alice Lake

Heart Lake

Big Sable River

900

Brand Lake

Big Sable River

McCarthy Creek

Pleasant Lake

HAMILTON RD

900

Twin Lakes

800

3 MILE RD

McCarthy Lake Campsite

800

Noud Lake

900

McCarthy Lake

1000

NCT

© The Countryman Press

ELEVATION PROFILE

1,000 ft
900 ft — Spur to Bear Track Campground
800 ft
700 ft
600 ft
500 ft

McCarthy Lake

| 2 | 4 | 6 | 8 | 10 | 12 miles |

of steep climbs and descents ending at McCarthy Lake.

HOW TO FIND

Bear Track Campground is accessed from the north by MI 55 by taking Udell Hills Road south to Campbell Road, crossing the Pere Marquette River, and immediately turning east (left) onto Riverside Drive. Take Riverside Drive about 4.0 miles to the entrance of Bear Track Campground. From the south and west (from US 31 between Scottville and Manistee) take Freesoil Road east through Freesoil; 8.0 miles from Freesoil, turn north on Tyndal Road. There is also a trailhead just before Tyndal Road where the North Country Trail crosses the road.

McCarthy Lake is best accessed with a high clearance, four-wheel-drive vehicle—although if recently maintained and you drive carefully, even a low-clearance vehicle can make it to the lake. From MI 37 10.0 miles north of Baldwin, turn west (left) onto Loon Lake Road. At the T-intersection 4.0 miles from MI 37, Loon Lake will go north and Brooks Road (gravel) will go south. Take Brooks Road south—it will bend to the southeast, then east, and as it bends to the northeast, look for an old road on the south side of the road. Drive in 0.25 mile to the lake or just pull to the side of the old road and walk in.

FACILITIES AND SERVICES

Backcountry camping is permitted in the national forest. There is a grocery store on 5 mile Road at the developed southern end of the southwestern-most lake of the chain, known as Sauble Lakes, just 0.3 mile east of the trailhead on 5 Mile Road. The private Leisure Time Campground has a camp store.

THE HIKE

Hiking in from Bear Track Campground using the trail spur, turn left onto the North Country Trail and hike mostly south through red pine and mixed forests. Cross Freesoil Road at the 2.4-mile mark, where there is a parking lot. Continue south and cross a few poorly maintained Forest Service roads over flat terrain.

At the 5.0-mile mark, cross 6 Mile Road to an unimproved road. The trail heads southeast over rolling, forested terrain for 0.4 mile and comes to an end as you turn left and continue on a 2.3-mile road walk on 5 Mile Road. You'll hike east on this fairly busy road with no shoulder. You'll pass Leisure Time Campground, a modern campground with 90 sites and full facilities, before the trail starts again by turning right into the woods at the 8.7-mile mark.

You'll immediately cross the Big Sable River in less than 0.1 mile, and then McCarthy Creek. At the 12.3-mile mark, cross 3 Mile Road and then progress downhill toward McCarthy Lake where there is a campsite on the north side of the lake. Use an access road to walk east 0.1 mile to reach the campsite (13.5 miles). You'll see what appears to be a beach and campsites are nearby. Most of the south side of the lake is surrounded by shrubs and marsh, making it inaccessible.

14

Pere Marquette River

START: McCarthy Lake

END: 76th Street

APPROXIMATE HIKING TIME: 8–18 hours

LENGTH OF SECTION: 27.7 miles

Your heavily forested scenery continues as the trail winds its way through more hilly terrain as you trek southwest, crossing the legendary Pere Marquette River. The northern part of this segment is high and dry between McCarthy Lake and US 10, so pack enough water to make it the nearly 10.0 miles between water resupplies.

After crossing US 10, hike the trail for about 2.0 miles until you come out to Wingleton Road, which will help you negotiate over the Pere Marquette River, a federally designated wild and scenic river. After crossing, continue winding through the woods; although not as hilly as the northern half of this segment, it is still noticeable that the landscape is rolling.

There are scant opportunities to load up on water on this stretch as well—there's a feeder creek just after the Pere Marquette River and Bowman Lake are on the trail, and also a spur trail to Bowman Lake Campground where there is potable water.

Around Bowman Lake, there is another trail system that is shared with bicycles. Although bikes are prohibited south of 56th Street, don't be surprised if you encounter the stray mountain biker. For the long-distance hiker, pay attention to wildlife sightings; the more northern species will start to drop out and more southern species will become more common. You'll notice from about US 10 until the end of the Manistee National Forest is dominated by red oak and red pine. You are just starting to enter a transition zone that separates the northern forests (dominated by evergreen) from southern forests (dominated by deciduous). The forested habitat dominated by red, jack, and white pines will slowly give way to more hardwood like oak and maple as

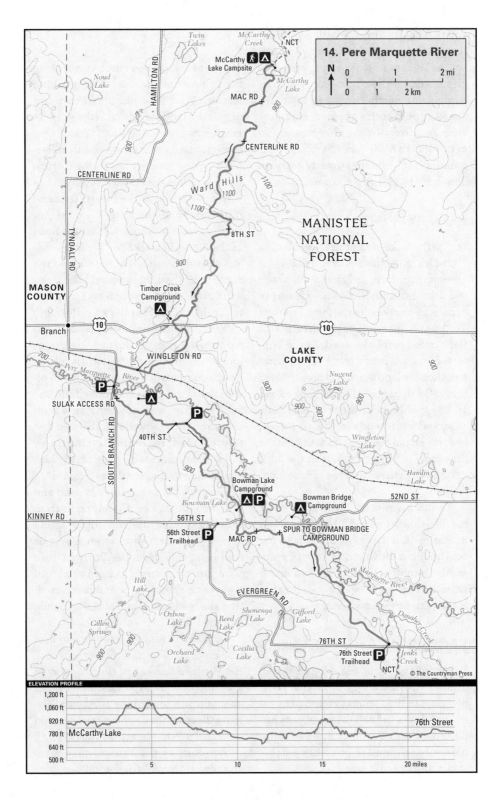

N

| 0 | | 1 | | 2 mi |
| 0 | 1 | | 2 km | |

Twin Lakes

McCarthy Creek

NCT

Noud Lake

McCarthy Lake Campsite

McCarthy Lake

HAMILTON RD

MAC RD

900

CENTERLINE RD

CENTERLINE RD

Ward Hills

1100

1100

1100

MANISTEE NATIONAL FOREST

TYNDALL RD

8TH ST

900

MASON COUNTY

Timber Creek Campground

Branch

10

10

LAKE COUNTY

Tank Creek

WINGLETON RD

Pere Marquette River

700

900

Nugent Lake

900

900

SULAK ACCESS RD

SOUTH BRANCH RD

40TH ST

900

Winghleton Lake

Hamlin Lake

Bowman Lake Campground

Bowman Lake

Bowman Bridge Campground

52ND ST

KINNEY RD

56TH ST

56th Street Trailhead

MAC RD

SPUR TO BOWMAN BRIDGE CAMPGROUND

Hill Lake

EVERGREEN RD

Shonenya Lake

Gifford Lake

Pere Marquette River

Gillen Springs

Oxbow Lake

Reed Lake

Cecilia Lake

Danaher Creek

900

Orchard Lake

76TH ST

76th Street Trailhead

Jenks Creek

NCT

© The Countryman Press

ELEVATION PROFILE

| 1,200 ft |
| 1,060 ft |
| 920 ft |
| 780 ft | McCarthy Lake |
| 640 ft |
| 500 ft |

76th Street

5   10   15   20 miles

you trek south. This transition will continue for about 100 miles as you head south. Typical northern indicator species would be the common raven, porcupine, and northern juncos. Southern species you'll notice are more common, such as tufted titmice, blue racers, and opossum. In addition, the black bear population diminishes greatly between here and the Grand Rapids area.

HOW TO FIND

McCarthy Lake is best accessed with a high-clearance, four-wheel-drive vehicle—although if recently maintained and you drive carefully, even a low clearance vehicle can make it to the lake. From MI 37 10.0 miles north of Baldwin, turn west (left) onto Loon Lake Road. At the T-intersection 4.0 miles from MI 37, Loon Lake Road will go north and Brooks Road (gravel) will go south. Take Brooks Road south—it will bend to the southeast, then east, and as it bends to the northeast, look for an old road on the south side of the road. Drive in 0.25 mile to the lake, or just pull to the side of the old road and walk in.

The 76th Street trailhead is 6.0 miles east of Baldwin on 52nd Street (it changes names to 56th Street as it winds to the south). Pass Bowman Bridge Campground (another trailhead) and about 1.0 mile from the campground entrance is the 56th Street trailhead.

FACILITIES AND SERVICES

Backcountry camping is permitted. Timber Creek Campground has potable water in the summer months and pit toilets. Upper Branch Bridge access has pit toilets, and Bowman Bridge Campground has campsites, pit toilets, potable water, and a picnic area.

THE HIKE

Leave the lake as you climb up out of the kettle back onto flat and slightly rolling terrain. Your forested hike continues across the landscape, and at the 5.7-mile mark you cross Mac Road. You'll continue to hike up and over small hills—heading southwest, then an abrupt turn to the southeast, and back southwest as you move through the forest. Descend into and cross a swampy area, reenter the dry forest, and cross Centerline Road at the 6.3-mile mark. You'll climb a relatively steep hill, level out, follow the contour of the hill, descend slightly to a flat area, and then descend a bit more to reach 8th Street at the 7.2-mile mark.

Your hike continues to rise and fall with the landscape. Just before a 200-foot climb up a hill, the trail will level out. Keep your eyes open for some small kettle holes at the climax of your climb. The trail will turn southeasterly on a high ridge and then move down about 50 feet to an old road. Your climbing efforts earlier will be rewarded as you slowly lose elevation winding southwest toward US 10 through the maturing red pine and jack pine forest. Less than 1.0 mile from the campground, the trail will use an old Forest Road for a short stretch. A spur trail is 0.1 mile from the Timber Creek Campground, a rustic campground with eight campsites. Just past this intersection is a trail kiosk, and at the 13.1-mile mark is US 10.

US 10 can be a busy highway, so take care crossing. The trail enters the woods 100 yards to the east of the driveway to the campground and provides hilly terrain going up and toward the southeast. The trail will turn to the southwest and descend into the flat Pere Marquette Valley.

At 15.0 miles, the trail will come out to and turn right on Wingleton Road, paralleling the railroad tracks in a nearly westerly direction. In 0.6 mile, turn left (south) on South Branch Road, a paved road. The North Country Trail will use this bridge to cross the Pere Marquette River. There is a public access on the south side of the bridge that previously had potable water (its future status is uncertain) and pit toilets.

At the 16.2-mile mark, look for a trailhead on the left (east) side of the road. The trail enters the woods, you'll descend slightly to river level with easy access to get water (and experience great fishing), then climb a steep hill on log steps to nice views above the river where the trail turns east and crosses Sulak Access Road. There are vehicle-accessible campsites along this road. Cross the road and continue southeast, with a reliable stream in about 1.0 mile.

At the 18.0-mile mark, you'll come to and bear right on 40th Street for a 0.5-mile road walk, then reenter the woods on your right, where there is parking. Almost immediately you will reach the junction with the Bowman Lake Loop Trail; pay attention to blue blazes. The trail will snake in a southeasterly direction over hilly terrain and through white pine and red oak forest. You'll climb in elevation and walk a ridge overlooking several old kettle holes. You have entered the Bowman Lake Semiprimitive Nonmotorized Area, with some of the most interesting glacial features of the region.

At the 21.1-mile mark, the trail merges with the Bowman Lake Trail, which is a 1.5-mile loop trail, and circles Bowman Lake. Bowman Lake Campground is on this loop, a rustic campground with four campsites.

At the 21.6-mile mark is an intersection with a spur trail to the 56th Street Trailhead. Continue, cross 56th Street and head south for 0.3 mile, and then head east—crossing Mac Road, then a Forest Service road, while your hike flattens out. Baldwin (full services) is 4.5 miles due east on 56th Street, which changes names to 52nd Street. Mountain bikes are prohibited south of 56th Street.

Another trail spur, at the 23.0-mile mark, heads to Bowman Bridge Campground. Turn left (north) onto the spur trail for the 0.5 mile to the campground, which is rustic with 24 campsites.

Continue to ramble in a southeasterly direction, and you'll notice a slight climb in elevation starting about 1.5 miles from the end of this segment. Use caution, as the trail is often wet through here. Cross a shallow creek at the top of a ravine, then take an old road where you can descend back to the northeast to the river for water. Descend to the 76th Street Trailhead and watch carefully for the spur turnoff to the trailhead—a wooded walk with stately red pine and several species of oak, interspersed with grassy openings.

The 76th Street Trailhead is at the 27.7-mile mark, which has parking (but no user fee is required). If headed north, be sure to follow the white blazes on the spur trail; look for a Carsonite post at the junction between the spur trail and the North Country Trail.

15

Northern Newaygo County

START: Cleveland Drive Trailhead

END: 6 Mile Road

APPROXIMATE HIKING TIME: 4–7 hours

LENGTH OF SECTION: 12.1 miles

This segment can make for a pleasant day hike over a rolling and mixed forest landscape. The forest continues its transition to its southern counterpart. Heading south, the terrain descends slightly to cross a couple of small creeks and traverse through another swampy area.

After crossing West Pierce Drive, your footing becomes dry and level, but only for a short distance, as the trail turns from a southerly to westerly direction to climb in elevation. You'll flatten out, circle a very small lake, and turn south again, headed through the maturing woodlands. The landscape takes on a kettle and kame appearance, and you'll then find a spur trail to Loda Lake Wildflower Sanctuary (staying on the main trail, you'll turn southwest). Loda Lake is a spectacular example of wildflower diversity. There are a couple of looped trails near the lake affording close-up views. Depending on the time of year, you can expect to find orchids and carnivorous plants. More information can be found at www.fs.fed.us/wild flowers/regions/eastern/LodaLake/index .shtml.

HOW TO FIND

Access the trail to the north at Cleveland Drive Trailhead, which is adjacent to Nichols Lake Campground. Between Baldwin and White Cloud, take 11 Mile Road west 4.2 miles to the entrance of Nichols Lake Campground, which is a trail access point. Continue 1.5 miles, turn north onto Warner Avenue for 2.0 miles, then east onto Cleveland Drive for 1.2 miles and trailhead parking.

South access is at 6 Mile Road, but park at Loda Lake and the interpretive trail parking area. Again, access is from MI 37; 5.0 miles north of White Cloud, turn west (right) onto 5 Mile Road for

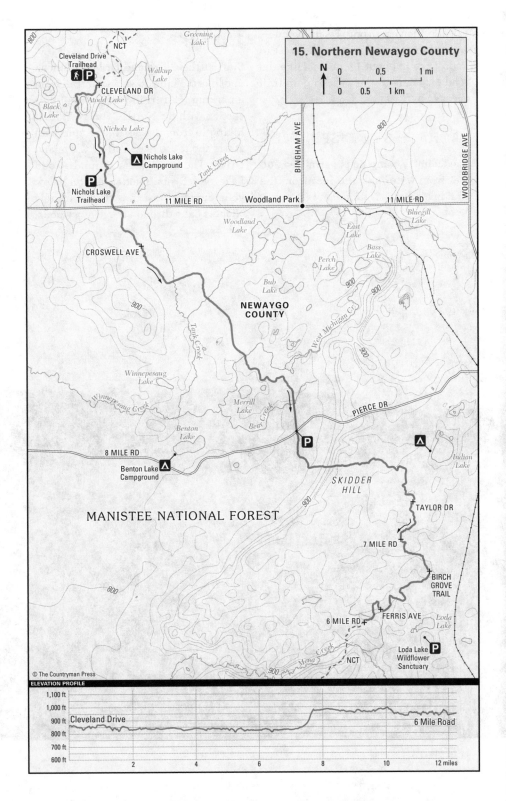

15. Northern Newaygo County

N

| 0 | | 0.5 | | 1 mi |
| 0 | 0.5 | | 1 km | |

NCT

Greening Lake

Cleveland Drive Trailhead

Walkup Lake

CLEVELAND DR

BINGHAM AVE

WOODBRIDGE AVE

900

Black Lake

Atodd Lake

Nichols Lake

Nichols Lake Campground

Tank Creek

Nichols Lake Trailhead

11 MILE RD

Woodland Park

11 MILE RD

Bluegill Lake

Woodland Lake

East Lake

Bass Lake

CROSWELL AVE

Perch Lake

Bub Lake

NEWAYGO COUNTY

900

West Michigan Cr.

900

900

Tank Creek

Winnepesaug Lake

Winnepesaug Creek

Merrill Lake

Bear Creek

PIERCE DR

Benton Lake

8 MILE RD

Benton Lake Campground

Indian Lake

SKIDDER HILL

MANISTEE NATIONAL FOREST

900

TAYLOR DR

7 MILE RD

800

BIRCH GROVE TRAIL

6 MILE RD

FERRIS AVE

Loda Lake

Mena Creek

900

NCT

Loda Lake Wildflower Sanctuary

© The Countryman Press

ELEVATION PROFILE

1,100 ft						
1,000 ft						
900 ft	Cleveland Drive				6 Mile Road	
800 ft						
700 ft						
600 ft		2	4	6	8	10	12 miles

1.0 mile, then north onto Felch Avenue—which bends and winds to the west to Loda Lake in about 1.5 miles. Hike the road 0.75 mile to the west to gain trail access.

FACILITIES AND SERVICES

Backcountry camping is permitted 200 feet from water and 100 feet from the trail in Manistee National Forest.

THE HIKE

Start at the Cleveland Drive Trailhead and hike 0.2 mile down a spur trail from a parking lot, turning left at the intersection with the North Country Trail. If hiking in from the north, the spur trail starts about 100 feet south of Cleveland Drive. The trail skirts around Atodd Lake, which sits in a depression below your current position, then parallels Nichols Lake through the heavy woods;

NICHOLS LAKE

Andrea Mack

you'll come down to the southern part of the lake.

The Nichols Lake Trailhead is at the 1.6-mile mark, and provides access to a parking lot via a short trail spur. At the parking lot, there is a user fee required. The trail uses a portion of the entrance road from the lot to 11 Mile Road. Nichols Lake is about 0.5 mile north on the paved entrance road. Climb out of the Nichols Lake basin and then descend again.

To reach the semimodern campground with 28 sites, take the parking access road left (east), then head north on Jerome Avenue. Otherwise, continue to cross 11 Mile Road (2.2 miles) and head into the woods. Cross Croswell Avenue (gravel) within 0.5 mile.

After crossing Croswell Avenue, cross Forest Road 9716, then the trail will parallel an ORV trail for about 0.4 mile, then will cross Forest Road 9716 a second time at the 3.0-mile mark. It will cross Tank Creek 0.1 mile after crossing FR 9716. Go east, and then bend right to the south to cross an unnamed creek and then parallel another ORV trail, which it parallels for about 2.0 miles, crossing West Michigan Creek, W. Nine Mile Road, and the headwaters of Bear Creek about 0.5 miles before crossing the next road, W. Pierce Drive. Benton Lake Campground (rustic, 24 sites) is 2.3 miles to your west.

Cross W Pierce Drive at the 6.8-mile mark, the trail then turns to the left and parallels W. Pierce Drive (on your north). As you head east, the trail climbs in elevation rather quickly and will then bend south to cross Forest Road 5431 (locally known as Taylor Drive).

Use Forest Road 5431 for about 0.2 mile, then head southwest into the forest, crossing 7 Mile Road at the 9.3-mile mark. Hike southeast and you'll come to an intersection with the Birch Grove Trail, which forks left, and takes you to Loda Lake Wildflower Sanctuary. Continue to the right, bend back to the southwest, and cross Ferris Avenue (a poor dirt road passable only by four-wheel drive) at the 11.7-mile mark. In 0.4 miles, this segment will end at 6 Mile Road, a gravel road. Loda Lake is 0.75 mile to your east and is the nearest place to park.

16

Southern Newaygo County

START: 6 Mile Road

END: Kimble County Park

APPROXIMATE HIKING TIME: 14–25 hours

LENGTH OF SECTION: 45.1 miles

For the long-distance hiker, your 100-mile-long hike through the Manistee National Forest will come to an end as you enter the unincorporated Croton on the Muskegon River and Croton Dam Pond. In fact, if you've hiked from the Wisconsin/Minnesota border, you've been hiking through areas where nature dominates the landscape around the trail and human impacts were incorporated into these wild areas.

The trail has been mostly intact and off-road. From here to the Ohio border, you'll be "island jumping" as the trail connects isolated natural areas mostly through game areas and county and state parks. There will be significant road walks for the long-distance hiker between trail segments.

The trail winds southerly from 6 Mile Road through the woods, crosses Mena Creek, then heads southerly to southeasterly over rolling terrain and through woods. At MI 20 there is parking, and the trail continues south through some bottomlands as you cross Rattlesnake Creek and the south branch of the White River. This is quite the scenic area, with swampland trees like ash and maple, a departure from the dominant oak and pine of the Manistee National Forest.

Shortly, you'll utilize Echo Drive for a road walk, then head back into the woods, crossing an intermittent but mostly reliable Coonskin Creek as you veer toward MI 37. There is a spur trail to MI 37, just north of where the trail actually crosses the state highway. There is a trailhead on 40th Street, just west of MI 37.

Immediately after crossing MI 37, a spur trail to a parking lot to the south and a set of railroad tracks converge. The spur trail takes you to a campground. There is another spur trail just to the east

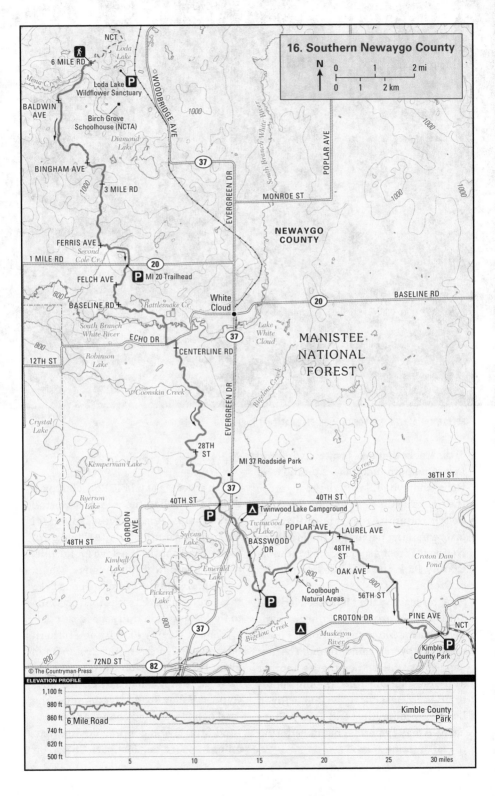

16. Southern Newaygo County

N

0   1   2 mi
0   1   2 km

NCT
Loda
Lake
6 MILE RD

Loda Lake
Wildflower Sanctuary   P

Mena Creek

WOODBRIDGE AVE

1000

BALDWIN
AVE

Birch Grove
Schoolhouse (NCTA)

Diamond
Lake

BINGHAM AVE

37

EVERGREEN DR

MONROE ST

POPLAR AVE

1000

NEWAYGO
COUNTY

1000

1000

1000

3 MILE RD

FERRIS AVE
Second
Cole Cr.
1 MILE RD

20

MI 20 Trailhead

FELCH AVE   P

800

BASELINE RD   Rattlesnake Cr.

White
Cloud

20   BASELINE RD

South Branch
White River

ECHO DR

CENTERLINE RD

37

Lake
White
Cloud

MANISTEE
NATIONAL
FOREST

800

12TH ST

Robinson
Lake

EVERGREEN DR

Bigelow Creek

Coonskin Creek

Crystal
Lake

Kemperman Lake

28TH
ST

MI 37 Roadside Park

Cold Creek

36TH ST

Ryerson
Lake

40TH ST

37

40TH ST

GORDON AVE

48TH ST

Sylvan
Lake

P

Twinwood Lake Campground
Twinwood
Lake
BASSWOOD
DR

POPLAR AVE   LAUREL AVE

48TH
ST

Croton Dam
Pond

Kimball
Lake

Emerald
Lake

800

OAK AVE

800

Coolbough
Natural Areas   56TH ST

Pickerel
Lake

P

Bigelow Creek

800

37

CROTON DR

Muskegon
River

PINE AVE   NCT

Kimble
County Park   P

72ND ST

82

© The Countryman Press

ELEVATION PROFILE

1,100 ft
980 ft
860 ft   6 Mile Road
740 ft
620 ft
500 ft

Kimble County
Park

5   10   15   20   25   30 miles

FOLLOW THE BLAZES THROUGH THE MANISTEE NATIONAL FOREST

Andrea Mack

of the tracks that takes you to Twinwood Lake Campground. It is a 2.0-mile road walk—then you'll leave the road, cross the tracks again, skirt east by the Coolbough Natural Areas, and utilize the last remaining patches of the Manistee National Forest as you come to Kimble County Park and then the community of Croton.

After leaving the Manistee National Forest, there are two significant gaps between the Manistee National Forest and a nearby trail campground. The first gap is sixty miles, then there's another 31.0-mile gap. Off-trail camping opportunities are possible in the Rogue River, Lowell, Middleville, and Barry State Game Areas by permit, but only during the fall hunting seasons.

HOW TO FIND

North access is at 6 Mile Road, but park at Loda Lake and the interpretive trail parking area. Again, access is from MI 37; 5.0 miles north of White Cloud, turn west (right) onto 5 Mile Road for 1.0 mile, then north onto Felch Avenue, which bends and winds to the west to Loda Lake in about 1.5 miles. Hike the road 0.75 mile to the west to gain trail access.

Kimble County Park is the southern terminus at Croton and the Croton Dam. From Howard City on US 131, take MI 82 west, turn north at Tift Corner onto Cypress Valley Road, drive 2.5 miles (the road bends west and changes names to 72nd Street) and continue another 2.0 miles into Croton. Just past Croton on

Croton Drive and after crossing the Muskegon River is Kimble County Park.

FACILITIES AND SERVICES

White Cloud has full services and is 1.5 miles from the trail when it crosses Echo Drive. Croton has a small motel and campground. Off-trail camping is permitted in the national forest.

There is a spur trail to the North Country Trail Schoolhouse (camping, indoor lodging, flush toilets, shower, and potable water). It is available for rent through the North Country Trail Association in Lowell.

THE HIKE

There is no trailhead at 6 Mile Road. Instead, park at Loda Lake 0.75 miles to the east. Hike the gravel 6 Mile Road west to the trailhead. Turn left (south) and hike a short stretch before entering the woods and descending into a shallow valley. Cross Mena Creek (0.6 mile), which can be unreliable in dry years. Climb up out of the valley and the trail will follow the top of a hill.

At the 1.7-mile mark, turn left at the intersection with a 1.5-mile-long spur trail to the North Country Trail Schoolhouse. From this point, the North Country Trail peels away in a southwest direction uphill into woods.

Cross Baldwin Avenue, and head south over flat terrain. The trail makes a fishhook back to the north and then crosses Bingham Avenue at the 2.6-mile mark. The trail then bends back to the south through rolling terrain, then east, then south. You'll cross the paved 3 Mile Road 1.0 mile past Bingham Avenue. The Manistee National Forest continues its characteristic rolling terrain to the

south. There is a maze of roads for the next 3.0 miles, so pay attention to your blazes.

At the 5.2-mile mark cross the gravel Ferris Avenue and bend east, cross an unimproved road, then bend south to MI 20, which is at the 6.6-mile mark.

The MI 20 trailhead has parking and requires a user fee to access the trail. Cross MI 20 and hike southwesterly as you use an unimproved road until it comes to Felch Avenue in 0.8 mile. Cross to the west side of Felch Avenue, hike in mature mixed forest within earshot of Felch Avenue, and the trail will cross over Felch Avenue to its east side at the 8.1-mile mark.

After crossing Felch Avenue, the trail makes easterly path as it follows a ridgeline, makes a hard right turn (south) to cross Rattlesnake Creek, and then takes a hard left (still easterly) for you to parallel the nearby south branch of the White River. The trail will turn right (south) in order to cross an impressive steel footbridge. The habitat is quite swampy, so be prepared for wet footing, especially after rain and in the springtime. The trail immediately climbs out of the river valley after crossing the creek and heads due south.

At the 10.3-mile mark you'll come to Echo Drive, a paved road. Turn left onto Echo Drive as a road walk east. White Cloud is about 1.5 miles east of here, and has full services. Turn right (south) on Centerline Road for about 0.5 mile before the trail leaves the road, as a left turn, directly across from Barry Drive (11.0 miles).

Habitats will change to mostly southern species such as sugar maple, beech, and red oak. Note that red pine and white pine are becoming sparser, and it has been quite a while since you've seen a jack pine. Cross a pipeline right-of-way, then Coonskin Creek 1.1 miles later; enjoy a flat walk as the trail snakes its way through the woods.

Cross East 28th Street (14.4 miles), then come to a trail intersection with a spur trail to a roadside park on MI 37. The North Country Trail goes straight; turn left to reach MI 37. Continue south, winding through the more open mixed forest to 40th Street, where there is a parking lot and a user fee is required.

Through the woods, you can hear the nearby MI 37, and the trail will veer southeasterly until the 18.0-mile mark where you cross MI 37; within 100 feet, you'll come to Basswood Drive—and across the street is Twinwood Lake Campground, which is rustic with five campsites. Hike south on Basswood Drive for 2.0 miles, which is mostly wooded and lightly traveled by vehicles.

The trail turns right to cross an active set of railroad tracks (20.1 miles), which will then bend west and then curl back east. The trail will cross the railroad tracks again to your left and take a northeast trek through the forest. There is a parking lot at the road and railroad intersection.

Thomas Funke

WILD LUPINE PREFERS THE OPEN HABITATS AND SANDY SOILS IN THE
SOUTHERN PART OF THE MANISTEE NATIONAL FOREST

In 0.8 mile you descend to cross Bigelow Creek, then ascend and, in about 0.2 mile, the trail will share part of the Coolbough Natural Areas trail system through rolling and forested terrain.

The trail will take an easterly turn, parallelling the boundary with a farm, then it crosses Poplar Avenue at the 24.1-mile mark. A slight descent to cross a small creek leads to a slight ascent to cross Laurel Avenue at the 25.2-mile mark.

After Laurel Avenue, hike in a southeasterly trajectory through long-ago harvested pine plantations, to cross 48th Street in about 0.8 mile. After crossing 48th Street, you'll see a variety of land uses, from those harvested pine plantations to ones that are nearing harvesting age, open fields, and natural second growth forest. You are coming to the end of the Manistee National Forest. Look for prickly pear, which is a native plant in Michigan.

Cross Oak Avenue (26.2 miles) and continue through a pine plantation, then use an old road through an open area to go south, then west through an open area, then southeast into another pine plantation. After crossing 56th Street (27.3 miles), jog east for 0.1 mile and then south on an old road. At 0.75 mile south of 56th Street, the trail will veer southeast to Croton Drive.

At 28.4 miles is the Croton Drive and South Pine Avenue intersection, which the trail crosses over (to the southeast) into your last patch of the Manistee National Forest. This hike can also be bittersweet because from here to the south, the landscape will be dominated by human activities. Your hike is a pleasant one through mostly oak and pine forest.

Your last trailhead (or first if hiking north) is Kimble County Park and Croton Dam (29.7 miles), which is on the north side of the road. The first lot to the north is parking for those fishing the dam, and taking the service drive north will take you to Kimble County Park.

For the long-distance hiker, it is a 14.9-mile road walk until the next segment, mostly through an open, rural, residential setting. The suggested road walk is as follows:

0.0 mile: Take Croton Drive to the north, then head right (east) onto 72nd Street.

0.8 mile: Turn right (south) on Elm Avenue.

5.9 miles: Cross MI 82.

6.4 miles: Head left (west) on 92nd Street.

7.4 miles: Head right (south) on Locust Street.

10.9 miles: Head left (west) on 120th Street.

11.4 miles: Head right (south) on Pear Street.

12.9 miles: Head left (west) on 128th Street.

14.9 miles: Head right (south) on Oak Avenue.

15.4 miles: Cross 22 Mile Road and continue on into the next segment.

II.

SOUTHERN LOWER PENINSULA

Rogue River State Game Area and White Pine Trail

START: 22 Mile Road

END: Rockford

APPROXIMATE HIKING TIME: 11–15 hours

LENGTH OF SECTION: 22.3 miles

Your last taste of the Northern Woods will be hiking south through the 6,136-acre Rogue River State Game Area. After that, you'll enter the farmlands and residential developments of the southern Lower Peninsula via road walks until you reach the Lowell area, where the trail picks up again—but only for a short distance.

The Rogue River has been designated as a Trout Unlimited Home River, meaning that funding is provided for habitat projects and protection. Interestingly, the original name was spelled a bit differently—Rouge River—but a mapmaker's error misspelled the name sometime in the 19th century and the new name stuck. The Rogue River has a historic importance as a travel route for traders and for floating timber to the Grand River and sawmills.

Today, the Rogue River is listed as a scenic river under Michigan's Natural Rivers Act. You'll experience this scenery, as most of the hike in the Rogue River State Game Area parallels the stream—although in many places it is in the upland, dryer areas, so as to keep your feet dry. Camping is allowed by permit between September 10th and May 15th. This area is open to hunting from September to March, and we recommend wearing hunter orange during this period—especially during firearm deer season from November 15th to 30th.

The Howard Christensen Nature Center, a former outdoor education camp for the Kent County Intermediate School District, has a network of trails across the street from the North Country Trail. Although the school district does not operate the center, they continue to own it and lease out its operation to a nonprofit organization.

Long-distance hikers have the option of cutting across to Cedar Springs, a

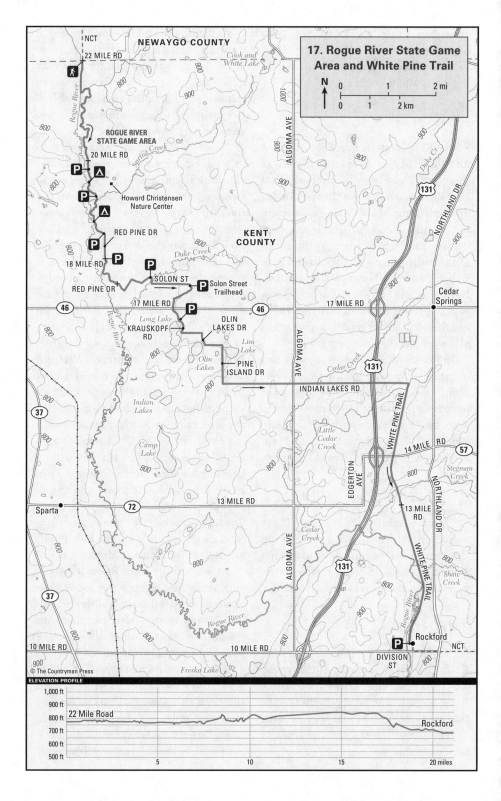

NCT

NEWAYGO COUNTY

22 MILE RD

Cook and
White Lake

17. Rogue River State Game Area and White Pine Trail

N

| 0 | | 1 | | 2 mi |

| 0 | 1 | | 2 km |

Rogue River

ROGUE RIVER
STATE GAME AREA

20 MILE RD

P

Howard Christensen
Nature Center

P

RED PINE DR

P

18 MILE RD

P

RED PINE DR

P

SOLON ST

P Solon Street
Trailhead

17 MILE RD

46

P

Long Lake

KRAUSKOPF
RD

OLIN
LAKES DR

Lim
Lake

Olin
Lakes

PINE
ISLAND DR

INDIAN LAKES RD

Indian
Lakes

Camp
Lake

13 MILE RD

72

Sparta

37

37

10 MILE RD

© The Countryman Press

Freska Lake

Spring Creek

Duke Creek

KENT
COUNTY

ALGOMA AVE

46

17 MILE RD

Cedar
Springs

131

NORTHLAND DR

Duke Cr

Cedar Creek

131

Little
Cedar
Creek

EDGERTON AVE

ALGOMA AVE

Cedar
Creek

131

WHITE PINE TRAIL

14 MILE RD

57

Stegman
Creek

13 MILE
RD

10 MILE RD

Rogue River

NORTHLAND DR

WHITE PINE TRAIL

Shaw
Creek

Rogue River

P Rockford

DIVISION
ST

NCT

ELEVATION PROFILE

1,000 ft				
900 ft				
800 ft	22 Mile Road			
700 ft				Rockford
600 ft				
500 ft				
	5	10	15	20 miles

small town with most services, then hopping onto the White Pine Trail south until the recommended road route begins again in Rockford.

HOW TO FIND

Rogue River State Game Area starts at 22 Mile Road, but there is no parking at this point. There is parking access off 20 Mile Road between Kent City and Cedar Springs. Using MI 46 from either town, turn north on Red Pine Drive Northwest, drive 1.0 mile, turn west (left) onto 18 Mile Road, jog back north onto Red Pine Drive, pass the Howard Christensen Nature Center (a trail access point) and continue to 20 Mile Road, turn west (left), and there is a feeder road that goes south about 0.2 mile to a parking area.

In Rockford, there is street-side and lot parking; inquire locally about overnight parking. Street-side overnight parking is not allowed November 15th to April 1st. Designated parking for White Pine Trail users is at 227 North Main Street and 99 Towers Drive in Rockford.

FACILITIES AND SERVICES

Rockford is a full service town. There are no organized camping areas along this segment of trail; however, dispersed camping is allowed in the game area, by permit, in the fall and winter months.

THE HIKE

Although marked trail begins at 22 Mile Road, there is no parking at this point. The trail squeezes between the Rogue River to your west and private land to the east along the boundary between the dryer, upland forests and the lowland floodplain forest.

At the 0.7 mile mark, cross the Rogue River on a small footbridge; the trail parallels the river to the east for about 0.1 mile, then turns south and continues to follow the edge of the riparian habitat. Keep winding through a mix of oak, pine, and swampy forest.

Cross 20 Mile Road, and a spur trail to a parking area is on your left. You continue hiking along the edge of the swamp, pass a bivouac location on the river, and soon after the trail peels away from the river habitat to your left and Red Pine Road, which has a parking area.

Immediately cross Spring Creek, and the trail treks southwest back to the edge of the riparian habitat; at the 5.0-mile mark, the trail comes to Red Pine Road and a trailhead with parking.

The nature center is across the street and has its own trail network. The North Country Trail comes to the Red Pine Drive parking lot, but does not connect with the nature center at this point. Use the street to hike north to connect with their trail network. Hike 0.6 mile south to 18 Mile Road, where there is a large parking lot. The North Country Trail heads into hardwood forest and then a pine plantation in a southerly direction. The trail turns east, leaves the pine plantation, and (0.5 mile past 18 Mile Road) heads southeast on an old road.

At the 6.1-mile mark, the trail merges with an old road through the woods, then heads northeast onto a pipeline right-of-way. Nearly 1.0 mile after merging with the old road, the pipeline walk ends, and you'll hike east into the woods.

At the 7.4-mile mark, you'll come to a parking lot at Division Avenue. Turn right and walk south on Division Avenue about 0.2 mile, then turn left (east) on Solon Street Northeast for 0.8 mile as a road walk to the Solon Street Trailhead.

From the Solon Street Trailhead, hike south, and about 0.2 mile in turn right to use an old road for a few hundred feet, then turn left (south) into the woods. In 0.25 mile you'll cross a utility right-of-way; in another 0.25 mile you'll come to MI 46. Long Lake Park is across the street and has parking.

For the long-distance hiker, you'll endure a 5.4-mile road walk to the White Pine Trail in Cedar Springs via MI 46. Then turn right (south) and take the White Pine Trail 1.6 miles to reunite with the certified North Country Trail at Indian Lakes Road, which is at the 16.7-mile mark.

You'll hike south on this flat, multiuse, paved trail open to bikes. At the 22.3-mile mark is East Bridge Street in downtown Rockford, which is where the North Country Trail leaves the White Pine Trail.

18

Central Kent County Parks and Trails

START: Rockford

END: Fallasburg Park

APPROXIMATE HIKING TIME: 10–20 hours

LENGTH OF SECTION: 32.5 miles

Rockford is a medium-sized city with full services, located along the Rogue River. From here, the White Pine Trail continues south to the northern suburbs of Grand Rapids. You'll be leaving this most extensive of Michigan state parks (90 miles between Grand Rapids and Cadillac) and heading southeast toward Lowell.

The Western Michigan Chapter has done an excellent job of piecing together several parks and multiuse trails between Rockford and Lowell. This will lessen the wear and tear, along with the dangers, of road walking. In any case, it will be open country of fields, houses, and farms for the majority of your road walk.

Right outside of Rockford, you'll cut through some private property hiking south before a road walk east and then a residential development south, utilizing a paved and boardwalked trail. Jog over to Warren Townsend Park for a short trail walk, then road walk through Cannonsburg. To the south, future trail development is planned in the Cannonsburg State Game Area, but for now it is a road walk until you reach the Ada Township multiuse trail. For the next 4.2 miles, utilize this paved trail to Seidman Park, then head east on another road walk until you turn north on the Flat River Valley Rail Trail. You'll have yet another road walk east, and then head south to Fallasburg Park.

HOW TO FIND

In Rockford, there is street-side and lot parking; inquire locally about overnight parking. Street-side overnight parking is not allowed from November 15th to April 1st. Designated parking for White Pine Trail users is at 227 North Main Street and 99 Towers Drive in Rockford.

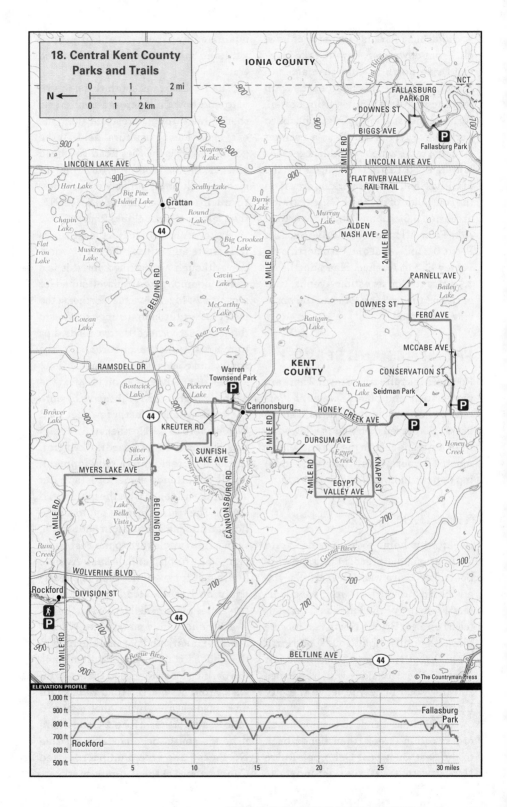

18. Central Kent County Parks and Trails

N ←

0   1   2 mi
0   1   2 km

IONIA COUNTY

NCT

FALLASBURG PARK DR

DOWNES ST

BIGGS AVE

3 MILE RD

LINCOLN LAKE AVE

P   Fallasburg Park

900

LINCOLN LAKE AVE

Slayton Lake

900

Hart Lake

900

Scally Lake

Big Pine Island Lake

Grattan

Chapin Lake

Round Lake

Byrne Lake

44

FLAT RIVER VALLEY RAIL TRAIL

Murray Lake

ALDEN NASH AVE

2 MILE RD

Flat Iron Lake

Muskrat Lake

Big Crooked Lake

PARNELL AVE

Bailey Lake

Gavin Lake

DOWNES ST

Cowan Lake

McCarthy Lake

Ratigan Lake

FERO AVE

BELDING RD

Bear Creek

MCCABE AVE

RAMSDELL DR

KENT COUNTY

Chase Lake

CONSERVATION ST

Bostwick Lake

Warren Townsend Park

P

Pickerel Lake

5 MILE RD

Seidman Park

P

Brower Lake

44

Cannonsburg

HONEY CREEK AVE

P

KREUTER RD

5 MILE RD

DURSUM AVE

Honey Creek

Silver Lake

SUNFISH LAKE AVE

4 MILE RD

Egypt Creek

MYERS LAKE AVE

Armstrong Creek

CANNONSBURG RD

Bear Creek

EGYPT VALLEY AVE

KNAPP ST

700

Lake Bella Vista

BELDING RD

Grand River

700

Rum Creek

10 MILE RD

700

100

WOLVERINE BLVD

Rockford

DIVISION ST

44

700

P

900

Rogue River

700

BELTLINE AVE

44

10 MILE RD

900

© The Countryman Press

ELEVATION PROFILE

1,000 ft
900 ft
800 ft
700 ft
600 ft
500 ft

Rockford

Fallasburg Park

5   10   15   20   25   30 miles

Fallasburg Park is just north of Lowell. From downtown Lowell, take Hudson Drive north (it changes names to Lincoln Lake Avenue Southeast as you leave town). At 3.2 miles from Lowell, turn northeast (right) onto Fallasburg Park Drive Northeast. Pass a parking lot at 0.4 mile, which has trail access. At Potters Road, turn east (right), cross the Flat River, and another parking area is on the south side of the road. Other parking areas are at Siedman Park, just north of Ada. From MI 21 and Pettis Ave SE, take Pettis 0.2 mile west and turn north onto Honey Creek Avenue. Head northeast 1.5 miles to Conservation Avenue, turn east, and the parking lot is on the north side of the road.

FACILITIES AND SERVICES

Rockford is a full service town. There are picnic areas and potable water at Warren Townsend, Seidman, and Fallasburg Parks. Dispersed camping is allowed in the state game area in the fall and winter months by permit only. There are lodging options in Lowell and Rockford.

THE HIKE

Rockford is home to Wolverine World Wide, a manufacturer of hiking and work boots. If you are wearing Merrells, you are hiking through their world headquarters. From the White Pine Trail, turn left (east) on East Bridge Northeast for one block, then turn right (south) on North Main Street Northeast, then head left (east) on East Division—which becomes 10 Mile Road once you leave the city limits.

10 Mile Road bends to the northeast, crosses Rum Creek, then bends back to the east. Just past Oakbrook Ridge Northeast, the trail turns right and starts again trending south (2.1 miles) into private land on an impressively maintained trail.

The trail zigzags south through private land, downhill to cross a small creek, then uphill through forest and along the east side of an agricultural field. At the 3.1-mile mark is the Kies Road Trailhead and parking lot. From here, turn right for a road walk of 4.2 miles west on Kies, turn left (south) on Blakely Drive NE, then left (east) on Belding Road/MI 44.

At Bella Vista Drive Northeast, a bike trail starts and utilizes the MI 44 corridor. Although not certified yet, this is a paved, nonmotorized trail well suited for bicycles. At Myers Avenue Northeast the trail crosses through the intersection to the southeast corner of the two roads, dips into a residential neighborhood to the south, and comes back to parallel MI 46.

Just past Silver Lake on MI 46 at the 7.3-mile mark, turn right (south) onto the trail, which is just a few feet past Wildermere Drive Northeast. Although this is a paved and boardwalked trail through a residential development, you'll experience some forests and a small lake mixed in with the manicured lawns. The trail will come out to a public road and make a straight shot south, then a right angle turn to the east. Turn right (south) on Sunfish Lake Avenue Southeast for 0.2 mile, then left (east) again on Kreuter Road Northeast for 0.75 miles to Ramsdell Drive Northeast.

At the 10.0-mile mark, enter Warren Townsend Park and parallel the road in the woods for about 0.5 mile, then come to a parking lot on Ramsdell Drive Northeast. From here, it is a road walk south on Ramsdell Drive; turn right (west) on 6 Mile Road Northeast for 0.25 mile where it bends south, becomes Joyce Drive Northeast, and enters unincorporated Cannonsburg at the 11.0-mile mark.

Jog left (east) onto Cannonsburg Road Northeast for a few hundred feet, then right (south) on Honey Creek Avenue Southeast for a 5.3-mile road walk, turn right (west) on 5 Mile Road Northeast, then left (south) on Dursum Avenue Northeast, left (west) on 4 Mile Road, and cross a small creek. Continue to Egypt Valley Road Northeast and turn left (south) to Knapp Street Southeast.

At Knapp Street Southeast (16.7 miles), take the Ada Township trail—a paved, multiuse route—for the next 4.3 miles. The trail will continue east on Knapp Street Northeast, then turn right (south) along Honey Creek Avenue Northeast. Seidman Park is on your left (east). Just north of Conservation Drive Northeast, the multiuse trail will turn into the park and bring you to a parking lot at the 20.9-mile mark.

From the Siedman Park parking lot is another road walk to your next trail segment. Turn left and take Conservation Drive Southeast east, turn left (north) on McCabe Avenue Northeast, then right (east) on Downes Street Northeast. Turn right (south) on Parnell Avenue South-east, then left (east) on McPhearson Street Northeast; 2.5 miles from the Parnell Avenue and McPhearson Street intersection, just after crossing Page Creek at the 27.6-mile mark, turn left (north) on the Flat River Valley Rail Trail, a paved, multiuse trail.

This is part of the Fred Meijer Trail System, which is a network of abandoned rail grades supported by an avid trail enthusiast, the late Fred Meijer. This segment winds gently north through second growth hardwood forest, then between agricultural fields on either side of you.

At the 30.7-mile mark turn right (east) onto 3 Mile Road Northeast for a 1.2-mile road walk, then right (south) onto Biggs Avenue Northeast. At the Y-intersection take the east (or left) fork onto Downes Street Northeast. You'll come to a T-intersection; turn right (south) and the trail will enter Fallasburg Park on the left (east) side of the road. Hike downhill, then bend to follow the Flat River to the southwest. There are several feeder creeks before you reach the Potters Road parking lot at Fallasburg Park and the 32.5-mile mark.

Grand and Flat Rivers

START: Fallasburg Park

END: Maher Audubon Sanctuary

APPROXIMATE HIKING TIME: 9–13 hours

LENGTH OF SECTION: 23.0 miles

Once you enter the Rogue River State Game Area, you are hiking in the largest watershed in Michigan, that of the Grand River. The Grand has many tributaries, and this hike will bring you along one of the larger watercourses emptying into the Grand, the Flat River.

It is in the Lowell area that you'll cross the Flat River, the Grand River, and find the headquarters to the North Country Trail Association. Not quite exactly at the halfway point on the entire North Country Trail, the national headquarters is conveniently located in the downtown business district just blocks from the trail. But don't let that be the highlight of hiking in the Lowell area, Fallasburg Park, and the Lowell State Game Area.

For the long-distance hiker, you'll notice that your hopscotching between trail and road walks continues, with considerably more asphalt than duff under your feet. Again, the countryside is varied—with farms, homesteads, and natural areas.

For the day hiker, connecting the Fallasburg Park and Lowell State Game Area segments makes for a nice walk. The trail enters the park and squeezes between a road and the Flat River, crosses the Flat on a bridge, and continues to follow the river. The trail will turn away from the river in an easterly direction, then cross Covered Bridge Road Northeast. Just to the west is one of only two covered bridges in Michigan open to standard vehicular traffic, the Fallasburg Covered Bridge. The bridge was built in 1871 for the sum of $1,500.

A road walk ensues on the east side of the Flat River, and then you'll enter the Lowell State Game Area. The trail winds through the woods until it exits onto Flat River Drive Northeast and uses it to cross back over into the game area. The trail winds until it crosses into the

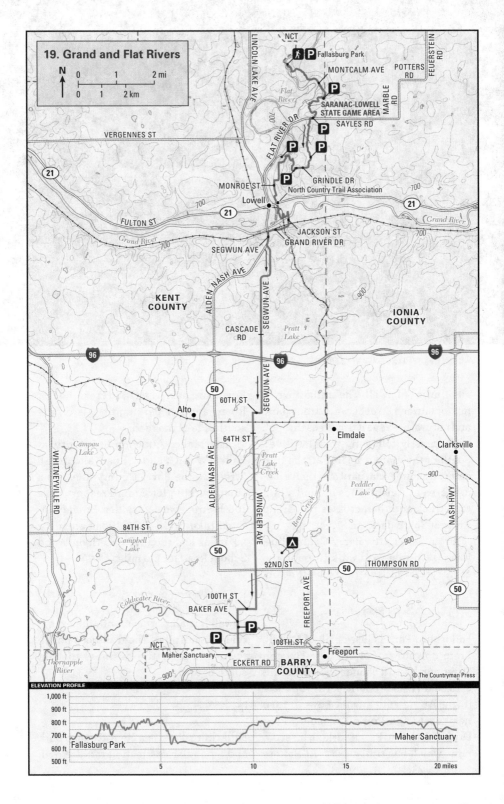

19. Grand and Flat Rivers

N

0   1   2 mi

0   1   2 km

NCT

Fallasburg Park

MONTCALM AVE

POTTERS RD

FEUERSTEIN RD

LINCOLN LAKE AVE

Flat River

MARBLE RD

SARANAC-LOWELL STATE GAME AREA

FLAT RIVER DR

700

SAYLES RD

VERGENNES ST

21

GRINDLE DR

MONROE ST

North Country Trail Association

Grand River

Lowell

700

21

21

FULTON ST

Grand River

700

700

JACKSON ST

GRAND RIVER DR

SEGWUN AVE

ALDEN NASH AVE

KENT COUNTY

SEGWUN AVE

CASCADE RD

Pratt Lake

IONIA COUNTY

900

96

96

96

50

60TH ST

SEGWUN AVE

Alto

64TH ST

Elmdale

Clarksville

Campau Lake

Pratt Lake Creek

900

WHITNEYVILLE RD

ALDEN NASH AVE

WINGEIER AVE

Peddler Lake

NASH HWY

84TH ST

Briar Creek

Campbell Lake

50

900

92ND ST

THOMPSON RD

50

50

100TH ST

BAKER AVE

FREEPORT AVE

Coldwater River

P

P

NCT

108TH ST

Freeport

Maher Sanctuary

ECKERT RD

BARRY COUNTY

Thornapple River

900

© The Countryman Press

ELEVATION PROFILE

1,000 ft
900 ft
800 ft
700 ft
600 ft
500 ft

Fallasburg Park

Maher Sanctuary

5   10   15   20 miles

WILDLIFE ON THE FLAT RIVER NEAR LOWELL

city limits of Lowell. The trail utilizes a mix of surface streets, waterfront park, and natural areas as it traverses through town, mostly following the Flat River. South of the main drag, MI 21, the trail enters a commercial park and then a natural area as it negotiates around a railroad track and then crosses the Grand River at South Jackson Street.

From here to the Barry County line, it is a 14.1-mile road walk through the countryside until the trail picks up again.

HOW TO FIND

Fallasburg Park is just north of Lowell. From downtown Lowell, take Hudson Drive north and it changes names to Lincoln Lake Avenue Southeast as you leave town. At 3.2 miles from Lowell, turn northeast (right) onto Fallasburg Park Drive Northeast. Pass a parking lot at 0.4 mile, which has trail access. At Potters

Road, turn east (right) and cross the Flat River; another parking area is on the south side of the road.

The Maher Audubon Sanctuary, at Baker/Wood School Road and 108th Street on the Barry County line, has a small parking lot. From Freeport, take 108th Street west 2.0 miles. From Hastings, take Stake State Road west for 3.5 miles and then turn north on Wood School Road for 6.0 miles.

FACILITIES AND SERVICES

Lowell has all services, with the exception of a hospital. The trail goes downtown and near the business district south of town.

THE HIKE

Fallasburg Park is a Kent County park and a popular destination for disc golf, picnicking, hiking, and of course its famous covered bridge. From the park, cross over McPhearson/Potters Road for 0.75 mile through the dryer portions of the floodplain forest along the Flat River, then through a mostly open field, and back into the woods to the intersection of Covered Bridge Road Northeast and Montcalm Avenue Northeast.

Cross over Covered Bridge Road Northeast and road walk south on Montcalm Avenue Northeast; in 1.0 mile, turn right into a small dirt parking lot at the Saranac-Lowell State Game Area. The trail becomes a natural tread through the woods, taking an immediate northwest trajectory that then bends southerly. As this is a state game area managed for hunting, wear hunter orange from September through March, especially in firearm deer season. You'll climb a steep hill, level out, and then follow the topography downhill through the woods into a ravine. The trail will climb out of the ravine, up to the top of another hill, then down to a parking lot. Cross Flat River Drive (with parking) and continue up and down through this hilly stretch of trail.

At the 4.6-mile mark cross Grindle Drive Northeast; the trail turns to the right (west) and comes back to Grindle as a westerly road walk for about 0.2 mile, then enters the woods at a bend in the road. The trail goes up, follows the contour of a modest hill clockwise, then starts a northerly, downhill progression toward the river.

At 5.3 miles you leave mature woods and enter Boy Scout property. The property line is well defined; as you leave the mature woods of the game area, you'll cross a utility right-of-way and then descend to the Flat River, walk along it for about 0.1 mile, then turn due south,

cross the right-of-way, and head into a pine plantation. The trail will go slightly uphill along the side of the hill and then descend to North Washington Road. To the north, there is parking on North Washington Road.

Turn left (south) onto North Washington Road and enter Lowell. This small town has all services and is home to the North Country Trail Association at 229 East Main Street. Take North Washington Road south, then head right (west) on Fremont. Oakwood Cemetery is to your west and north. Turn left on North Monroe Street and turn right (west) onto King Street, which ends in one block at the Lowell Riverwalk—turn left on this paved, multiuse trail.

The riverwalk comes to Main Street (MI 22) and crosses the Grand River at the 6.0-mile mark. The North Country Trail Association is a few doors down on the north side of the road to your left (east). You'd be amiss not to stop in and say hello, especially if you were on a long-distance hike! Cross MI 22 and get back onto the trail, hiking along the edge of the Flat River, then through some open fields, and back into the woods—where you'll come to the Grand River. Hike east, then north along the railroad tracks (and under a trestle), and south back to the river, where you'll hike in the woods 0.1 mile to a road, which you'll have to hike a few hundred feet north to get up to grade.

Hop onto Jackson Street (8.5 miles) by turning right (south), and use the road's bridge to cross the Grand River. For the long-distance hiker this is a milestone of sorts, having hiked halfway across Michigan's largest watershed. It won't be until you are in southern Barry County that you will leave the watershed.

From here, it is a 15.6-mile road walk

AN EASTERN BOX TURTLE HIKES THE WIDTH OF THE TRAIL

through an agricultural landscape until you reach the next trail segment in Barry County. After crossing the Grand River, turn right onto Grand River Drive Southeast, hike west, and then turn left (south) on Segwun Avenue Southeast/ Alden Nash. Segwun Avenue splits off to the east, makes a bend to the west, takes a straight shot south 3.5 miles, crosses I-96, and jogs to the right (west) on 60th Street Southeast for 0.1 mile before heading left (south) on Wingeier Avenue SE. Although this stretch of road walk seems as high and dry as it is hilly, there are several streams that cross the road where you can resupply on water. Turn right (west) onto 100th Street Southeast and then left (south) onto Baker Avenue Southeast. Cross the reliable Coldwater River (a trout stream), then head right (west) onto 108th Street Southeast. This is the boundary between Barry and Kent Counties.

At 21.0 miles, hike west along the Barry/Kent County line and the north boundary of the Maher Audubon Sanctuary. Although the trail does not go through the Maher Audubon Sanctuary, it is a good side trip with parking access. Hike west on 108th Street Street 2.0 miles to North Harris Creek Road.

Barry County

START: Maher Audubon Sanctuary
END: Kalamazoo County line at Baseline Road
APPROXIMATE HIKING TIME: 12–16 hours
LENGTH OF SECTION: 38.7 miles

For the long-distance hiker, the Northern Woods are a distant memory, and you are coming to terms with long stretches of road walking. Pounding the pavement may be painful at times, but the rolling topography and rural agricultural scenery should make up for it. It is important to note that the North Country Trail does not isolate the hiker from the surrounding land uses. To some, walking through the countryside is as or even more rewarding than walking through a wilderness.

Many years ago the tourism pitch for Barry County compared this rural, little-populated (59,173 at last census) county with the Upper Peninsula. You'll get a sense of the UP as you trek though the mixed pine and hardwood of the Yankee Springs Recreation Area and the Barry and Middleville State Game Areas. The soils are dry and droughty, encouraging the growth of white pine and oak—mostly white, red, and black. You'll also notice more northern trees growing in the swamps, like yellow birch, red maple, black ash, and tamarack. Don't be surprised if you see the occasional cedar, hemlock, or balsam fir, all of which are found in the area.

The trail starts at the Maher Audubon Sanctuary, owned by the Grand Rapids Audubon Club. Currently there is a trail system at the sanctuary, but the North Country Trail does not utilize it at the moment. It makes for a nice side trip. The trail follows the Kent and Barry County lines before heading southwest toward Middleville through the Middleville State Game Area. In Middleville it is a road walk until you cross Main Street, then the North Country Trail utilizes the Paul Henry Thornapple Trail for 3.7 miles, followed by a 2.0-mile road walk until it enters the Barry State Game Area.

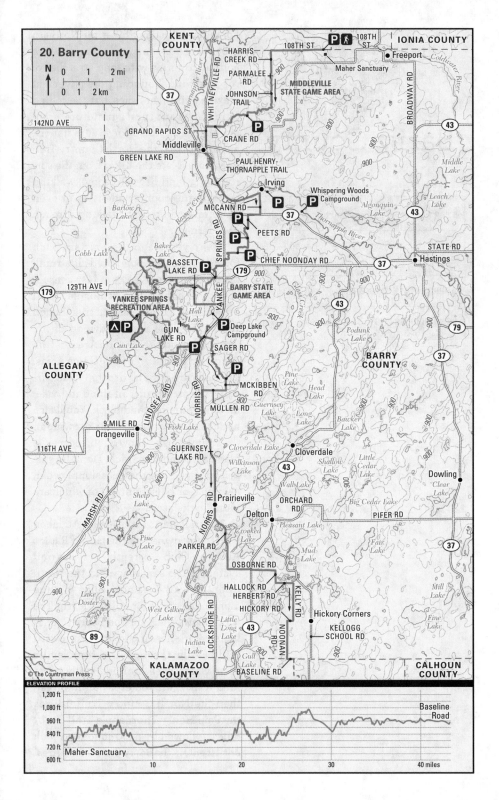

20. Barry County

N

0　1　2 mi

0　1　2 km

KENT COUNTY

IONIA COUNTY

Freeport

Middleville

Hastings

Orangeville

Cloverdale

Dowling

Delton

Prairieville

Hickory Corners

ALLEGAN COUNTY

BARRY COUNTY

KALAMAZOO COUNTY

CALHOUN COUNTY

142ND AVE

HARRIS CREEK RD

108TH ST

108TH ST

PARMALEE RD

JOHNSON TRAIL

Maher Sanctuary

MIDDLEVILLE STATE GAME AREA

GRAND RAPIDS ST

CRANE RD

GREEN LAKE RD

PAUL HENRY-THORNAPPLE TRAIL

Irving

Whispering Woods Campground

Algonquin Lake

Leach Lake

Middle Lake

MCCANN RD

PEETS RD

CHIEF NOONDAY RD

STATE RD

BASSETT LAKE RD

129TH AVE

BARRY STATE GAME AREA

YANKEE SPRINGS RECREATION AREA

GUN LAKE RD

Gun Lake

Hall Lake

Deep Lake Campground

SAGER RD

MCKIBBEN RD

MULLEN RD

Podunk Lake

Pine Lake

Head Lake

Long Lake

Guernsey Lake

Baucker Lake

9 MILE RD

116TH AVE

Fish Lake

GUERNSEY LAKE RD

Wilkinson Lake

Cloverdale Lake

Shallow Lake

Little Cedar Lake

Big Cedar Lake

Clear Lake

Wall Lake

ORCHARD RD

PIFER RD

Pleasant Lake

Crooked Lake

Mud Lake

Fair Lake

PARKER RD

OSBORNE RD

HALLOCK RD

HERBERT RD

HICKORY RD

KELLOGG SCHOOL RD

NOONAN RD

Little Long Lake

Indian Lake

Gull Lake

BASELINE RD

Mill Lake

Fine Lake

Lake Doster

West Gilkey Lake

Pine Lake

Shelp Lake

MARSH RD

LINDSEY RD

NORRIS RD

LOCKSHORE RD

KELLY RD

YANKEE RD

SPRINGS RD

WHITNEVILLE RD

BROADWAY RD

Thornapple River

Bassett Creek

Thornapple River

Coldwater River

Glass Creek

Barlow Lake

Cobb Lake

Baker Lake

37

37

37

37

37

43

43

43

43

43

179

179

179

79

89

© The Countryman Press

ELEVATION PROFILE

1,200 ft

1,080 ft

960 ft

840 ft

720 ft

600 ft

Maher Sanctuary

Baseline Road

10　20　30　40 miles

Thomas Funke

A ROAD WALK IN BARRY COUNTY

Then it heads southeast into the Yankee Springs Recreation Area, southwest back into the Barry State Game Area, then over a 15.0-mile road walk until the next trail segment just over the Barry County line in Kalamazoo County.

HOW TO FIND

The Maher Audubon Sanctuary at Baker/Wood School Road and 108th Street on the Kent and Barry County line has a small parking lot. From Freeport, take 108th Street west 2.0 miles. From Hastings take W. State Road west 3.5 miles, then turn north on Wood School Road for 6.0 miles.

The nearest parking to the southern end of this segment is a small lot for a W. K. Kellogg Biological Station interpretive trail on B Avenue just west of 39th Street. Another option is in the suburb of Hickory Corners, which is less than 1.0 mile to the east of the road walk on Hickory Road. From MI 89 between Richland and Battle Creek, take 40th Street north to B Avenue, turn east, and drive about 1.0 mile. Continue north 2.5 miles to Hickory Corners.

FACILITIES AND SERVICES

The trail and road walks pass by several communities with services, including Freeport, Hastings (full services), Delton, Hickory Corners, and Richland. The trail does pass through Middleville, which has most services except medical and lodging.

Middleville was the first "trail town"

designated by the North Country Trail Association. The downtown district of Middleville has restaurants, information at the township and village halls, and a hardware store. If you take Main Street west to the stoplight and turn north, you'll find groceries and financial services. Turn south, and the post office is on the right.

The Gun Lake area has groceries, sporting goods, financial services, and lodging on the west side of the lake.

Prairieville has a café and a gas station with limited groceries and supplies.

Hastings is the nearest full-service town, with a hospital, laundromats, hardware, lodging, outfitting supplies, and groceries.

Thomas Funke

A SIGN OF GOOD TRAILS TO COME

THE HIKE

Park at the Maher Audubon Sanctuary and hike west on 108th Street, cross the gate at Solomon Trail, and after 2.0 miles turn left (south) on North Harris Creek Road. This segment is composed of a gravel road walk along the Kent and Barry County lines. Enter the Middleville State Game Area in 1.0 mile at Parmalee Road. Cross over Parmalee Road and take the old road, locally known as Johnson Trail, south into the game area. The walk is hilly and rolling as you head south, crossing a small creek along the way.

At 4.4 miles, leave Johnson Trail and turn right and head west through the heart of the Middleville State Game Area. The topography is kettle and kame, and the habitat is mature oak forest with some openings.

Come to North Robertson Road (5.8 miles), turn left, and walk south 0.1 mile as a road walk to a parking lot, then west into the woods through quite hilly terrain. In the spring, this is an excellent place to hear and see migrating and nesting woodland birds like wood thrushes, scarlet tanagers, and even the rare cerulean warbler.

The trail will merge with West Crane Road at the 7.0-mile mark as it comes in from your left. Hike 0.8 mile as a road walk east through a residential neighborhood. Turn left (south) onto Whitneyville Road/Grand Rapids Street and enter Middleville, which has most services except lodging and medical.

At 8.6 miles, turn southwest (right) onto East Main Street. Walk the main drag west, where you'll find a hardware store and a couple of restaurants. Just before the Thornapple River at 8.8 miles, turn left (south) when you see (just before the bridge crossing the Thornapple River) a gazebo with a stagecoach underneath, which is the beginning of a short jaunt on the Thornapple/Paul Henry Trail.

The Paul Henry Trail was a relatively long-lived railroad which was in active use from 1869 to 1983. Today, the trail is a multiuse, paved trail that is heavily used by locals. It is important to note that a section of this trail is closed during the firearm deer season and the Paul Henry portion of the trail is closed all of November. The trail follows and crosses the Thornapple River through floodplain forest and is flat. Keep your eyes open for redheaded woodpeckers, which are common in the area.

After hiking 3.7 miles on the paved trail, turn right (south) on McCann Road (12.5 miles) as a road walk. Just east 1.9 miles is Irving Road, where there is the modern Whispering Waters Campground. Turn right (west) onto MI 37 for 0.5 mile, then left (south) onto Peets Road (13.9 miles).

Walk through a rural residential setting for 0.6 mile until you come to a trailhead with a parking lot on the right (west) side of the road. Take the trail into the woods for 0.5 mile back to Peets Road and use the road to cross Glass Creek trout stream; then head 0.4 mile south until the trail reenters the woods to the right (west) side of Peets Road. The trail heads west through pine plantations before heading south to Bowens Mill Road (14.9 miles).

Turn right onto Bowens Mill Road, which is a road walk west to circumvent private property and to cross an intermittent stream. The trail turns left (south) into woods in 0.5 mile, curls around the east side of a field, heads south to Yankee Springs Road through pine forest, and then turns left (south).

There is a parking lot about 100 feet south of where the trail crosses the road. The trail goes into the forest, turns southwest, then heads south to MI 179 (with parking) to cross Turner Creek. Continue hiking through heavy woods, mostly oak with a mix of pine. The trail follows the contour of a hill to the south, then bends west and rises in elevation before leveling out.

At 17.5 miles, you'll cross Bassett Lake Road. Although there isn't any sort of grand entrance, you are crossing over from the Barry State Game Area into Yankee Springs Recreation Area. Combined, the two properties account for 22,000 acres of habitat, making this the second-largest natural area in the southern Lower Peninsula. Only Allegan State Game Area is larger. Your heavily wooded walk continues west through rolling terrain to Norris Trail. Camping is available by taking the Long Lake Trail east 2.0 miles to a modern campground.

At 18.5 miles, look for a trail intersection with the Deep Lake Trail as that can take you 2.0 miles to the east to a rustic campground. The trail makes a southerly turn, and works its way south through hilly, forested terrain. The habitat contains more oak, especially white oak, through this stretch. Turn easterly and cross a couple of rough and little used gravel roads, then head south and hug the west shore of Hall Lake. The trail is heavily used here as it is part of a popular loop trail.

At the 21.0-mile mark, cross the paved Gun Lake Road and pay attention to trail signage as the area has a horse trail that intermingles with the North Country Trail. You will cross the horse trail and continue hiking through mixed oak and pine forest uphill to the Yankee Springs Road trailhead (22.5 miles).

Cross over the paved road and back into the Barry State Game Area. The ter-

Thomas Funke

TALL SUNFLOWERS GROW IN MOIST HABITATS

rain is hilly and heavily forested. Hike east, then south, cross Sager Road, and then head southeast to McKibben Road (24.3 miles). In 2016, the new trail will utilize the east side of the Circle Pines property, coming out on Mullen Road, and skipping the road walk until you reach Guernsey Lake Road.

A road walk commences until you reach Kalamazoo County, through rolling countryside filled with farms, fields, and forests. You'll go south on McKibben Road, right (west) on Mullen Road, and left (south) on Norris Road. Be advised around Guernsey Lake Road that there isn't much of an apron and little space between the guardrail and the road.

Prairieville (31.5 miles) is a cross-roads with a gas station/party store and a restaurant. Norris Road splits off to the right; you need to hike Parker Road to the left (south). The road splits Middle Crooked Lake and Crooked Lake, and is a reliable water source. You are now in the Kalamazoo River watershed.

Turn left (east) onto Osborne Road (gravel) (33.7 miles), right (south) onto Hallock Road, left (east) on Herbert Road, right (south) on South Kelly Road, right (west) on Hickory Road, then left (south) onto Noonan Road. Noonan Road ends at the county line at Baseline Road. Hike Baseline east 0.3 mile, where it turns right (south) and enters Kalamazoo County at North 39th Street (40.1 miles).

Battle Creek

START: Baseline and 38th Street

END: C Drive North and 15 Mile Road

APPROXIMATE HIKING TIME: 14–20 hours

LENGTH OF SECTION: 38.2 miles

Less than 1.0 mile after crossing the Barry/Kalamazoo County line, the trail enters the W. K. Kellogg Biological Station, owned by Michigan State University. This agricultural research station has an experimental forest, automated dairy farm (open to the public), bird sanctuary, and biological field station bordering Gull Lake. This field station was founded by W. K. Kellogg of Kellogg cereal fame.

The trail in the biological station skirts along a couple of lakes and parallels then crosses Augusta Creek, a trout stream. After leaving the station, it utilizes private property until it reaches the village of Augusta. It is important to note for the long-distance hiker that there are no trailside camping opportunities anywhere on this segment of trail. One will have to utilize the Fort Custer State Recreation Area or motels in the Battle Creek and Marshall area.

From Augusta, the trail enters the Fort Custer National Cemetery and exits across from the Battle Creek Veterans Administration Hospital as a short road walk until the Battle Creek Linear Park, which takes the hiker through the heart of downtown while hugging the Kalamazoo and Battle Creek Rivers. You'll cross some railroad tracks and utilize a few side streets to enter the Ott Biological Preserve, part of the Calhoun County park system. Bring your plant identification book, as this preserve has hundreds of species of plants—making it one of the most biologically diverse places in southern Michigan.

The trail utilizes a chain of three county parks in total—besides the Ott, there are Kimball Pines and the Historic Bridge Park. Cross under the railroad tracks, and it is nearly a 10.0-mile walk to the next segment of trail in Marshall.

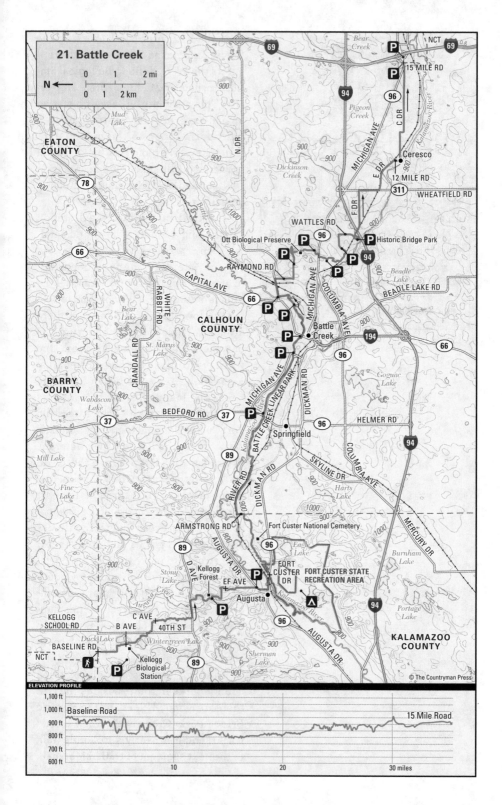

21. Battle Creek

N ←

| 0 | 1 | 2 mi |
| 0 | 1 | 2 km |

EATON COUNTY

Mud Lake

Bear Creek

NCT

15 MILE RD

Pigeon Creek

Dickinson Creek

Ceresco

12 MILE RD

WHEATFIELD RD

Ott Biological Preserve

WATTLES RD

Historic Bridge Park

RAYMOND RD

CAPITAL AVE

Battle Creek

Beadle Lake

BEADLE LAKE RD

CALHOUN COUNTY

WHITE RABBIT RD

Bear Lake

CRANDALL RD

St. Marys Lake

BARRY COUNTY

Wabascon Lake

BEDFORD RD

BATTLE CREEK LINEAR PARK

Springfield

Goguac Lake

HELMER RD

Mill Lake

Fine Lake

Harts Lake

ARMSTRONG RD

SKYLINE DR

Fort Custer National Cemetery

Eagle Lake

Burnham Lake

MERCURY DR

Stony Lake

Kellogg Forest

EF AVE

EFORT CUSTER DR

FORT CUSTER STATE RECREATION AREA

Augusta

Portage Lake

KELLOGG SCHOOL RD

C AVE

B AVE

40TH ST

AUGUSTA DR

KALAMAZOO COUNTY

Duck Lake

BASELINE RD

Wintergreen Lake

NCT

Kellogg Biological Station

Sherman Lake

© The Countryman Press

ELEVATION PROFILE

1,100 ft	
1,000 ft	Baseline Road
900 ft	
800 ft	
700 ft	
600 ft	

15 Mile Road

10   20   30 miles

You will pass through the unincorporated Ceresco—which is on the Kalamazoo River and, up until recently, had an impoundment.

HOW TO FIND

The nearest parking to the western end of this segment is a small lot for a W. K. Kellogg Biological Station interpretive trail on B Avenue just west of 39th Street. Another option is in the suburb of Hickory Corners, which is less than 1.0 mile to the east of the road walk on Hickory Road. From MI 89 between Richland and Battle Creek, take 40th Street north to B Avenue, turn east, and drive about 1.0 mile. Continue north 2.5 miles to Hickory Corners.

The eastern trailhead is a Michigan Department of Transportation carpool lot at C Drive North and 15 Mile Road at I-94, on the western side of Marshall.

FACILITIES AND SERVICES

Battle Creek is a full-service town. Most services are found within 1.0 mile of the trail. Downtown Battle Creek has food and outfitting services. The hospital complex is found less than 1.0 mile from the trail by hiking north on Capital Avenue, then north on North Avenue. There is also taxi and bus service in Battle Creek.

Augusta has a post office, hardware store, and restaurants. Fort Custer State Recreation Area has a concession and camp office with limited supplies, and is open from spring through fall.

THE HIKE

From the intersection of North 39th Street and Baseline Road, hike south through an agricultural setting and enter the W. K. Kellogg Biological Station by turning left (east) at the 0.25-mile mark, take the dirt road east within the biological station another 0.25 mile, and then the trail will head south along the west edge of a field. Continue past Duck Lake to B Avenue (1.2 miles).

Continue your trail hike to a kiosk at the bird sanctuary driveway. Hike along the edge of a field to 40th Street, where the trail enters woods (2.6 miles), follows inside the woodlot near an agricultural field full of test plots to the east, and then turns south to the next road.

At C Avenue (3.2 miles) you'll enter private property and enjoy the heavily wooded walk south over rolling terrain; at MI 89 (4.5 miles), turn left, using the highway to hike east to cross the trout stream Augusta Creek. Turn right into the W. K. Kellogg Experimental Forest (5.1 miles), which has a maze of trails through a forest where it is obvious there has been artificial tinkering with different forest types, ages, densities, and species. Hike uphill and then descend to cross Augusta Creek, follow along a service road south, and turn east and cross a covered bridge built by local volunteers. Turn south and follow the river. The trail will make a right angle east and go along a line of trees before reentering the woods. The trail will make a hairpin turn going north and then immediately head south onto private property (7.1 miles).

Hike through the woods to EF Avenue East, turn right (west) for a few hundred feet as a road walk, then left (south) onto private land. You'll climb slightly to the top of a small hill, level out and hike along the edge of the woods and an open field, then descend to the next road (Augusta Drive) at the 9.3-mile mark. There is parking to either side of a locked gate; try not to block it if parking here.

Turn right and hike south into Augusta (9.8 miles).

Augusta has all services but medical to the east of the intersection of Augusta Drive and MI 96. Turn left and hike east on MI 96, crossing the Kalamazoo River and then railroad tracks. Turn left (north) on Fort Custer Drive. Across from this intersection is the entrance to Fort Custer State Recreation Area.

Immediately on your right, look for the trail and a kiosk which enters Fort Custer National Cemetery (11.3 miles) and cross Whitman Creek to another kiosk, then follow the boundary between the forest and the large marsh complex to the south. Utilizing dikes, it zigzags over some wet areas, then continues in a northeasterly direction through the woods. Come out to Armstrong Road and turn left to walk north 0.25 mile to River Road, where you turn right (east). River Road (14.3 miles) is a road walk past a few industries, joining the Battle Creek Linear Park, just before crossing the railroad tracks at the Battle Creek Wastewater Treatment Plant.

Battle Creek Linear Park starts at the 16.0-mile mark. This multiuse, paved trail is a city park that has several loops and spurs throughout the Battle Creek area. You'll follow the Kalamazoo River (on your north) through floodplain forest.

The MI 37/Helmer Road/Bedford Road (18.2 miles) Trailhead and parking is to the north side of the Kalamazoo River. The paved trail continues to follow the river while paralleling the nearby Jackson Street. Your hike gets noticeably more urban and residential as you head east.

At 20.6 miles, cross MI 89/North Washington Avenue and enter the downtown district and start to follow the Battle Creek River. Cross Michigan Avenue West, then McCamly Street North,

then Capital Avenue SW. All services are within a few blocks, including medical and the post office. Cross MI 66/Division Street, and the trail crosses to the south side of the Battle Creek River and follows its south bank, crossing Elm Street, then using Union Street to cross back to the north bank while paralleling Wagner Drive through an urban residential setting. There are several parking lots along Wagner Drive.

At Emmett Street (23.4 miles) the multiuse trail goes straight (north), but you'll turn right (east) and use Emmett Street to cross a series of railroad tracks where a new section joins the Calhoun County Trailway multiuse path after crossing Raymond Road. Enter a parking lot for the Ott Biological Preserve.

At 24.7 miles, turn east onto East Jameson Avenue and walk through a small neighborhood. In 0.5 mile, walk into a parking lot for the Ott Biological Preserve. The local trail chapter has worked with Calhoun County Parks and Recreation and other trail partners to develop a multiuse trail system in this preserve. The Ott Biological Preserve is rich in biological and geological features—take time to slow down to enjoy the surroundings. Follow the North Country Trail through the preserve—on eskers, through swamps, and across a historic bridge that was set in place by a helicopter. Exit the Ott Biological Preserve, rejoining the Calhoun County Trailway, then cross MI 96/Michigan Avenue (27.3 miles).

Continue on the shared Calhoun County Trailway and North Country Trail well past the McDonald's, then head south to a junction where the trails separate. Follow the North Country Trail, and it will rejoin the Calhoun County Trailway in Kimball Pines. Continue on the shared trail. Cross Wattles Road and the

THE TRAIL CROSSES AND PARALLELS THE KALAMAZOO RIVER SEVERAL TIMES

Calhoun County Trail will break north and enter Historic Bridge Park (29.4 miles).

The Calhoun County Road Commission acquired several historic bridges and placed them in this park that sits on the Kalamazoo River. The trail utilizes several of these bridges as its trajectory takes a hairpin turn and crosses under the railroad tracks while heading north, then comes to a paved road, F Drive North, which is used to cross I-94.

At 31.4 miles, start a road walk to Marshall. Turn right on 11 Mile Road and head south, then left (east) on the gravel E Drive North, right (south) on 12 Mile Road, and left (east) on C Drive North. Your hike is through mostly agricultural and rural residential territory, even though the Kalamazoo River is less than 1.0 mile away. Take C Drive North, which bends north to Michigan/MI 96, which is used to reach to 15 Mile Road about 0.2 mile to the east.

At the 38.2-mile mark is the intersection of 15 Mile Road and Michigan Avenue. There is a carpool lot 0.2 mile to the east, just past the on-ramp to I-69.

22

Calhoun County Countryside

START: 15 Mile Road and C Drive North

END: Hillsdale and Calhoun County line

APPROXIMATE HIKING TIME: 11–20 hours

LENGTH OF SECTION: 33.2 miles

Creating a hiking trail through mostly private land is challenging. One must link together numerous cooperative private landowners to avoid long road walks, which is the current situation between Battle Creek to the state line. For now, your hike will mostly consist of road walking. However, the local trail chapter, working with municipal park districts, has identified a corridor that would utilize the Kalamazoo River. Currently there are only three small trail segments and many road miles as it hopscotches from Marshall to Albion down to Homer near the source of the Kalamazoo.

The Marshall River Walk is about 0.75 mile long and has the Kalamazoo River as its setting. For the long-distance hiker there is another road walk to Albion, where there is a 0.2-mile trail in Victory Park. This is one of the first steps in completing the long-term plan for Calhoun County Parks and Recreation—to create a trail along the Kalamazoo River between Battle Creek and Albion the North Country Trail can utilize. Until then, the long-distance hiker will have road walks to look forward to. From Albion, it is almost a 9.0-mile road walk to Homer, where another short trail segment awaits in the form of a bike path and nature trail. Then it is another road walk for 6.0 miles until the Hillsdale County line.

For the long-distance hiker, the countryside setting is getting quite agricultural. The soils are fertile and the terrain is rather flat, making for excellent conditions for growing crops, mostly corn and soybeans in these parts.

Marshall is a modest tourist town with all services and many choices for lodging, including several B&Bs. Albion also has all services and Homer has all but medical. Other than these three short

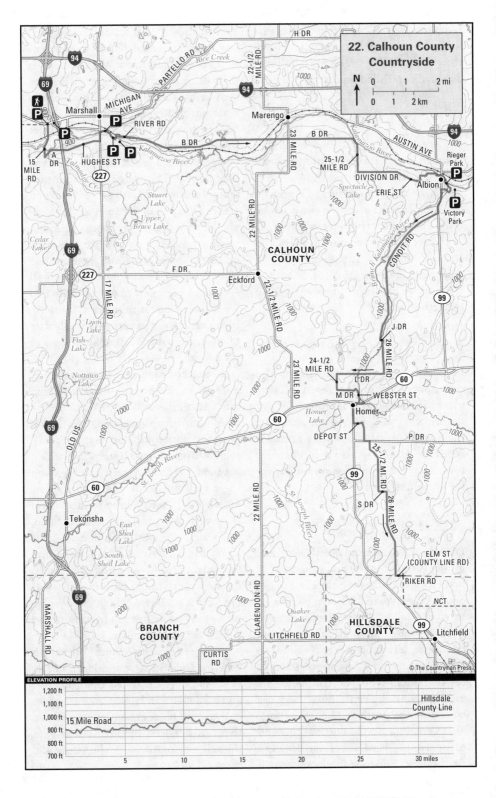

segments of trail, long-distance hikers will need to enjoy the rural character of their road walk between Marshall and Jonesville in Hillsdale County.

HOW TO FIND

The western trailhead is a Michigan Department of Transportation carpool lot at C Drive North and 15 Mile Road at I-94, on the western side of Marshall.

The trail at the southern end is a road walk. The nearest trail access points are in Homer, which has parking lots and street-side parking. In Hillsdale County, Jonesville is the nearest town that the trail passes through that has parking opportunities.

FACILITIES AND SERVICES

Marshall is a full-service town. The downtown district has nearly all services, including a hospital. West of downtown you'll find most services, including outfitting supplies at major retailers. Albion is also a full-service town. Homer has most services, except for a hospital.

THE HIKE

From the intersection of 15 Mile Road and MI 96, turn left (east) and hike 15 Mile Road to the south, then turn left (east) onto A Drive West (which changes names to West Hughes Street after it crosses I-69) and enter Marshall. The road route continues left (north) on Kalamazoo Street, crossing the Kalamazoo River to the Marshall Riverwalk Trailhead (3.2 miles) on the right. You'll find all services by continuing north to Michigan/Business Loop I-94. To the north at this end of the river walk is Dark Horse Brewery. At the fountain in the roundabout, you'll find the downtown district to the east and the commercial district to the west.

The Marshall River Walk is a series of boardwalks, paved paths, and bridges that bring you along the shore of the Kalamazoo River. Cross Jones Street (which has parking), then the outlet of Rice Creek; at the 0.5-mile mark where the trail forks, continue on the east (right). The trail becomes a nice walk through the forest before you walk through the grounds at the Marshall Recreation Department (parking), cross a small bay on a footbridge, then come to South Marshall Avenue. The river walk continues across Marshall Avenue, which makes a great side trip for the long-distance hiker. Otherwise turn north; walk past the hydroelectric plant, and cross the Kalamazoo River to the north.

Cross the Kalamazoo River at the 3.2-mile mark. For the long-distance hiker, it is a 12.2-mile walk until Victory Park in Albion. Turn right (east) on Clinton Street, right (south) on Maple Street, then left (east) onto River Road which turns into B Drive North upon leaving the city limits as it bends to the left (east). You'll have a long road walk on B Drive North until you reach Albion, and you'll cross the Kalamazoo River along the way. At 25.5 Mile Road and the Kalamazoo River, turn right (south) on the county road and turn left (east) onto Division Drive, which changes its name to West Erie Street upon entering Albion at the 15.6-mile mark.

Albion has most services. Turn north on West Gale Street, enter Harris Park, veer east, and cross the Kalamazoo River and hike its north bank. Cross the river to the south bank at South Eaton Street, then turn left (east) onto West Cass, pass the building for Albion Public Safety, and cross MI 99.

At Market Place, veer southeast through a developed park on the Albion River Trail, a multiuse trail which follows the Kalamazoo River. Cross East Erie Street into Rieger Park and continue on the paved trail toward Victory Park.

Upon crossing the south branch of the Kalamazoo River, enter Victory Park (16.6 miles). Continue on the paved trail until you come to a large pavilion, which you'll follow around clockwise onto a service drive, then onto Veterans Way, then west (right) onto Haven Road—crossing the south branch of the Kalamazoo River (16.9 miles) on a road bridge.

For the long-distance hiker, your road walk begins here to the city of Homer 8.9 miles away. A nice feature of this road walk is that it is lined with trees. Take River Street west, then head left (south) on MI 99 to cross the Kalamazoo River yet again, and turn right (west) onto Condit Road, which bends to the south. Cross the Kalamazoo River on Condit Road, which changes names as it makes a jog left through the J Drive South intersection to 26 Mile Road, and you'll turn right onto 26½ Mile Road. In 1.0 mile you'll turn right (west) onto L Drive South and then left (south) onto 24.5 Mile Road.

Enter Homer and turn left onto the Homer Linear Path (25.8 miles). Use the Homer Linear Path, a paved, multi-use trail skirting the north side of this small town. The multiuse trail parallels M Drive South and goes east into the forest when the road bends to the south. Hike through the river-lined forest, come to the south branch of the Kalamazoo River, follow it for several hundred feet, then turn right (south) on North Webster Street, which brings you to the downtown district.

The trail jogs left (east) at MI 60, goes under the bridge, and then takes a hard right onto South Byron Street to downtown Homer. Turn right (west) on Main Street, left (south) on MI 99 for 8 blocks, left (east) on Depot Street, and right (south) on 25.5 Mile Road—which bends to the east and changes its name to S Drive South for 0.2 mile before turning right (south) again and changing names to 26 Mile Road. 26 Mile Road makes a jog at North Elm Street at the Calhoun and Hillsdale County line. You are now on the boundary between the Kalamazoo and St. Joseph watersheds.

At the 33.2-mile mark is the Hillsdale County line. There are a couple of options to consider for long-distance hikers. The recommended road route continues in the next chapter; however, long-distance hikers have used MI 99 to hike south through Litchfield to save a few miles and have a resupply point.

23

Hillsdale County

START: Hillsdale and Calhoun County line

END: Ohio state line

APPROXIMATE HIKING TIME: 10–25 hours

LENGTH OF SECTION: 41.7 miles

Hillsdale County is mostly an agricultural community with few publicly owned natural areas compared to the rest of Michigan's counties. That being said, the North Country Trail utilizes a bike trail, an abandoned railway, and a trail system through the Lost Nation State Game Area through about half of the county. What road walking there is, if you are taking the recommended road route, will be light in traffic and scenic in nature. If you are road walking, there are many open fields that are not in production that produce some of the best grassland bird watching you'll have in Michigan.

From the county line, if you take the recommended road route, you'll bypass Litchfield to the east. What few long-distance hikers there have been, including myself, utilize MI 99 headed south out of Albion to Litchfield (8.5 miles), then continue a road walk to the MI 99 bike path which starts at the north end of Jonesville, saving 1.5 miles of a road walk and giving you more opportunities to resupply and lodge.

In Jonesville, connect with the MI 99 bikeway. Although this isn't a hiking trail through the woods but a bike path, you'll be comfortable with the hike as it keeps you off the road. Once you reach Hillsdale, use sidewalks on surface streets until the Baw Beese Trail starts on an abandoned rail grade and takes you about 5.0 miles to Osseo. This segment takes you through mostly natural areas.

In Osseo, utilize surface streets for 1.5 miles before entering the Lost Nation State Game Area. The trail will hopscotch from road walk to trail headed southeast. This hike is best enjoyed in the springtime, when the ephemeral flowers are at their peak. Bloodroot, spring beauties, trout lily, and a host of other flowers give

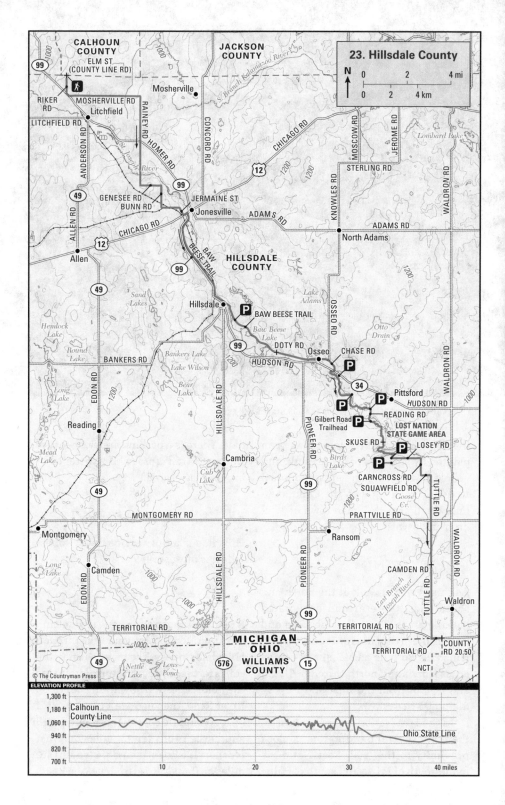

ELEVATION PROFILE

CHESTNUT-SIDED WARBLER NEST IN LOST NATION STATE GAME AREA

Thomas Funke

the impression that the forest has been painted by splashes of white, pink, and yellow. Leave the game area and it is a 10.0-mile road walk to the Ohio state line. You'll pass the small town of Waldron on the west.

HOW TO FIND

As this is a road walk at the north and south ends, there are no designated parking areas. There is street-side and lot parking in the cities of Jonesville and Hillsdale. Both lie on MI 99 and can be accessed via the north through Albion and I-94 or from the west and I-69 by taking US 12 east.

In the Lost Nation State Game Area, there are several parking lots in close proximity to the trail. Lost Nation is found south of MI 34 and south of Hills-

dale. There is a parking area just east of where the trail crosses MI 34 after leaving the Osseo area.

FACILITIES AND SERVICES

Hillsdale is a full-service town. Jonesville has most services.

THE HIKE

If road walking in an agricultural setting is for you, you'll enjoy your hike through Hillsdale County. The terrain is flat, the soil is fertile, and agriculture dominates the landscape. Start by hiking south on Riker Road, then use a left turn onto MI 99 for 0.1 mile to connect eastbound with another left turn for 3.4 miles on West Mosherville Road, then right (south) 4.0 miles on Rainey Road to Genessee Road.

Take Genessee Road right (east) a mile, then head right (south) on North Bunn Road 1.0 mile to Jonesville Road and turn left (east) on a road that bends south and changes names to Jermaine Street.

At the 11.8-mile mark in Jonesville, turn left (northeast) onto US 12 and then immediately turn right to start hiking on the paved, multiuse Baw Beese Trail, which parallels MI 99. Baw Beese was a local Potawatomi chief who lived in the area until he was forcibly removed in 1840 due to the Indian Removal Act. He ruled about 150 in his tribe, and they raised maize and other crops in the area.

The multiuse trail is in close proximity to the highway and the St. Joseph River. The trail enters the city of Hillsdale on the north and heads through commercial and residential areas, splits from MI 99 at Carlton Road East, and uses sidewalks to East Bacon Street in Hillsdale (17.1 miles).

The Baw Beese Trail jogs right (east) at Bacon Street and MI 99, where you'll find most services. Cross West Bacon Street and continue south on the paved, multiuse trail. You may park at the intersection of Barnard and Griswold Streets. The trail becomes more natural and country residential and less agricultural as it follows the north shore of Baw Beese Lake. Pass the lake on your right (south), and the terrain will rise slightly as you cross Doty and South Lake Pleasant Roads. About 0.5 mile past crossing South Lake Pleasant Road, the multiuse trail ends and becomes a road walk on Beecher Road; the name changes to Chase Road, and it comes to MI 34 at Osseo (23.4 miles).

Osseo is unincorporated with no services. There is a small parking lot 0.4 mile to the southeast. Lost Nation State Game Area is 2,500 acres of hilly, heavily forested countryside bisected by the east

Thomas Funke

GIANT TRILLIUM IS A COMMON WILDFLOWER IN WOODED AREAS LIKE LOST NATION STATE GAME AREA

branch of the St. Joseph River. The area is known for its spring wildflowers.

Cross MI 34, hike downhill, follow the edge of a swamp, cross two small creeks, climb uphill, and start a road walk at 1.2 miles, which utilizes a little-used and rough game area gravel road for 1.4 miles. There is a parking lot and a small creek where the road turns left into the woods at the 26.0-mile mark.

The trail continues through forested, hilly topography, mostly on a hilltop, then descends to cross the outlet of Lake Number Five and to connect to a parking lot at South Rumsey Road (27.2 miles). Turn right onto Rumsey Road, hike south, descend to cross the east branch of the St. Joseph River, then continue south on the road (it will change names to Gilbert Road after East Reading Road).

The Gilbert Road Trailhead (27.8 miles) has a parking lot—the trail starts from here, turns left into the woods, winds southeast through forest, and passes the shallow and weedy Lake Number Eight on the south. You'll climb uphill, level out, then descend to cross Skuse Road. The trail will loop east, then downhill to cross a small creek, then back east. You'll experience a steep ascent to the top of another hill, then a steep descent to South Pittsford Road, where there is an intermittent stream.

Turn right at South Pittsford Road (30.9 miles); there is a parking lot 0.2 mile south of where the trail crosses the intersection with Losey Road. For the long-distance hiker, a road walk ensues to the Ohio state line through heavily agricultural areas. Thankfully, there are multiple stream crossings along the way. Turn left onto Losey Road and hike 1.7 miles, then south (right) on Carncross Road for 0.75 mile, then left (east) 0.5 mile on Squawfield Road—where an intermittent stream crosses twice. Turn right for a straight shot due south 7.4 miles on Tuttle Road to Territorial Road, where you will turn left (east) for 0.5 mile. At the intersection with County Road 20.50 (CR 20.50) and Territorial Road is the Ohio state line (41.7 miles).

III.

WISCONSIN

24

MacQuarrie Wetlands and Pattison State Park

For the long-distance hiker, your adventure starts not in the wilds of a northern Wisconsin forest but during a long and arduous road walk through the country-side. The first segment of trail is a detour off County Route C/W (CR C/W) to access a foot trail that winds through the MacQuarrie Wetlands, artificial ponds created by the Wisconsin Department of Transportation to replace wetlands filled in due to the construction of the nearby US 53. These wetlands are now managed by the University of Wisconsin–Superior for outdoor learning and research. The trail then enters the Douglas County Forest, where several overlooks provide views of the Nemadji River Valley.

For the day hiker, Pattison State Park makes for a nice day hike and is set up to accommodate walk-in campers who wish to use the trails in the park for day trips while not having to move their campsite every day.

Pattison State Park's history started about a billion years ago, when ancient lava flowed over the landscape. Today's basalt is the remnant of this volcanic activity. Over the next billion years, many geological activities shaped the park. Oceans covered the area and left sediments, creating sandstone. A fault that formed during that period, known today as the Douglas Fault, can be seen at the base of the Big Manitou Falls (the southern section rose to a 50 degree angle). As the earth rose over the eons, breccia was created, due to all the heat and pressure of the bedrock rubbing and pushing against itself. These faults, cracks, and fissures have been explored since prehistoric times for minerals such as copper.

Then in recent times (geologically speaking), glaciers a mile thick scraped away the soil and loose bedrock, such as the sandstone that was created after

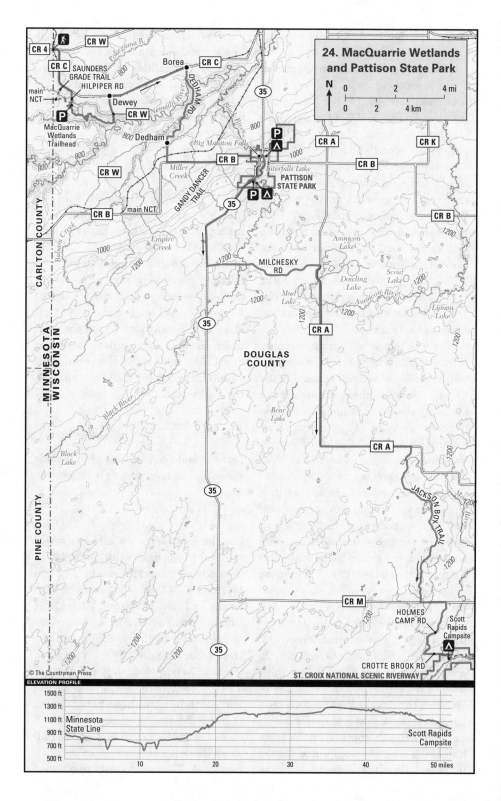

24. MacQuarrie Wetlands and Pattison State Park

N

| 0 | | 2 | | 4 mi |

| 0 | 2 | | 4 km |

CR 4

CR W

CR C

Borea

CR C

Pokegama R.

800

SAUNDERS GRADE TRAIL HILPIPER RD

35

main NCT

Dewey

CR W

P

MacQuarrie Wetlands Trailhead

DEDHAM RD

Menadji River

800

Dedham

Fish River

800

800

P

Miller Creek

Big Manitou Falls

CR B

Interfalls Lake

1000

CR A

CR K

CR B

CARLTON COUNTY

CR W

GANDY DANCER TRAIL

P

PATTISON STATE PARK

35

CR B

main NCT

Balsam Creek

Empire Creek

1000

1200

MILCHESKY RD

1200

1200

Amnicon Lake

Dowling Lake

Scout Lake

1200

CR B

1200

35

Mud Lake

1200

Amnicon River

Lyman Lake

MINNESOTA WISCONSIN

Black River

1200

CR A

DOUGLAS COUNTY

1200

Black Lake

Bear Lake

35

CR A

1200

JACKSON BOX TRAIL

PINE COUNTY

1200

35

1200

1200

1200

CR M

1200

HOLMES CAMP RD

Scott Rapids Campsite

CROTTE BROOK RD

ST. CROIX NATIONAL SCENIC RIVERWAY

© The Countryman Press

ELEVATION PROFILE

| 1500 ft |
| 1300 ft |
| 1100 ft | Minnesota State Line |
| 900 ft |
| 700 ft |
| 500 ft |

Scott Rapids Campsite

10   20   30   40   50 miles

the oceans retreated. This exposed the basalt we see today.

The first signs of humans occurred about 9,000 years ago. Following the retreating glaciers, Native Americans from the Archaic and Old Copper Complex lived here until about 1,500 years ago, when Woodland Native Americans replaced them. The forests had rebounded after having several thousand years to recover from the glaciers that scraped the landscape clean. Ojibwe were here when Europeans arrived. The Ojibwe believed they could hear the voice of the Great Spirit, Gitchi Manitou, in the falling water. They mined rocks and quartz to make points and tools. Today the park is still rich in Native American artifacts.

The first record of European copper exploration in northwestern Wisconsin was below Big Manitou Falls and in the Copper Creek (northeastern) section of the park between 1845 and 1847. Mining has continued on and off over the years, usually driven by the price of copper. Various prospectors visited the area and created many test pits and holes in the rock throughout the park. Even gold and sliver were found here, and mining was active up through the Civil War. After the war, prices fell and mines were abandoned, but prices rebounded after the turn of the last century. However, the mines never became self-sustaining and were finally abandoned.

Pattison State Park is named for Martin Pattison, an early lumber man and miner. Pattison learned of a plan to build a power dam on the Black River, which would have destroyed Big Manitou Falls. To block the development, he secretly purchased 660 acres along the river from a number of landowners. With the donation of the land in 1918, Pattison saved the waterfall and the property surrounding it; Wisconsin dedicated this land as its sixth state park on January 20, 1920. Until 1935, facilities at Pattison were few. The Civilian Conservation Corps, during the Great Depression, built the majority of the facilities and infrastructure you see today.

HOW TO FIND

The University of Wisconsin–Superior MacQuarrie Wetlands are found by taking WI 35 south of Superior and then heading west onto CR C. After 7.0 miles, pass Barnes Road, turning onto Hilpiper Road to find the trailhead. Pattison State Park is 12.0 miles south of Superior on WI 35. For the West Mail Road Trailhead, take US 53 south of Solon Springs for 3 miles, then west onto CR M for 6.5 miles, then south onto West Mail Road for about 3.0 miles to the trailhead.

FACILITIES AND SERVICES

Pattison State Park has camping, potable water, and an interpretive building.

THE HIKE

For the long-distance hiker, a set of railroad tracks marks the beginning of your adventure at Minnesota CR 4 and Wisconsin CR C/W. Walk east into Wisconsin and turn right (south) onto CR C, which eventually bends east. Turn right (south) on the Saunders Grade multiuse trail. After 0.6 mile, the open ponds of the MacQuarrie Wetlands are reached. The trail follows the wetland dikes east and south to a trailhead parking area (3.6 miles).

At the MacQuarrie Wetlands Trailhead, there is parking and an information kiosk. The trail follows an old road south across a small bridge, turns briefly west, and then south and east while following wetland dikes. Look for waterfowl and other wetland wildlife in the ponds. After 0.7 mile the trail descends from the dike system in a southeasterly direction, entering the Douglas County Forest. It approaches the north rim of the Mud Creek valleys and Nemadji River. Follow the rim eastward through aspen forest past several overlooks. The trail descends and follows a small ridge out to CR W at the 6.2-mile mark.

Turn left (north) and follow CR W uphill 1.3 miles to the intersection with CR C at Dewey (which has no services). Turn right (east) and follow CR C 3.2 miles to Dedham Road. Turn right (south) on Dedham Road, which is a narrow gravel road that winds south, cross the Nemadji River, and finish after 4.4 miles at CR B, where you'll turn left (east) and walk 3.9 miles east to Pattison State Park.

Turn left (north) on WI 35 and enter the state park (15.2 miles) on your right through a picnic area. Follow the lightly blazed trail to the Beaver Slide Nature Trail, which follows the impoundment along its shore to the south; the trail then splits. To the left, the Logging Camp Trail takes you to a walk-in campground with several loops that make for an excellent base camp for a weekend of hiking, perfect for the day-tripper or weekend hiker. For the long-distance hiker, bear right; continue on the Beaver Slide Nature Trail, cross the Black River, follow its bank on the Little Falls Hiking Trail, and end up at the day use area at Little Manitou Falls. Exit the park here, and you'll end up back at WI 35. Pattison State Park has 17 modern, 38 semimodern, and 3 walk-in sites.

At 16.1 miles you'll leave Pattison State Park for a long road walk of 31.9 miles until you reach the St. Croix National Scenic Riverway. Water is limited to one lake, a few streams, and several stretches of wetland. There are no facilities or public lands, or any place to obtain refreshments or supplies.

Hike south on WI 35, then turn left (east) onto Milchesky Road, where you'll come to the intersection with CR A. Amnicon Lake is on the east side of CR A. Turn right and hike CR A south, then east. At 3.5 miles past where CR A makes the 90 degree turn to the left and heads east, turn right (south) onto the gravel road Jackson Box Trail and hike south through wetlands and somewhat hilly terrain. Turn left (east) onto CR M for 1.1 miles, then right (south) on Holmes Camp Road. Wind 2.4 miles south to an intersection with East Crotte Brook Road, and turn left (east). The road will intersect with West Mail Road; turn right (southeast) and take the entrance road (with a metal gate sporting a North Country Trail emblem and a foot bridge immediately behind the gate) to Scott Rapids Campsite (3 primitive sites, 8 people maximum) and enter the St. Croix National Scenic Riverway. Cross the Moose River to reach the campsite at the 48.0-mile mark.

25

St. Croix River and Solon Springs

START: South Mail Road at entrance to Scott Rapids Campsite

END: CR A Trailhead

APPROXIMATE HIKING TIME: 10–15 hours

LENGTH OF SECTION: 20.3 miles

The St. Croix River is a designated National Wild and Scenic River, one of the original eight designated when the corresponding legislation was passed in 1968. Downstream, the river becomes the common border between Minnesota and Wisconsin before it empties into the Mississippi River. Although the national park is over 250 miles in length, your hike in this national park is a short one of about 2.5 miles before it enters the Douglas County Forest.

Although you may only be hiking a few miles in the park, you'll hike plenty along and in the vicinity of this historic river upstream, and this segment will end near its headwaters. After a mostly wooded walk in the national park and county forest, you'll notice a drastic change in scenery when you cross East Prairie Lane. You'll leave the county forest and enter the Douglas County Wildlife Area. Except for a couple of patches of forest, it will be an open savanna hike through pine barrens, an area managed for a prairie/shrub ecosystem, with scattered trees and open fields until Solon Springs.

After crossing US 53, follow an off-road trail to South US Business 53, then surface streets to Lucius Woods County Park, where there is ample shade and camping along the scenic Upper St. Croix Lake. The trail continues to parallel the lake, which is really a wide spot in the St. Croix River, north of town, as it meanders through forests while utilizing some surface streets. The trail descends into the wet footing of the river valley to cross the St. Croix Creek, utilizing about 0.75 mile worth of boardwalk to negotiate the boggy and swampy footing. After leaving the forested wetland, the trail follows the contour to the parking lot at County Route A (CR A).

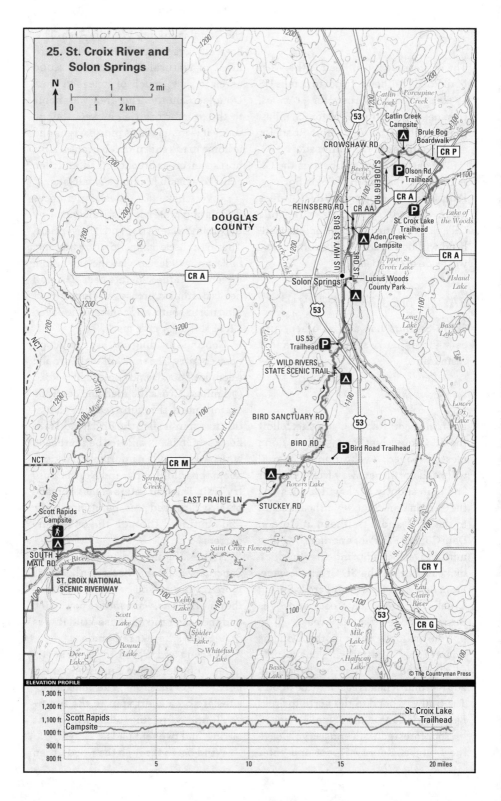

25. St. Croix River and Solon Springs

N

0   1   2 mi

0   1   2 km

1200

1200

1200

1100

Catlin Creek

Porcupine Creek

53

Catlin Creek Campsite

Brule Bog Boardwalk

CROWSHAW RD

CR P

Beebe Creek

SJOBERG RD

Olson Rd. Trailhead

1100

CR A

REINSBERG RD

CR AA

St. Croix Lake Trailhead

Lake of the Woods

Aden Creek Campsite

DOUGLAS COUNTY

US HWY 53 BUS

3RD ST

Upper St. Croix Lake

CR A

Park Creek

CR A

Island Lake

Solon Springs

Lucius Woods County Park

1200

1200

53

Long Lake

1100

Bass Lake

1200

US 53 Trailhead

WILD RIVERS STATE SCENIC TRAIL

Leo Creek

Lord Creek

1100

1100

53

Lower Ox Lake

1100

BIRD SANCTUARY RD

NCT

1200

1100

BIRD RD

Bird Road Trailhead

NCT

CR M

Spring Creek

Rovers Lake

St. Croix River

EAST PRAIRIE LN

STUCKEY RD

Scott Rapids Campsite

1100

SOUTH MAIL RD

St. Croix River

Saint Croix Flowage

CR Y

ST. CROIX NATIONAL SCENIC RIVERWAY

1100

Eau Claire River

1100

Webb Lake

1100

1100

53

CR G

Scott Lake

Spider Lake

One Mile Lake

1100

Deer Lake

Round Lake

Whitefish Lake

Bass Lake

Halfway Lake

© The Countryman Press

ELEVATION PROFILE

1,300 ft				
1,200 ft				
1,100 ft	Scott Rapids Campsite			St. Croix Lake Trailhead
1000 ft				
900 ft				
800 ft				
	5	10	15	20 miles

HOW TO FIND

The westernmost trailhead is the West Mail Road Trailhead. To get to it, take US 53 south of Solon Springs for 3.0 miles, then head west onto CR M for 6.5 miles, then south onto West Mail Road for about 3.0 miles to the trailhead.

The easternmost trailhead is the CR A Trailhead just north of Solon Springs. From Solon Springs, take CR A 1.5 miles north. CR A will split, going south, while CR P starts at the intersection; the trailhead will be immediately south on the west side of the road.

FACILITIES AND SERVICES

Solon Springs has a post office, grocery store, bank, some motels, and a restaurant.

THE HIKE

From the Scott Rapids Campsite, follow the St. Croix River for 2.5 miles along mostly wooded, level ground. The trail will head northeast away from the river and gain slightly in elevation (passing the Gordon Dam Spur, which heads south to the river and a trailhead at Gordon Dam County Park) for another 1.75 miles until it overlooks Spring Creek, which makes a bay on the St. Croix Flowage. From here, head north and cross Spring Creek; the trail bends east and goes through wooded swampy areas.

You are now deep in the Douglas County Forest. The trail will come out onto a lightly used gravel road; use it for about 200 feet until it heads east into the woods. The trail will bend to the north to cross East Prairie Lane at the 6.3-mile mark.

Your forested walk ends as you leave the Douglas County Forest and enter the Douglas County Wildlife Area. This area, managed by the Wisconsin Department of Natural Resources, is 4,000 acres in size, much of it leased from Douglas County. The area was home to the greater prairie chicken, though today it is managed as pine barrens and is home to the sharp-tailed grouse. Hike northeast, cross Stuckey Road, and then come to a basin holding a small lake.

Rovers Lake (7.7 miles) experiences fluctuating water levels influenced by the groundwater's rise and fall over time. There is a rustic campsite with a fire ring, table, and wilderness latrine—and room for tents at three separate pads. The trail heads northeast, crosses an old road running north-south, and comes to the paved CR M at the 8.4-mile mark.

Continue heading northeast, through open country. The trail will snake around a couple of ponds and come to Bird Road (9.1 miles). Cross the road and continue 0.2 mile north through a red pine plantation to a spur trail to the Bird Road Trailhead, which is 0.3 mile to the southeast, with parking and an informational kiosk about the wildlife area and North Country Trail. The trail enters a small acreage of fairly large red pine, bends northerly, and continues through the open pine barrens.

At the 9.8-mile mark you'll cross Bird Sanctuary Road and the terrain becomes more rolling as you head north. Leave the pine barrens, walk under a power line and then over the multiuse Wild Rivers State Trail, a former rail grade.

Descend and cross Leo Creek at 11.3 miles. Look for rustic campsites on the north side of the creek. The main campsites are on a short spur to the right—you'll find a fire ring, table, wilderness latrine, and two tent pads.

Wind north through the woods, then

Thomas Funke

GIANT CLOVER GROWING WHERE THE TRAIL CROSSES
US 53 IN SOLON SPRINGS

follow the base of an embankment, which is the Solon Springs wastewater ponds. A short spur trail connects to the US 53 Trailhead to your left at the 12.8-mile mark. The US 53 Trailhead has ample parking and an information kiosk. The trail descends, bears right through woods and heads east, then crosses US 53 using South Holly Lucius Road. The trail winds north through land owned by Solon Springs, crossing an access road to the village transfer station. Exit onto South Holly Lucius Road close to its intersection with US Business 53.

At 13.5 miles into this segment, hike into Solon Springs on South US Business 53. Solon Springs is an official North Country Trail town with a grocery store, post office, bank, motels, and a restaurant. The trail comes to and uses US Business 53 as a road walk for 0.6 mile, then turns right over a set of railroad tracks and continues left (north) on Railroad Street another 0.3 mile to a park, Lucius Woods County Park (14.4 miles). This park has 13 modern and 11 semimodern campsites and is open Memorial Day through the second weekend in September.

From the park entrance drive, turn right and hike into the woods off the west side of the drive. Immediately you'll see the check-in station for the campground. This heavily wooded (but open understory) park is on a wide part of the St. Croix River. The trail winds to the bottom of a hill, then hairpins due north to the park perimeter and comes out onto East Main Street at the 14.8-mile mark.

Turn left (west) on Main Street, right (north) on South 3rd Street East, then cross CR A into the woods by stepping over a highway guardrail (15.4 miles). You are leaving Solon Springs and getting back to the soft underfooting of the trail. The trail heads north into the woods, crosses Dudeck Creek on a truss bridge located above a series of fish ladders, and parallels the railroad tracks for a while. Aden Creek Campsite, in an oxbow of the creek, is just before another truss bridge; it is a rustic campground with a fire ring, table, wilderness latrine, and two tent pads.

Hike 0.1 mile north to the end of South Reinsberg Road, and turn right (north), then turn right (east) onto CR AA at 15.6 miles. Hike east on East CR AA, then turn left (northeast) onto CR A; at the 16.7-mile mark, bear left (north) on Sjoberg Road, cross Beebe Creek, then take an uphill walk to bear right at a fork in the road onto East Crowshaw Road, then right onto South Olson Road. The trail leaves this road to the left (north) in 0.2 mile. There is parking at the end of this little-traveled road.

The South Olson Road Trailhead (18.3 miles) is the start of another heavily wooded walk northeast, paralleling the wetland that forms the headwaters of both the Brule and St. Croix Rivers. The trail takes an easterly trajectory and crosses Catlin Creek. Catlin Creek

Campsite (rustic, fire ring, table, wilderness latrine, and two tent pads) is 0.1 mile northeast of the bridge.

At the campsite, the trail enters the Brule River State Forest. After 0.3 mile, it turns southeast and enters the Brule Glacial Spillway State Natural Area. The trail crosses Porcupine Creek, following an abandoned beaver dam. It enters a cedar swamp on what is locally known as the Brule Bog Boardwalk. About 0.75 mile of this segment is boardwalk as it negotiates the beautiful old-growth white cedar and mixed conifer swamps and bogs southeast to cross CR P (19.4 miles).

Your hike continues using a mix of boardwalk and trail, through a swampy setting, crossing St. Croix Creek—the headwaters of the St. Croix River. Leave the swamp and follow the contour of a hill to South County Road A (CR A). The trail comes to the road, crosses the highway on a spur that leads 0.2 mile to the St. Croix Lake Trailhead (20.3 miles). The trailhead, part of a boat landing, has parking, an information kiosk, pit toilets, and an artesian well for potable water.

Bois Brule River and Portage Trail

START: CR A St. Croix Lake Trailhead	
END: Samples Road Trailhead	
APPROXIMATE HIKING TIME: 6–9 hours	
LENGTH OF SECTION: 18.1 miles	

The history of this area started with the retreat of the glaciers about ten thousand years ago. Water flowed south out of Lake Superior, carving out the valley whose ridge you will walk along while looking down on the conifer swamps and the headwaters of the St. Croix and the Bois Brule Rivers. Although not obvious, the cedar swamp separation between the St. Croix flowing to the south and the Bois Brule flowing to the north is the divide between the Great Lakes and Mississippi River watersheds.

The Brule is a mere 44 miles long, but drops an average of 10 feet a mile as it makes its way to Lake Superior. Voyagers, explorers, and even contemporary people have used this 2.0-mile-long "Portage Trail" to make their way from Lake Superior to the Mississippi River.

Although Native Americans have used this portage for centuries, the first written record was by Daniel Greysolon Sieur du Lhut in 1680. He is the namesake for Duluth, and was a diplomat sent by the French government to make peace between the Chippewa and Sioux in order to facilitate trade in furs. Interestingly, du Lhut, although having "solon" as part of his name, is not the namesake for Solon Springs. That honor goes to Tom Solon, who invented a water-dispensing vending machine; the name of the town at the time, White Birch, was changed to Solon Springs.

Along the trail, eight boulders commemorate other explorers and travelers who have used the trail, each having their name and year of first travel on the Portage Trail inscribed into the rock. In addition to du Lhut, Pierre Lesueur (1693), Jonathan Carver (1768), Michel Curot (1803), Jean Baptiste Cadotte (1819), Henry Schoolcraft (1820),

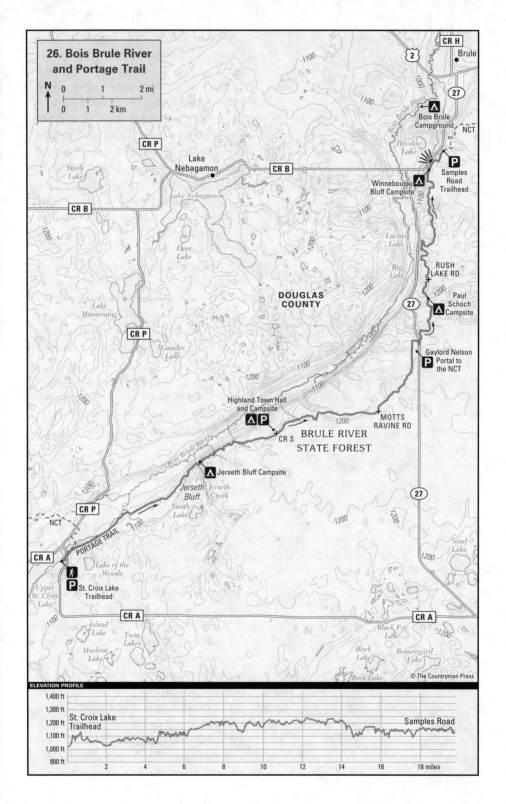

26. Bois Brule River and Portage Trail

N

0   1   2 mi

0   1   2 km

CR H
2
Brule
27
Bois Brule Campground
NCT
CR P
1100
1000
1100
Lake Nebagamon
CR B
1100
Hoodoo Lake
Bois Brule River
P
Samples Road Trailhead
Winneboujou Bluff Campsite
Steele Lake
Lake Nebagamon
CR B
1100
Lucius Lake
Deer Lake
1200
1200
Big Lake
RUSH LAKE RD
1200
Paul Schoch Campsite
Lake Minnesuing
DOUGLAS COUNTY
27
Gaylord Nelson Portal to the NCT
P
CR P
Gander Lake
1200
1100
1100
1200
Highland Town Hall and Campsite
1100
MOTTS RAVINE RD
CR S
BRULE RIVER STATE FOREST
27
Bois Brule River
Jerseth Bluff Campsite
Jerseth Bluff
Jerseth Creek
Smith Lake
Sand Lake
NCT
CR P
PORTAGE TRAIL
1100
1200
1200
CR A
Lake of the Woods
St. Croix Lake Trailhead
P
Upper St. Croix Lake
1100
CR A
Island Lake
Twin Lakes
Black Fox Lake
CR A
1200
Muskrat Lake
Rock Lake
Beauregard Lake
Boot Lake

© The Countryman Press

ELEVATION PROFILE

	1,400 ft
	1,300 ft
St. Croix Lake Trailhead	1,200 ft
	1,100 ft
	1,000 ft
	900 ft

Samples Road

2   4   6   8   10   12   14   16   18 miles

George Stuntz (1852), and Nicholas Jr. and Joseph Lucius (1886) are all recognized on the trail. The local chapter has produced a good brochure on this segment and its history and it is worth reading as you start learning about the incredible events that have taken place on this short stretch of the North Country Trail.

Except for a very short permanent easement, all of this trail winds through the Brule River State Forest. You will experience a variety of landscapes, both artificial and natural. When standing at the Schoolcraft rock, look to the north and west horizons. In the summer of 2000, a devastating, baseball-sized-hail storm struck the Brule valley, killing most of the trees in a 5,000-acre-area of the state forest. Although fire would be nature's way of taking care of the dead trees, the Wisconsin Department of Natural Resources salvaged what they could and knocked over the rest to make way for forest regeneration both by natural processes and planting of seedlings.

HOW TO FIND

The westernmost trailhead is the St. Croix Creek Trailhead on CR A just north of Solon Springs. From Solon Springs, take CR A 1.5 miles north; CR A will split, going south while CR P starts at the intersection, and the trailhead will be immediately south on the west side of the road.

The easternmost trailhead is at Samples Road, off Troy Pit Road just off WI 27 south of Brule. From Brule, drive south 1.5 miles and turn east onto Troy Pit Road, then immediately head to the right onto Samples Road, and the trailhead is at the top of the hill.

FACILITIES AND SERVICES

Backcountry camping in the Brule River State Forest, including the designated campsites along the North Country Trail, requires a free permit from the forest headquarters (6250 South Ranger Road, Brule, WI 54820).

THE HIKE

From the parking area across from the information kiosk, follow the spur trail 0.2 mile across CR A to the trail junction. The trail heads northeast and uphill into the forest and starts hugging the edge of the valley of the St. Croix and Bois Brule Rivers. The Portage Trail, as it is locally known, interprets the trail history through the use of stones with the names and dates of each explorer known to have used the trail—the start of the trail is also marked by a large stone. The first stone you'll reach is the Lucius stone, and the last one is for du Lhut. At the Carver stone, look in the foreground for a thin stream thread, which is the St. Croix. In the background to the north and a bit west, using binoculars, you might be able to see the Bois Brule River. You are looking over the divide between the Great Lakes and the Mississippi River watersheds.

At 2.2 miles, you'll come to an intersection on your left with a spur trail down to the east fork of the Bois Brule River that helps you access water. This trail leads to the canoe landing used by explorers and traders. The trail continues northeast, following a gated woods road parallel to the river. Where the road turns east, the trail leaves it and continues northeast on higher ground.

At 4.3 miles is Jerseth Bluff, where the trail skirts around the northwest side of a

THE PORTAGE TRAIL COMMEMORATES EXPLORERS WHO

hillside, which rises in elevation to your south and east. You'll descend to Jerseth Creek and cross on a bridge. After several short sections of puncheon, you'll ascend the valley slope to a campsite. The Jerseth Bluff Campsite is at the 4.5-mile mark—a rustic camp with fire ring, table, wilderness latrine, and two tent pads.

Continue northeast through open woods; the trail uses the contour of the valley, while negotiating the small side valleys created on the hillside to your southeast. Some of these small valleys have very intermittent sources of water. Pass a gigantic white pine, then ascend to the uplands and head east away from the Bois Brule River valley.

At the 7.0-mile mark is the CR S and Highland Town Hall Trailhead and parking. Just north of CR S, a spur trail leads to the Highland Town Hall (which has water available from a spigot). The trail continues 0.2 mile northeast through a red pine plantation to the Highland Campsite, which is rustic and has the usual fire ring, table, and wilderness latrine—but only a few tent pads.

Continue your ramble through the woods and experience the ups and downs of several small valley crossings. The

trail passes through the Mott's Ravine State Natural Area, a glacial outwash channel featuring perched prairie with dryland plants and flowers. The trail will clip Mott's Ravine Road on your right, head due north, and then continue its northeasterly trajectory, eventually becoming northerly.

At the 12.2-mile mark, another intersection with a trail spur, you'll head 0.1 mile to your right to the Gaylord Nelson Portal to the North Country Trail Trailhead and WI 27. There is an information kiosk and an interpretive monument about Gaylord Nelson, former governor and United States senator from Wisconsin and ardent trail supporter and founder of Earth Day. This is a beautiful location that commemorates one of America's great environmental leaders. He was instrumental in getting the North Country Trail designated as a National Scenic Trail.

Continue north, then east, and then southeast for 0.7 mile. Cross WI 27, trek about 0.7 mile through private land to the

A WHITE PINE DWARFS
THE AUTHOR'S HIKING STICK
IN THE BRULE STATE FOREST

north, and then head west. The trail will then turn north and reenter the Brule River State Forest. Winding north through hilly terrain, the trail reaches the Paul Schoch Campsite on a small rise above a ravine. The campsite contains a plaque in memory of Paul Schoch, a longtime member of the Brule–St. Croix Chapter of the North Country Trail Association. There is one tent pad, a table, fire ring, and wilderness latrine. Water is obtained from a pipe jutting out of the side of the nearby ravine.

In 1.0 mile the trail crosses Rush Lake Road and continues to negotiate through hilly and forested terrain. Several overlooks give glimpses of Big Lake, a natural widening of the Brule River in a deep, glacial valley.

At 18.1 miles is the Winneboujou Bluff, which gives a sweeping view of the countryside to the west. This is yet another rustic campsite with five tent pads, fire rings, a table, and a wilderness latrine—with a spur trail to the Little Bois Brule River to access water.

The North Country Trail follows the bluff, passing two overlooks of the Brule Valley and Hoodoo Lake. After 0.9 mile, a short spur trail leads to the Samples Road Trailhead at the 18.8-mile mark, which has plenty of parking and an information kiosk.

Bayfield County Forest

START: Samples Road Trailhead	
END: CR A Lake Ruth Trailhead	
APPROXIMATE HIKING TIME: 4–7 hours	
LENGTH OF SECTION: 11.4 miles	

With great foresight the citizens of Wisconsin, through their legislature, enacted several laws that created county forest systems. This was brought about in hindsight, after Wisconsin was essentially logged by a booming forest industry that thrived from about 1860 to 1910. Once grand forests, which covered the northern reaches of the state, were reduced to stumps and slash and experienced frequent forest fires until modern management practices were implemented in the Great Depression, which continue today. There were 52,000 acres originally enrolled in 1932, mostly from taking title on tax-delinquent properties. Today Bayfield County owns and manages just over 165,000 acres, making it the fourth largest of the county forests in Wisconsin.

Over 90 percent of the area is forested, although much of it is second growth. Mixed coniferous and deciduous forest along with oak and pine barrens composes most of the forest. The area has some open fields and prairies.

Your hike will be mostly a forested one. Leaving the Brule River State Forest at South Shore Road, this is where you'll enter the county forest. The only noticeable change between ownerships is a straight, due-east hike into the county forest, which starts at the county line. Then you'll have a slightly southeast trek winding through the rolling forest along and around several water sources.

HOW TO FIND

The westernmost trailhead is at Samples Road, off Troy Pit Road just off WI 27 south of Brule. From Brule, drive south 1.5 miles and turn east onto Troy Pit Road, then immediately to the right onto Samples Road; the trailhead is at the top of the hill.

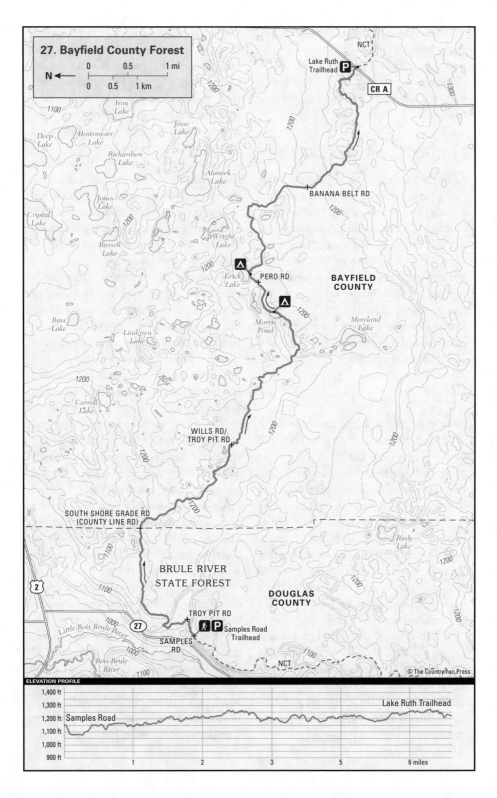

27. Bayfield County Forest

N ←

| 0 | 0.5 | 1 mi |
| 0 | 0.5 | 1 km |

NCT

Lake Ruth
Trailhead P

CR A

1200

1300

1100

Iron
Lake

Deep
Lake

Hostrauser
Lake

Jesse
Lake

Richardson
Lake

Ahmeek
Lake

BANANA BELT RD

1200

1200

Jones
Lake

Crystal
Lake

Wright
Lake

1200

Russell
Lake

PERO RD

BAYFIELD
COUNTY

Erick
Lake

1200

1200

Moreland
Lake

Bass
Lake

Lindgren
Lake

Morris
Pond

1200

Carroll
Lake

1200

1200

WILLS RD/
TROY PIT RD

1200

1200

1200

SOUTH SHORE GRADE RD
(COUNTY LINE RD)

Rush
Lake

1200

1100

BRULE RIVER
STATE FOREST

DOUGLAS
COUNTY

1200

2

1100

1200

27

TROY PIT RD

P Samples Road
Trailhead

1000

Little Bois Brule River

SAMPLES
RD

1000

1100

NCT

Bois Brule
River

1100

© The Countryman Press

ELEVATION PROFILE

1,400 ft				Lake Ruth Trailhead
1,300 ft				
1,200 ft	Samples Road			
1,100 ft				
1,000 ft				
900 ft				
	1	2	3	5	6 miles

The eastern trailhead is at CR A and the Lake Ruth Trailhead. From Iron River and US 2, drive 4.5 miles south on CR A; just past the southern intersection between CR A and Bradfield Road is the trailhead.

FACILITIES AND SERVICES

Brule, 3.0 miles north of the trailhead, has a convenience store, restaurants, a bank, and a post office. Backcountry camping in the Brule River State Forest, including the designated campsites along the North Country Trail, requires a free permit from the forest headquarters (6250 South Ranger Road, Brule, WI, 54820). Camping in the Bayfield County Forest does not require a permit, but is allowed only at the Morris Pond and Erick Lake Campsites.

THE HIKE

Your start point is the Samples Road Trailhead, but you'll hike a short spur trail to the North Country Trail. Turn right at the trail intersection, head northeast, and cross Samples Road; hike downhill to cross Troy Pit Road in 0.3 mile. Hike through a red pine plantation over flat terrain, then start a climb. A spur trail to the west will lead to a state forest campground nearly 2.0 miles away. The trail will crest, descend a small valley, turn east, and head in an easterly direction over rolling, forested terrain.

South Shore Grade Road (2.2 miles) marks the boundary between Douglas and Bayfield Counties, and between the Brule River State Forest and the Bayfield County Forest. Turn southeast and continue through rolling forest with a few openings.

At 4.2 miles cross to the southeast through the intersection of Wills and Troy Pit Roads. The forest will thicken, then, about 0.75 mile from crossing the road, you'll hike through a large opening with some scattered trees, then back into forests of varying ages and compositions. The trail will track southeast, then cross an abandoned road and head to the northeast, passing Morris Pond on the northwest. Morris Pond has a rustic campsite with a fire ring, table, wilderness latrine, and one tent pad. The campsite is near an abandoned farmstead. Look for a root cellar protruding from a hillside.

From the campsite the trail crosses Pero Road, then angles across the entry to a county trail system and heads downhill and northeast 0.3 mile to Erick Lake, which marks the 7.2-mile mark into your journey. Two campsites with fire rings, a table, and wilderness latrine on a wooded lake welcome you to a potential camping opportunity.

The trail enters an open canopy and oak/pine barren, then heads back into the forest and continues this pattern for about 1.0 mile before turning south and back into more mature forest. The trail takes a southeasterly turn, follows the perimeter between the maturing forest and an open canopy forest, then finds an old road heading south to Banana Belt Road (9.2 miles).

Cross the road and a power line corridor. Head southeast and reenter a young forest. The trail will slowly turn to the northeast in a counterclockwise direction through a variety of forest types and ages. The terrain continues to be rolling but not hilly. Continue east and then southeast toward the Lake Ruth Trailhead (11.4 miles). East of here lies the Chequamegon-Nicolet National Forest.

Chequamegon-Nicolet National Forest– Rainbow Lake Wilderness

START: CR A

END: US 63

APPROXIMATE HIKING TIME: 10–15 hours

LENGTH OF SECTION: 20.7 miles

The Chequamegon (Ojibwe for "shallow water") is an 865,000-acre national forest, created in 1993 and co-managed with the Nicolet since 1993. Most of its old-growth forests were logged off nearly a century ago and sold to homesteaders who tried to farm the droughty soils. They quickly found the area was better suited for growing trees—today the second growth is maturing within a matrix of bogs, fields, muskeg, lakes, and many wild rivers. The national forest hosts most of the wildlife that makes it a truly wild place: wolf, bear, bald eagle, and common loon. The area is also known for its human history, especially with the numerous Civilian Conservation Corps camps that dotted the area during the Great Depression.

The trail heads in a southwest direction, towards the village of Drummond. This segment lent its name to the entire trail; long before the North Country National Scenic Trail was established, this segment was known simply as the North Country Trail. The topography has been influenced by long-ago volcanic activity, and the current landscape is crisscrossed by abandoned rail grades and roads, so paying attention to the trail markers is of paramount importance.

For about 7.5 miles, the trail cuts diagonally across the 7,000-plus-acre Rainbow Lake Wilderness. Designated in 1975, this wilderness is popular with various user groups and has several trails that are well worn and used. The main attractions are the 15 lakes and numerous unnamed ponds that attract canoers and kayakers.

If through hiking, this will be your first wilderness area of several, and it is important to note that trail markers are not permitted—nor is mechanized equipment, even to clear the trail of

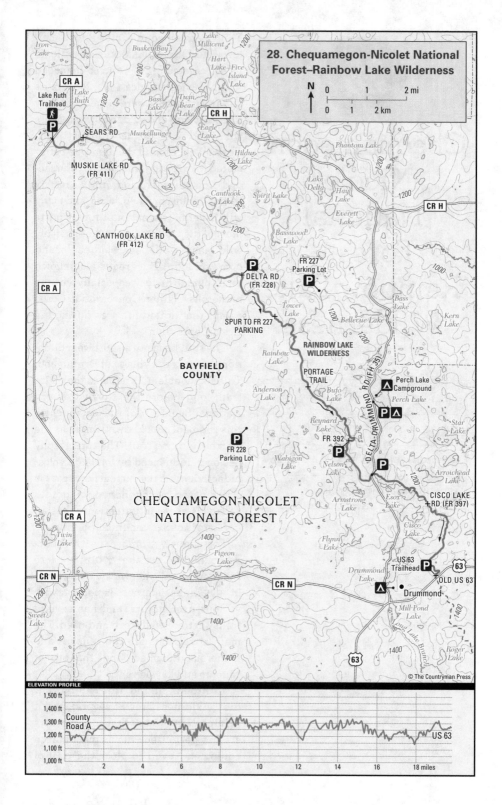

28. Chequamegon-Nicolet National Forest–Rainbow Lake Wilderness

N
0   1   2 mi
0   1   2 km

Iron Lake
Busken Bay
Lake Millicent
1200
Hart Lake
Five Island Lake
CR A
Lake Ruth Trailhead
Lake Ruth
1200
Bass Lake
Twin Bear Lake
CR H
Eagle Lake
Phantom Lake
SEARS RD
Muskellunge Lake
Hildur Lake
1200
MUSKIE LAKE RD (FR 411)
Canthook Lake
Spirit Lake
Lake Delta
Hay Lake
1200
CR H
1200
Everett Lake
CANTHOOK LAKE RD (FR 412)
1200
Basswood Lake
1000
Bass Lake
Kern Lake
CR A
P
DELTA RD (FR 228)
FR 227 Parking Lot
P
Tower Lake
1200
Bellevue Lake
SPUR TO FR 227 PARKING
RAINBOW LAKE WILDERNESS
BAYFIELD COUNTY
Rainbow Lake
PORTAGE TRAIL
Anderson Lake
Bufo Lake
Perch Lake Campground
Perch Lake
Star Lake
Reynard Lake
P
FR 392
P
FR 228 Parking Lot
Wabigon Lake
Nelson Lake
P
Arrowhead Lake
1200
CHEQUAMEGON-NICOLET NATIONAL FOREST
Armstrong Lake
Esox Lake
CISCO LAKE RD (FR 397)
Cisco Lake
CR A
1200
Twin Lake
1400
Flynn Lake
US 63 Trailhead
P
63
Pigeon Lake
Drummond Lake
OLD US 63
CR N
CR N
Drummond
Mill Pond Lake
Sweet Lake
1200
1400
Long Lake Branch
1400
Roger Lake
63
1400
© The Countryman Press

ELEVATION PROFILE

1,500 ft
1,400 ft
1,300 ft — County Road A
1,200 ft
1,100 ft
1,000 ft
                2   4   6   8   10   12   14   16   18 miles
                                                                                    US 63

downfall. At the 4.2-mile mark after entering the wilderness, a major portage trail—the Anderson Grade—crosses the North Country Trail. If you do get turned around, the wilderness area is bordered on all sides by roads. Utilize the roads to get back on track if necessary.

This segment ends at US 63, just outside of Drummond, which has limited services. Along the way, there are plenty of places to trailside camp and water is plentiful. This area is prone to forest fire, so inquire with the local US Forest Service district office for an update on conditions before hiking.

HOW TO FIND

Access and parking opportunities abound in the Chequamegon-Nicolet National Forest. One can usually rely on pulling off to the side of a lightly used Forest Service road, finding a pullout, or using an abandoned logging road to park.

The western trailhead is at CR A and the Lake Ruth Trailhead. From Iron River and US 2, drive 4.5 miles south on CR A; just past the southern intersection between CR A and Bradfield Road is the trailhead.

The eastern (or southeastern) access point is just outside of the village of Drummond on US 63. From Drummond, drive 1.0 mile east on US 63 and double back on Old US 63 west; the trailhead is a few hundred feet from the intersection.

Other trailheads include Forest Road 231 (FR 231); drive south 8.6 miles from Iron River on CR A, then turn east onto West Delta Road which changes names to FR 231; the trailhead is 4.2 miles from the intersection. This is the northern access to the Rainbow Lake Wilderness.

The southern access is on FR 392. Take Delta-Drummond Road north 4.0 miles, turning west (left) onto FR 392;

about 0.75 mile from the intersection is a trailhead.

Along the way to the previous trailhead, you'll drive by the Delta-Drummond Road Trailhead, which is about 0.75 mile south of the intersection of Delta-Drummond Road and FR 392.

FACILITIES AND SERVICES

Drummond has financial services, a grocery store, a restaurant, a modern campground, and sporting goods.

THE HIKE

Your hike starts off on an old logging road in the Bayfield County Forest; 0.75 mile from the trailhead, you'll cross over into the Chequamegon-Nicolet National Forest. It should be noted that the North Country Trail has significant gaps between roads in the Chequamegon-Nicolet, many of which are miles apart, especially paved and/or regularly used gravel roads. The trail heads south over heavily forested and rolling terrain. At the 1.0-mile mark you'll cross Sears Road, at 2.5 miles Muskie Lake Road, and at 4.9 miles Canthook Lake Road. After crossing Canthook Lake Road, the trail will wind between several small ponds, lakes, and wetlands in a southeast then easterly direction.

At the 7.4-mile mark, cross FR 228 and enter the Rainbow Lake Wilderness—a federally designated wilderness popular with anglers. There are several portage and spur trails in the wilderness, along with many social trails created by exploring anglers, hunters, and hikers looking for that perfect campsite. Note that the trail heads southeast and the wilderness area is surrounded on all four sides by regularly used Forest Service roads. If you get turned around, you should end up on a road and be able to reconnoiter back to the trail from there.

At the 9.0-mile mark, cross a spur trail, which you could take to a parking lot 1.6 miles to the east on FR 227. Pass Tower Lake on your north, then Rainbow Lake on your south and west.

At 12.6 miles, and without any signage, cross a portage trail. This trail leads to a parking lot on FR 228 that is 2.1 miles to the west; Perch Lake Campground is 1.8 miles to the east. Continue southeast and take note of the lack of any forestry activities as the trees around you continue to grow and the forest recovers from the logging that took place here over one hundred years ago. Pass Bufo Lake immediately past the intersection on the east, then Reynard Lake on your west, then Wishbone Lake on the east less than 0.25 mile from the next road.

At 14.7 miles, cross FR 392, a gravel Forest Service road, and leave the Rainbow Lake Wilderness. The trail will use an old railroad grade south of Stratton Ponds for about 1.0 mile.

At Delta Drummond Road (16.1 miles) the topography becomes noticeably different as the lakes you pass by are sitting in depressions and the landscape becomes hillier. Hike by Rana and Esox Lakes, then pass by a small, unnamed lake.

At 18.0 miles, cross FR 397/Cisco Lake Road. Continue hiking southeast through maturing forest. The trail turns southerly and crosses a small stream. A side trail to the Drummond Interpretive Trail indicates you are about 0.5 mile from a parking lot on Old US 63, where the interpretive trail makes its start. The area making up the interpretive trail was spared the ax during the logging boom. There are trees well over two hundred years old—including basswood, hemlock, and pine.

You'll reach the US 63 trailhead at the 20.7-mile mark, just outside the village of Drummond, 1.0 mile to the east. There is a modern campground on Drummond Lake; find it by turning north on Drummond Lake Road in Drummond.

Chequamegon-Nicolet National Forest– Porcupine Lake Wilderness

START: US 63

END: Beaver Lake Campground

APPROXIMATE HIKING TIME: 10–15 hours

LENGTH OF SECTION: 28.4 miles

The topography becomes noticeably hilly, due to the past volcanic and glacial activity, as you hike eastward on this segment. The trail continues its southeast trajectory until Lake Owen, where it turns easterly, winding through the lakes, forests, rivers, and wetlands of the Chequamegon-Nicolet.

You'll cross Porcupine Lake Road and enter the 4,000-acre Rainbow Lake Wilderness. Again, as a wilderness area, trail markers are not allowed—nor is machinery to clear the trail. So when you walk through what appear to be treetops on either side of the trail, thank the hard work of the Forest Service and the local trail chapter. This area was devastated by a storm in 1999 and the effects of the storm are still noticeable. There are several resources that indicate bears live here at a higher than normal density, and I even saw one when I hiked through this segment—although it hightailed it away from me.

Cross CR D and leave the 7.0-mile hike through the wilderness behind, and continue to negotiate the rolling topography eastward. The trail crosses several Forest Service roads, and there continue to be plenty of places to camp and find water.

Long Mile Lookout is 2.5 miles from CR D, and sits on a rock outcropping giving a great view to the east. After Old Grade Road, enter the Marengo Semi-primitive Nonmotorized Area and pass through "Swedish Settlement," a remnant of a farm abandoned in the 1930s. These farms were settled by immigrants from Sweden, but abandoned during the Great Depression—probably due to several factors, one being the poor soils. The local trail chapter and national forest have cleaned up the areas of trees and brush taking over the ruins to allow for better viewing, as this is an

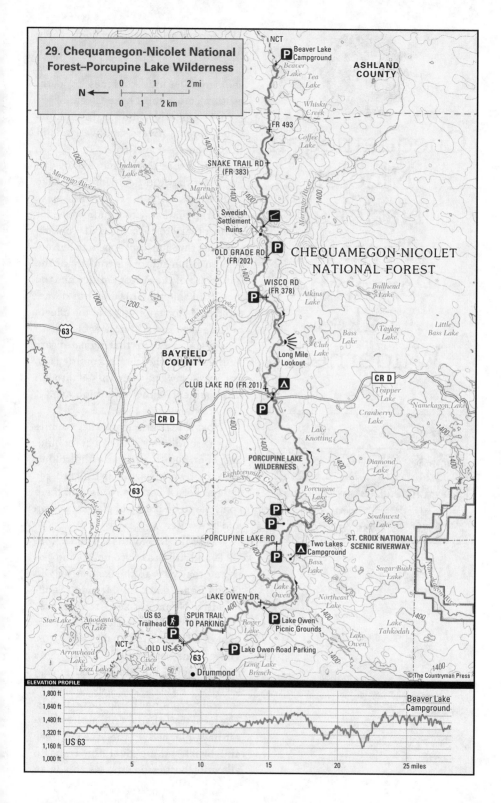

29. Chequamegon-Nicolet National Forest–Porcupine Lake Wilderness

N ←

0   1   2 mi
0   1   2 km

NCT

P Beaver Lake Campground

ASHLAND COUNTY

Beaver Lake
Tea Lake

Whisky Creek

FR 493

Coffee Lake

SNAKE TRAIL RD (FR 383)

Indian Lake

Marengo River

Marengo Lake

1400

1400

1400

Swedish Settlement Ruins

P CHEQUAMEGON-NICOLET NATIONAL FOREST

OLD GRADE RD (FR 202)

1000

WISCO RD (FR 378)

P

Atkins Lake

Bullhead Lake

Marengo River

1200

Twentymile Creek

Bass Lake

Taylor Lake

Little Bass Lake

63

BAYFIELD COUNTY

Long Mile Lookout

Club Lake

1000

CLUB LAKE RD (FR 201)

△

CR D

Trapper Lake

Namekagon Lake

P

CR D

Cranberry Lake

Lake Knotting

PORCUPINE LAKE WILDERNESS

Eighteenmile Creek

Diamond Lake

1400

1400

Porcupine Lake

1400

1400

P

Southwest Lake

ST. CROIX NATIONAL SCENIC RIVERWAY

P

PORCUPINE LAKE RD

1000

Two Lakes Campground △

Bass Lake

Sugar Bush Lake

63

P

Namekagon River

Lake Owen

LAKE OWEN DR

1400

Northeast Lake

US 63 Trailhead

SPUR TRAIL TO PARKING

P Lake Owen Picnic Grounds

Roger Lake

Lake Owen

Lake Tahkodah

Star Lake

Anodanta Lake

P OLD US 63

NCT

63

P Lake Owen Road Parking

1400

1400

Arrowhead Lake

Cisco Lake

• Drummond

Long Lake Branch

Esox Lake

1400

© The Countryman Press

ELEVATION PROFILE

| | | | | | Beaver Lake Campground |

1,800 ft
1,640 ft
1,480 ft
1,320 ft
1,160 ft
1,000 ft

US 63

5   10   15   20   25 miles

important archeological resource worth preserving.

A trail shelter is located just past the settlement; keep hiking the hilly terrain eastward, crossing several more Forest Roads, then follow the shore of Beaver Lake on the north to the campground.

HOW TO FIND

The westernmost access point is just outside of the village of Drummond on US 63. From Drummond, drive 1.0 mile east on US 63 and double back on Old US 63 west; the trailhead is a few hundred feet from the intersection.

The eastern trailhead for the segment is at Beaver Lake Campground. From the east and Mellen, take CR GG west 7.0 miles, turn north onto Forest Road 188 (FR 188)/Hanson Road, drive less than 1.0 mile, then turn west onto FR 187/ Mineral Lake Road. When Mineral Lake Road turns north, continue straight on FR 198. Just past the intersection with FR 387, look for signs directing you into Beaver Lake Campground.

From the west and Drummond, drive north on US 63. At Grandview, turn south on CR D; in about 4.5 miles, turn east onto FR 201/Club Lake Road for 3.0 miles, then north onto FR 202 for less than 1.0 mile, then east onto FR 198 for about 5.0 miles to Beaver Lake.

FACILITIES AND SERVICES

Drummond has financial services, a grocery store, a restaurant, a modern campground and sporting goods.

THE HIKE

The trailhead at Old US 63 and US 63 links to the Drummond Interpretive Trail. The village of Drummond is about 1.0 mile to the west. You'll continue southeast, immediately cross US 63, then head through noticeably hilly and forested terrain. The trail bisects and is part of the Drummond Ski Trail System, which takes advantage of the hilly and scenic terrain. A side trail to your right takes you to the east about 0.5 mile to a parking area on Lake Owen Road. The ski area stretches to the next road and parking area at Lake Owen.

The Lake Owen Picnic Grounds are 3.3 miles into this segment's hike. This developed picnic and day use area has toilets, picnic shelters, and potable water. Hike south, counterclockwise along Lake Owen, cross Porcupine Lake Road, and parallel the road in forested and hilly terrain. The trail comes back to the road for the Porcupine Lake Wilderness Trailhead (7.9 miles).

There are a couple of parking areas just to the east of this trailhead that have spur trails to the North Country Trail, which is within the Porcupine Lake Wilderness. No trails are marked in the wilderness, and you'll have to ford any stream crossings. There is also quite a lot of beaver activity in here, so be prepared to orienteer around these obstructions. A right turn on a spur trail in 0.2 mile will lead to the Two Lakes Campground about 0.5 mile from the trail. Another left turn on a spur trail awaits at 0.5 mile, which takes you back to Porcupine Lake Road; another left turn on a spur trail, at the northern tip of Porcupine Lake, nearly 3.0 miles past the trailhead, will take you back to Porcupine Lake Road. This wilderness area is surrounded by roads on all sides, so if you end up on another trail, you'll have to figure out which road you ended up on and correct yourself by using these roads to get back to the North Country Trail.

At 14.9 miles, cross CR D and you'll notice your hike continues to get more rugged, hilly, steep, and noticeably rocky in places. Immediately pass Davis Lake and cross FR 1750/Club Lake Road, head east past Long Mile Lookout, and continue up on higher ground with the occasional view.

At 19.2 miles you'll cross FR 378/Wisco Road, continue a northeasterly trek to a stream crossing, then hike easterly to cross FR 202/Old Grade Road at the 20.9-mile mark. This is an exceptionally scenic area, and to make it more special you'll pass through the Swedish Settlement about 1.0 mile from the road before crossing the Marengo River at 1.2 miles. About 0.1 mile east of the river crossing is a trail shelter.

The forest continues to impress as you'll probably have the next several miles to yourself and your thoughts. Cross FR 383/Snake Trail Road at the 25.2-mile mark, then FR 493 (26.3 miles)—a little used forest road—before reaching Beaver Lake Campground (28.4 miles). Look for a spur trail leading to the campground on your right.

30

Chequamegon-Nicolet National Forest and Copper Falls State Park

START: Beaver Lake Campground

END: Copper Falls State Park entrance

APPROXIMATE HIKING TIME: 10–15 hours

LENGTH OF SECTION: 27.5 miles

The hilly terrain pocketed with lakes and surrounded by maturing forest continues eastward toward this segment's terminus. Although there are no wilderness areas to traverse, the wilderness feel of the trail continues. You'll continue to wind around lakes and Forest Roads until you come out to CR GG to cross a tributary of the Bad River. It is a short road walk, then back into the woods northward where the Chequamegon-Nicolet segment of the trail ends at Kornstead Road.

A road walk on Kornstead leads you to the city of Mellen, which has most services. Utilize surface streets and sidewalks, which are blazed, through town and then into a natural area on the north side of town out to WI 169 on a multiuse trail. Take WI 169 to the entrance of Copper Falls State Park.

For the long-distance hiker, Copper Falls State Park is an out-and-back side trip of 18.4 miles. If you can, camp in this fascinating state park bursting at the seams with scenery and history. It is thought to have started about six thousand years ago with people of the Old Copper Complex, who lived here and mined copper for centuries; then the area was abandoned, and later the Sioux and Ojibwe found their way here. Exploratory mining by European and American miners started in earnest in the 1860s; a small village popped up and a mine shaft was drilled, which yielded little copper. The company even lowered the Bad River in order to temper the quickly rising waters flooding the shaft. Still, no copper was found worth mining, and the area was abandoned in the early 1900s.

The state park was established in 1929. Much of the infrastructure that still exists today was created by the Civilian Conservation Corps during

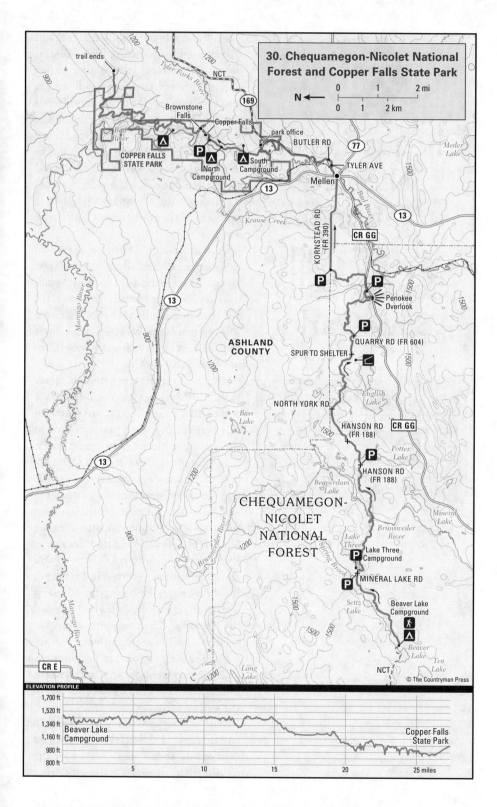

30. Chequamegon-Nicolet National Forest and Copper Falls State Park

N ←

0   1   2 mi
0   1   2 km

trail ends

Tyler Forks River

NCT

1200

900

169

Brownstone Falls

Copper Falls

park office

BUTLER RD

77

Meder Lake

1500

Bad River

COPPER FALLS STATE PARK

North Campground

South Campground

13

Mellen

TYLER AVE

13

Bad River

Krause Creek

KORNSTEAD RD (FR 390)

CR GG

1500

1500

Penokee Overlook

QUARRY RD (FR 604)

SPUR TO SHELTER

1500

ASHLAND COUNTY

Marengo River

900

1200

1500

Bass Lake

NORTH YORK RD

English Lake

HANSON RD (FR 188)

CR GG

Potter Lake

HANSON RD (FR 188)

13

1200

Beaverdam Lake

CHEQUAMEGON-NICOLET NATIONAL FOREST

Mineral Lake

Brunsweiler River

Lake Three

Lake Three Campground

Brunsweiler River

Spring Brook

MINERAL LAKE RD

900

1500

1500

Seitz Lake

Beaver Lake Campground

1500

Beaver Lake

Tea Lake

CR E

1200

Long Lake

NCT

© The Countryman Press

ELEVATION PROFILE

| 1,700 ft |
| 1,520 ft |
| 1,340 ft |
| 1,160 ft |
| 980 ft |
| 800 ft |

Beaver Lake Campground

Copper Falls State Park

5   10   15   20   25 miles

THE CIVILIAN CONSERVATION CORPS CREATED MUCH OF THE INFRASTRUCTURE
AT COPPER FALLS STATE PARK

Thomas Funke

the Great Depression. The park has a great trail network and concession building. From the state park, there is active trail development toward the north end of the park and into an area designated as the Scattered Wildlife Area, where the trail will dead end. In the near future, the trail will continue from here east toward Hurley. For the long-distance hiker, it is a road walk to the next segment about 15.0 miles to the east in Iron County.

HOW TO FIND

The western trailhead for the segment is at Beaver Lake Campground. From the east and Mellen, take CR GG west 7.0 miles, turn north onto Forest Road 188 (FR 188)/Hanson Road, drive less than 1.0 mile, then turn west onto FR 187/ Mineral Lake Road. When Mineral Lake Road turns north, continue straight on FR 198. Just past the intersection with FR 387, look for signs directing you into Beaver Lake Campground.

From the west and Drummond, drive north on US 63. At Grandview, turn south on CR D; in about 4.5 miles, turn east onto FR 201/Club Lake Road for 3.0 miles, then north onto FR 202 for less than 1.0 mile, then east onto FR 198 for about 5.0 miles to Beaver Lake.

Copper Falls State Park is the eastern access point, about 1.0 mile north of Mellen. Take WI 13 less than 1.0 mile north, then veer to the right onto WI 169; in about 1.0 mile is the park entrance.

FACILITIES AND SERVICES

Mellen has all services, except medical. Off-trail camping is allowed in the national forest.

THE HIKE

Leave the Beaver Lake Campground behind and continue northeast over hilly and sometimes rough terrain. At 1.7 miles, overlook Seitz Lake, and continue your hilly hike. At 2.4 miles is the Mineral Lake Road Trailhead; the Lake Three Campground entrance is 0.1 mile to the north—turn left on Mineral Lake Road and the rustic campground with three campsites is on your right.

You'll come to a valley and switchback down in elevation to cross an outlet to Beaverdam Lake on the Brunsweiler River via an impressive bridge. Follow the base of the hill, then climb back up in elevation with views of Beaverdam Lake to the north. The trail dips into a valley and then back up to the next road crossing (at the 6.0-mile mark), Hanson Road.

From FR 188/Hanson Road, the trail crosses a small, intermittent stream, and crosses FR 188 to the north side. The trail is slightly rolling by this point, when it comes to North York Road (7.6 miles).

The terrain continues to be heavily forested, and it becomes a little more rolling in topography. Descend to cross a stream and then ascend slightly; at about 2.0 miles in you'll come to an intersection with the Penokee Mountain Ski Trail system. A trail shelter is found by taking the first spur south to FR 1382, then turning north on the entrance road—the shelter is on the west side of the road.

At 9.8 miles is Quarry Road and a trailhead which the North Country Trail shares with the Penokee Mountain Ski Trail system for the next 1.0 mile; there are several trail intersections, all marked. Due to the gentle grades in this area, this is a popular ski trail. The North Country Trail deviates from these grades as it brings you up to the Penokee Overlook

for a view to the south, then downhill to a parking lot. The trail comes to CR GG to negotiate over a tributary of the Bad River, turns left onto the road, then left again back onto trail, which then shoots north uphill to the final trailhead in the Chequamegon-Nicolet National Forest at Kornstead Road (13.5 miles).

For the long-distance hiker, congratulations are in order, as you have hiked across your first national forest. From this point, it is a 2.3-mile road walk to Mellen. Turn right onto Kornstead Road and hike it into the city of Mellen, which is reached at the 15.8-mile mark as you cross WI 13. Turn left (north) on WI 13, and one block north turn right (east) onto East Bennett Street, where you will find the post office. Turn right onto East Tyler Avenue, then left (north) onto Butler Road.

You'll bear left onto a multiuse trail (16.6 miles) and hike north along the Bad River, cross over, and turn right onto WI 169; continue to walk along the state highway toward Copper Falls State Park.

The Copper Falls State Park entrance is at the 18.3-mile mark for the long-distance or road walker. However, for the day hiker, this park makes for an exciting hike with its waterfalls, views, winding trails, and overall scenery. For the long-distance hiker, it is an out-and-back, because although there is active trail development, it dead-ends in the woods.

The current total trail distance is 9.2 miles from the park entrance until the trail dead-ends in the park. Pass the park office at 0.4 mile and walk the road for about 0.1 mile before the trail goes left off-road and parallels the road for about 0.5 mile before crossing a pathway to the campgrounds. The group sites are to the east, as is the South Campground. Another 0.4 mile and you'll pass through the North Campground; another 0.4 mile farther leads to the parking lot.

The Doughboys Trailhead starts at the parking lot, and, with a series of three bridges, crosses over the Bad River and a tributary, the Tyler Forks River. Stay right and go counterclockwise to cross the Tyler Forks and observe Copper Falls and then Brownstone Falls. At the Devil's Gate, the Doughboy Trail goes along the river, and the North Country Trail turns north; you'll cross Little Creek.

At the 4.3-mile mark from the park entrance, there is a spur trail to a backpacker campsite a short 0.1-mile jaunt toward the river. From this point until where the trail ends, you'll likely have the trail to yourself. At 9.2 miles from the park entrance, the trail will end in the woods—but not before giving you an excellent hike through rugged and wooded terrain.

For the long-distance backpacker, it is a 13.8-mile road walk from the park entrance until the next trail segment. Take WI 169 east and north through the countryside, turning right (east) on Vogues Road (28.4 miles). Vogues Road goes east, then bends clockwise to a southeasterly direction to an intersection with Sullivan Fire Lane. Across the street on the south side of the intersection is the trailhead for your next trail segment.

31

Iron County

START: Vogues Road

END: Copper Peak Trailhead

APPROXIMATE HIKING TIME: 15–25 hours

LENGTH OF SECTION: 36.2 miles

For the long-distance hiker, the paved road comes to an end at Vogues Road. The trail will head east, then double back on itself in a southwesterly direction, where it makes a hairpin turn east at Sullivan Fire Lane. At this point, an old road heads south to the next segment of trail in the Iron County Forest, where it intersects with a trail spur to a primitive camp on the Tyler Forks River. Along the way, pass Wren Falls, a very popular day hike for those interested in waterfalls.

The trail meanders east over the rough topography and forest, crosses Casey Sag Road, then descends on a snowmobile trail to Upson Lake to use Upson Lake Road on the south, where there is a trail shelter. After passing the lake, the road route continues off Upson Road onto a ATV trail skirting Skye Golf to Weber Lake Road, where there is a campground.

From here the main North Country Trail route continues west toward Lake Superior. The old Uller Trail is still in use, though, and offers a unique experience. Although it is mostly used as a Nordic ski trail, this segment is open to mountain bikes. Knowing that, keep your eyes open for bicyclists and you'll see why this is a popular ski-hike-bike trail, with its rugged topography and great views to the south. Dispersed camping is allowed and there are plenty of water sources even though you are hiking through the higher elevations of the surrounding landscape. Descend to cross a tributary of Alder Creek and walk along the lower elevations and a large wetland complex to your south.

Cross North Valley Road, and utilize a snowmobile trail until you reach North Harma Road. Hike south and then east on South Drive to cross the Montreal

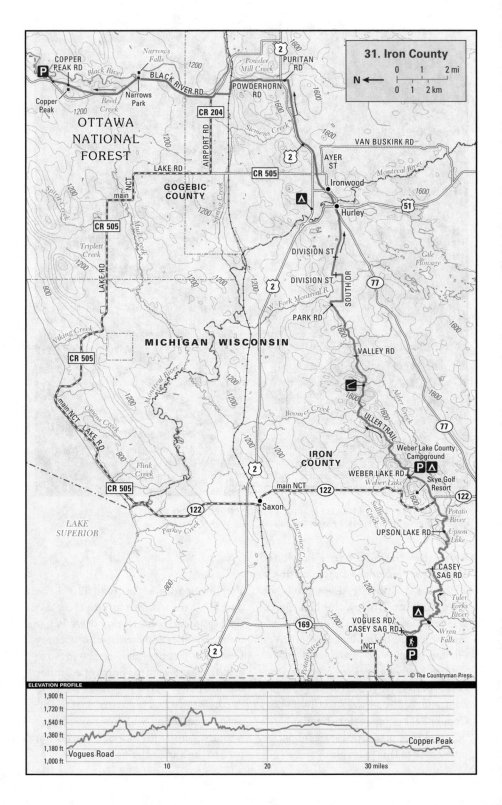

31. Iron County

N ◀

0   1   2 mi

0   1   2 km

COPPER PEAK RD

Narrows Falls

Black River

Powder Mill Creek

PURITAN RD

POWDERHORN RD

BLACK RIVER RD

Copper Peak

Reed Creek

Narrows Park

CR 204

Siemens Creek

OTTAWA NATIONAL FOREST

AIRPORT RD

LAKE RD

CR 505

NCT

main

GOGEBIC COUNTY

VAN BUSKIRK RD

AYER ST

Montreal River

Ironwood

Hurley

51

Spirit Creek

Mud Creek

Spring Creek

CR 505

Triplett Creek

LAKE RD

DIVISION ST

DIVISION ST

SOUTH DR

77

W. Fork Montreal R.

PARK RD

Gile Flowage

Viking Creek

CR 505

MICHIGAN WISCONSIN

Montreal River

VALLEY RD

Adler Creek

main NCT

LAKE RD

Owens Creek

Boomer Creek

ULLER TRAIL

77

Flink Creek

IRON COUNTY

Weber Lake County Campground

WEBER LAKE RD

Weber Lake

Skye Golf Resort

P ⛺

122

LAKE SUPERIOR

CR 505

122

Saxon

main NCT

Parker Creek

Lawrence Creek

Sullivan Creek

UPSON LAKE RD

Upson Lake

Potato River

CASEY SAG RD

Tyler Forks River

169

Potato River

VOGUES RD/ CASEY SAG RD

NCT

Wren Falls

⛺

P

2

© The Countryman Press

ELEVATION PROFILE

1,900 ft	
1,720 ft	
1,540 ft	
1,360 ft	
1,180 ft	Copper Peak
1,000 ft	

Vogues Road

10   20   30 miles

CLIMB TO THE TOP OF COPPER PEAK FOR THE BEST, UNOBSTRUCTED VIEW OF THE MIDWEST. ON A CLEAR DAY, YOU CAN SEE ISLE ROYALE AND CANADA

River; then the road bends north and comes to an abandoned railroad grade, which is a multiuse trail open to bikes. Hike this into Hurley, the last city in Wisconsin, and utilize the old rail grade into Ironwood before heading north on Puritan Road.

This road changes its name to Powderhorn Road as you cross US 2, and is an unmarked road walk until you pass Copper Peak—the western hemisphere's tallest ski jump; the trail starts about 0.5 mile north of this marvel.

HOW TO FIND

Vogues Road and Sullivan Fire Lane parking is the western terminus for this trail segment; from Hurley drive WI 77 west 20.0 miles and turn north on County Line Road. County Line Road bends west at 3.8 miles then turns north at 4.8 miles onto WI 169. Drive 5.3 miles winding northeasterly and then turn east (right) onto Vogues Road, which curls around to a southwesterly direction. At an abrupt turn to the east is the parking area.

The easternmost trailhead is in the Black River Harbor Recreation Area north of Ironwood, Michigan. From Ironwood, take US 2 east about 5.0 miles and turn north onto Powderhorn Road. The road will jog around a set of railroad tracks, and then through Auvinen Corner. Continue north, past Copper Peak, and the road will end at Black River Harbor, which is about 15 miles from US 2. Hurley and Ironwood have street-side parking and parking lots.

FACILITIES AND SERVICES

Hurley and Ironwood are full-service towns. The trail goes through their downtowns and near the commercial districts.

THE HIKE

Start your hike from Vogues Road, a lightly used gravel road to hike south through the forest on an old road. Wren Falls is 1.5 miles south on the old road. At 1.5 miles, you can turn right on a trail spur to a bivouac campground on the Tyler Forks River.

Your hike will start a trend of many ups and downs through forested and very hilly terrain. About 0.2 mile past the spur trail intersection you'll cross a branch of the Tyler Forks River using the road, then head back into the woods to zigzag through the forest, up and down many hills, mostly making an easterly trajectory.

At 3.2 miles, you'll cross Casey Sag Road; in another 1.0 mile, the trail begins to use Upson Lake Road, which passes Upson Lake on the south. About 0.7 mile past the lake, the trail turns off the road onto an old road, crosses a small creek, and continues northeast to cross WI 122 at the 4.0-mile mark.

Cross the state highway and proceed on an old road as it parallels a county road to the southeast with a large hill to the northwest, which comprises the Skye Golf resort. You'll cross several service and entry roads to the resort and hike through a parking lot, going north, to Iron County Forest public campground, a semimodern campground with 11 campsites.

Continue past the campground to Weber Lake Road (8.5 miles) and the trailhead for the Uller Trail. The Uller Trail is a ski trail used as a temporary connector while the local chapter creates new trail in the area. Less than 1.0 mile onto the trail is a trail shelter that sleeps six persons.

At the 9.9-mile point you'll cross Sullivan Creek by descending a small valley, then heading uphill and follow-

Thomas Funke

TRAILHEAD TO
BLACK RIVER HARBOR

ing the valley for about 0.2 mile. You'll head up a ravine where it levels off, crosses another creek, and has a slow, uphill climb followed by a descent down a valley to a creek bottom—where you'll parallel Boomer Creek before crossing it at 12.2 miles. You'll use a saddle to negotiate between two large hills, then down to another creek crossing before coming to another trail shelter, which sleeps six.

The trail will cross an Alder Creek tributary (13.4 miles) and squeeze into a swampy area and then to more rugged topography. It will be another 1.0 mile to a trail shelter, again sleeping six persons.

You'll follow a rutted forest road that is a snowmobile trail in winter, marked as Snowmobile Trail #6. This trail hugs the wetlands and offers some great views of a very large marsh complex. This would be an excellent place to look for marsh birds like American bitterns, soras, and Virginia rails. At Valley Road and the 14.2-mile mark, continue to enjoy your wetland view to the south and the uplands to your north before your next road crossing at Park Drive (16.6 miles).

Hike south before the road bends east and changes names to South Drive. The road will bend north, pass Division Street, and 0.1 mile past the intersection you'll find a multiuse trail on an abandoned rail grade.

At 18.5 miles, start your flat ramble on the abandoned rail grade, which will cross Park Street and take you into Hurley, on the Wisconsin-Michigan border.

The trail will start in the woods and become residential, then enter the city proper (21.3 miles). Hurley has most services. There is a post office just south of the intersection with the trail and 5th Street. Turn south on 5th Street and then left onto Silver (WI-77). About 0.1 mile past, you'll cross the Montreal River and enter Michigan.

At 26.5 miles you'll turn left (north) on Puritan Road. As you cross US 2, the name changes to Powderhorn Road. Powderhorn Road merges with Black River Road in 3.0 miles. Keep your eyes open on your right for Narrows Park (32.7 miles), which is an unassuming, small roadside park with a pit toilet and bivouac camping. There is a steep drop to the Black River and Narrows Falls, which are more like rapids in the summer months.

Continue north on the paved road to Copper Peak (35.7 miles), the world's tallest ski jump. From the top of the structure, which is over 1,700 feet above sea level, you have an unobstructed view. On a clear day, you can see Canada, Isle Royale, Minnesota, and Wisconsin. A small museum at the base of the hill interprets its history. You can purchase a lift ticket to take the ski lift to the base of the hill. Then, take an elevator ride to about 2/3 of the way up the tower. If you are brave, walk all the way to the top.

Hike the gravel road north back to the paved road; less than 0.2 mile on your right (east) is the Copper Peak Trailhead (36.2 miles).

IV.

UPPER PENINSULA

Black and Presque Isle Rivers

START: Mouth of the Black River

END: Summit Peak parking lot, Porcupine Mountains Wilderness State Park

APPROXIMATE HIKING TIME: 9–20 hours

LENGTH OF SECTION: 27.4 miles

Leaving the bustling Black River Harbor, the trail crosses the Black River on a suspension bridge. You'll climb a steep set of stairs and follow the trail around to the right to an overlook over the Rainbow Falls. Since most hikers to this point turn around after viewing the falls, the tread becomes thin and overgrown at times as it goes into a little-used segment of the Ottawa National Forest, thick with thimbleberries and black bears. The trail is a straight shot, mostly on old logging roads, until it ends at a small parking area on County Route 519 (CR 519).

The trail crosses over to the east side of the road, continues south a short distance, and then turns east across a short section of private land before entering the Porcupine Mountains Wilderness State Park. The trail continues east on an old logging road, passing by a spur (with white blazes) that takes you to a campsite by Lepisto Falls. Continue north, following the Presque Isle River for a while, before crossing a ravine on a 20-foot bridge and then climbing to the top of the plateau using a rope assist through a ravine. The trail travels through the forest and reconnects with the Presque Isle River a short distance before reaching South Boundary Road. You'll cross South Boundary Road and continue your hike on the high banks of the Presque Isle River until you reach a day-use area with a semimodern campground just beyond.

Porcupine Mountains Wilderness State Park is Michigan's largest state park, at 60,000 acres. It is home to one of the few remaining old growth forests, plenty of trout streams, and many waterfalls. These features attract many thousands of backpackers, campers, hikers, and day-trippers from all over the midwest. Even in the backcountry, the

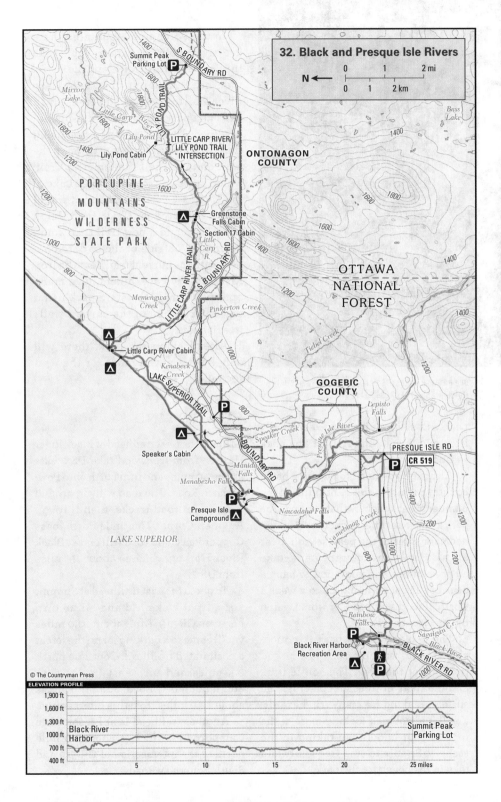

32. Black and Presque Isle Rivers

N ←

| 0 | 1 | | 2 mi |
| 0 | 1 | 2 km | |

Summit Peak
Parking Lot

S BOUNDARY RD

Mirror
Lake

Little Carp River

LILY POND TRAIL

Lily Pond

Lily Pond Cabin

LITTLE CARP RIVER/
LILY POND TRAIL
INTERSECTION

PORCUPINE
MOUNTAINS
WILDERNESS
STATE PARK

ONTONAGON
COUNTY

Bass
Lake

Greenstone
Falls Cabin

Section 17 Cabin

Little
Carp
R.

LITTLE CARP RIVER TRAIL

S. BOUNDARY RD

OTTAWA
NATIONAL
FOREST

Memengwa
Creek

Pinkerton Creek

Tiebel Creek

Little Carp River Cabin

LAKE SUPERIOR TRAIL

Kenabeek
Creek

GOGEBIC
COUNTY

Lepisto
Falls

Speaker's Cabin

S. BOUNDARY RD

Speaker Creek

Presque Isle River

PRESQUE ISLE RD

CR 519

Manido
Falls

Manabezho Falls

Nawadaha Falls

Presque Isle
Campground

Namebinag Creek

LAKE SUPERIOR

Rainbow
Falls

Sagaigan Cr.

Black River

Black River Harbor
Recreation Area

BLACK RIVER RD

© The Countryman Press

ELEVATION PROFILE

1,900 ft						
1,600 ft						
1,300 ft						Summit Peak
1000 ft	Black River					Parking Lot
700 ft	Harbor					
400 ft		5	10	15	20	25 miles

OLD GROWTH FOREST IS COMMONPLACE AT PORCUPINE MOUNTAINS WILDERNESS STATE PARK

In the Porcupine Mountains there is a myriad of trail names. You'll take the Lake Superior Trail along the shore, then head inland on the Little Carp River Trail to the Lily Pond Trail, which ends at a parking lot on South Boundary Road. There is a plan to stop using the current southern route through the park and use the Lake Superior Trail, which takes you to the popular Lake of the Clouds Overlook. The trail would use the Escarpment Trail, then Union Lake Trail, and a new trail that would be created outside of the park to connect with the current trail near the Iron River. In any case, hikers have many options to cross the state park using any combination of the current trails in existence.

After leaving the park, there will only be two paved roads for the next 100 miles.

HOW TO FIND

To get to the west trailhead at Black River Harbor, from Ironwood take US 2 east about 5.0 miles and turn north onto Powderhorn Road. The road will jog around a set of railroad tracks, then through Auvinen Corner. Continue north, pass Copper Peak, and road will end at Black River Harbor, which is about 15 miles from US 2.

To get to the east trailhead at Summit Peak, from Wakefield and MI 28 turn north on CR 519. After about 10.0 miles you'll come to a parking lot on the left at a designated trailhead. Continue north 2.5 miles and turn east (right) onto South Boundary Road. Summit Peak is about 12.0 miles from this intersection.

Another trailhead is at Presque Isle Campground, which is about 1.0 mile north of the intersection of CR 519 and South Boundary Road.

park will seem quite busy—especially from mid-July to mid-August, the peak season.

Although you need to pay for a backcountry permit, there are no limits to the number of backpackers that can be in the park at any one time. Expect full shelters and campsites in the peak season. Bear are also problematic in the park—take all precautions and know how to hang a bear bag or face waking up to a week's worth of food scattered (or worse, eaten by the local bears).

The geology of the park is noticeable—tough, volcanic rock is exposed throughout the area. The soil is thin, and the roots of trees creep across the surface, making for many trip hazards. You'll find yourself looking more at the tops of your boots than taking in the scenery. Be sure to stop frequently and take in the beauty of the park.

FACILITIES AND SERVICES

At the Black River Harbor Recreation Area you can find a phone, water, harbor, concessions, bathrooms, picnic tables, and a covered picnic pavilion. Wilderness camping is permitted between Black River Harbor and CR 519 in the Ottawa National Forest. The nearest full-service city is Ironwood.

THE HIKE

The Black River Harbor Recreation Area consists of a day use area, campground, and marina at the mouth of the Black River in the Ottawa National Forest. Take the suspension bridge over the Black River, making sure to take in the wonderful view of the river mouth. Go up the steps and follow the signs for RAINBOW FALLS to the right.

Rainbow Falls (0.9 mile) is about 100 feet lower than the overlook. The trail turns to a light tread from here to CR 519. From here, you are basically climbing the side of a hill, crossing the contour at a slight diagonal. Hiking through second-growth hardwood forest, you will cross several small intermittent streams. If heading east, a small old road will come in from your left within 0.5 mile of CR 519. From here to CR 519, wilderness camping is permitted, though water is unreliable because of the many intermittent streams. The paved CR 519 (5.8 miles) is the main road accessing Porcupine Mountains Wilderness State Park from the west. When you get to CR 519 there is a gravel parking lot with room for about four vehicles, and a gate blocking car access to the old road you were just hiking.

The trail crosses CR 519 (6.4 miles), turns hard left (north), and squeezes between CR 519 and the Presque Isle River. This segment is a lightly used portion that is an easy, relatively flat hike along a raging river with some waterfalls. Maple hemlock forest, although far from mature, makes for a beautiful hike.

You'll enter the Porcupine Mountains Wilderness State Park by crossing South Boundary Road at the 10.9-mile mark. Hike along the west bank of the Presque Isle River. Enjoy three waterfalls and massive trees reaching into the sky but keep your eye on your footing—the substrate can be loose and on the edge of a steep escarpment.

Hike into the parking area for the Presque Isle Campground (10.3 miles), which has a backpacker registration station. This is a modern campground, with 88 campsites giving you your first views of Lake Superior. Park regulations require backpackers to register, even if you are thru-hiking. This parking lot is adjacent to the campground registration station. You must utilize the park campgrounds, backcountry campsites, and trail shelters.

The North Country Trail segment in the Porcupine Mountains Wilderness State Park is probably the most heavily backpacked segment of the North Country Trail along its 4,600-mile length. The trail is marked at intersections with small signs, and is marked with blue painted diamonds. The trail is rough and lined with roots and rocks courtesy of the prevalent Canadian Shield. This segment of trail, although heavily used, is also a spectacular hike. Virgin hemlock and white pine fill the forest. Wildlife abounds, and the scenery is just amazing. You will encounter four waterfalls along the way. The Summit Peak tower gives the hiker a view from 40 feet above the ground and over 1,900 feet above sea level.

At 12.3 miles, you'll cross the mouth

VIEWING DECK AT SUMMIT PEAK

of Speaker's Creek. By this point, you've been hiking along the Lake Superior shore for a while. Speaker's Creek is just one of many small wilderness streams you will encounter in this area. There is a cabin available via advance reservations at this spot.

Continue heading east, and turn right off Lake Superior Trail onto Little Carp River Trail (16.2 miles). The trail in this section parallels the Little Carp River, offering several views of waterfalls. Your footing continues to be roots and rocks. Another cabin, the Little Carp River Cabin, is available with advance reservations.

Your wilderness hike continues with spectacular scenery. You will start a gradual climb for the next couple of miles through mature forest, and you'll pass the Section 17 cabin in 5.8 miles; Greenstone Falls Cabin will be in another 0.5 mile (21.3 miles). Both are available through advance reservations with the state park.

At the 24.4-mile point, you'll reach the Lily Pond Trail intersection and another cabin. Lily Pond is actually a trout lake! Virgin pine surround the area. From either direction, you'll climb a large hill only to descend back to your original elevation. Take note that this will be your last maintained camping opportunity for almost 50.0 miles to the east.

Hike down to the Summit Peak parking lot (27.4 miles), and the trail will then cross South Boundary Road and become lightly used as it leaves the state park and enters the Ottawa National Forest.

33

Gogebic Ridge Trail

START: Forest Road 250 (FR 250)

END: North Country Trail

APPROXIMATE HIKING TIME: 5–6 hours

LENGTH OF SECTION: 8.6 miles

The Trap Hills are a remnant of a rugged ancient mountain that has eroded over the 1 billion years or so since it was created. Most recently (geologically speaking), this area was eroded by glaciers then covered with glacial till, all of ten thousand years ago. The name of the trail comes from the nearby Lake Gogebic.

There is great debate on what exactly the word *Gogebic* means. The word is thought to be derived from the Ojibwe word *akogib* or *akogibing*, which may refer to *someone, something,* or *somewhere*. Although there are many claims for the origin and definition to the word *Gogebic*, the debate has gone on for over one hundred years and is far from settled.

One local translation comes from a Ojibwe word meaning *where trout rising to the surface makes rings on still waters*. As this is the largest lake in the Upper Peninsula and it is known for its great walleye fishery, who could argue with that translation?

The first known attempt at finally getting to the origin of the word and its meaning started the same year that the railroad came into the area, made by the editor of the local newspaper, the *Ontonagon Miner*. An editorial printed various meanings of the word *Gogebic* such as *green lake, little fish, place of the falling leaves, porcupine lake, bear in the water,* and *body of water hanging on high*. I think we can agree that the true origin and meaning of *Gogebic* is lost in the pages of time.

The Youth Conservation Corps constructed the Gogebic Hiking Trail in 1977. Parts of this trail closely follow the Lake Gogebic–Iron River Indian Trail that was used more than one hundred years ago.

If you enjoy bird watching, look and listen in the woods for warblers, vireos,

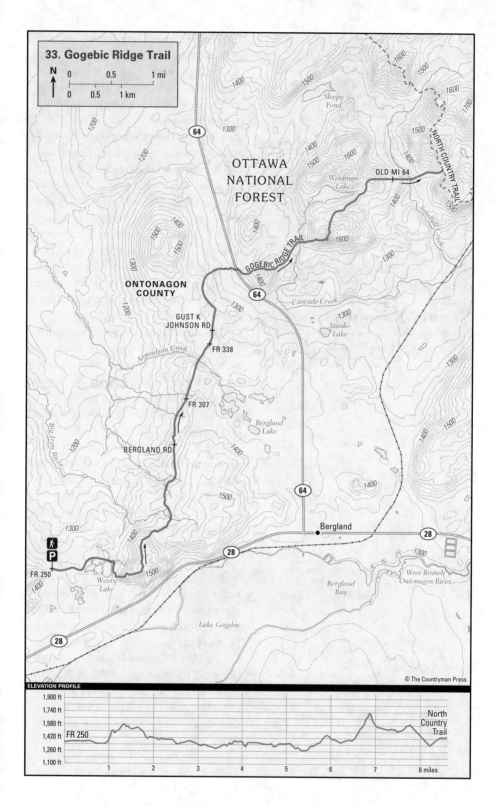

33. Gogebic Ridge Trail

N

| 0 | 0.5 | 1 mi |
| 0 | 0.5 | 1 km |

OTTAWA
NATIONAL
FOREST

Sleepy
Pond

Weidman
Lake

OLD MI 64

NORTH COUNTRY TRAIL

Sandhill Creek

GOGEBIC RIDGE TRAIL

ONTONAGON
COUNTY

Cascade Creek

Stanko
Lake

GUST K
JOHNSON RD

FR 338

Amundson Creek

FR 307

Bergland
Lake

BERGLAND RD

Bergland

FR 250

Weary
Lake

Bergland
Bay

West Branch
Ontonagon River

Lake Gogebic

© The Countryman Press

ELEVATION PROFILE

1,900 ft								
1,740 ft								
1,580 ft								
1,420 ft	FR 250							North Country Trail
1,260 ft								
1,100 ft								
	1	2	3	4	5	6	7	8 miles

and thrushes. Along water, keep a look-out for bald eagles and peregrine falcons, which are known to nest in the area.

HOW TO FIND

The south trailhead is found west of Bergland by taking MI 28 and turning north on FR 250; the trailhead is about 1.0 mile up the road. There isn't a vehicle-accessible trailhead at the north end where it intersects with the North Country Trail. However, another trailhead and parking is on MI 64, about 4.0 miles north of Bergland.

FACILITIES AND SERVICES

None, though trailside camping is permitted.

THE HIKE

Start your hike at the FR 250 parking lot—trekking west, circling a couple of small lakes on the north, then clockwise to the south, to the base of a hill at the 1.0-mile mark. Climb up this steep hill and it levels out for a view to the west. The hike becomes heavily wooded, as you'll be surrounded by sugar maple, hemlock, and white pine. At 2.8 miles you'll cross an intermittent stream in deep woods and in a low area.

In 0.4 mile you'll cross Bergland Road, a Forest Service road. The trail follows a contour and you ascend and descend several small valleys as you head north through the forest.

After crossing FR 307 (3.7 miles) you'll descend into a stream valley—listen for northern waterthrushes, wood thrushes, and other deep forest birds. The waterthrush, although a warbler, is found running along fast-moving streams, foraging for bugs. Look for this bird as you cross Amundsan Creek (4.2 miles), which is a reliable creek and may make a good bivouac.

In 0.2 mile you'll cross FR 338 and in another 0.1 mile Gust K. Johnson Road. You'll circle clockwise along a contour, then head down to cross a swampy area. Climb up to MI 64 at the 5.6-mile mark, cross the highway, then continue your climb up to the top of what seems to be a small hill—but is really a rather noticeable knob of hard, volcanic rock—before descending to cross Cascade Creek (6.6 miles).

You'll climb a second knob to over 1,500 feet in elevation, enjoy the view, then lose most of the elevation you've gained in the next mile as you approach Weidman Lake at the 7.7-mile mark. This may make a nice bivouac in a wooded setting along the lake. Ascend up a ravine to cross Old MI 64 at the 8.0-mile mark.

If you haven't already noticed, a trend has formed of climbing then descending. This time, descend and hike into a saddle where you intersect the North Country Trail at the 8.6-mile mark.

It is 8.0 miles to the north on the North Country Trail to Old MI 64, or 8.4 miles to FR 400 (which can be hiked back to M28, then to FR 250, to make a loop of 22.0 miles).

Big Iron River

It is amazing that in the span of 200 feet you leave a well-worn and wide path, cross the parking lot, and enter a trail that is used more by deer and bear than people. For the first 1.0 mile the trail is still in the state park and little used. This is a very remote section of trail, crossing several large rivers, and it is recommended that you have advanced to expert orienteering skills. In case the bridge at the Big Iron River is out, you must know how to ford a large river—which may be impassable, especially in the spring—or take a lengthy detour.

There is a light tread, a decent lane, and sparse blue painted rectangles mark the trail. Recent trail maintenance has raised the confidence level of hikers. Rocky outcrops exposing the Canadian Shield offer spectacular scenery. It is a rare occurrence if one backpacker encounters another in this section. From Black River Harbor, you are in the middle of a 110-mile segment with no services and only three paved road crossings. There are several old logging roads and active off-road vehicle/snowmobile trails, so keep your eyes peeled for trail markings. There is wilderness camping only between here and Old Victoria, over 30 miles to the east.

Covering nearly 1 million acres, the Ottawa National Forest stretches from the south shore of Lake Superior to the Wisconsin-Michigan state line. Heavily forested with both hardwood and softwood, the Ottawa is an outdoor person's paradise. Three wilderness areas composing 50,000 acres, 500 named lakes, and over 2,000 miles of rivers and streams pull in people from all over the midwest. Although the Ottawa National Forest has the resources, you'll find that if you get away from pavement and developed areas, you'll have the whole place to yourself.

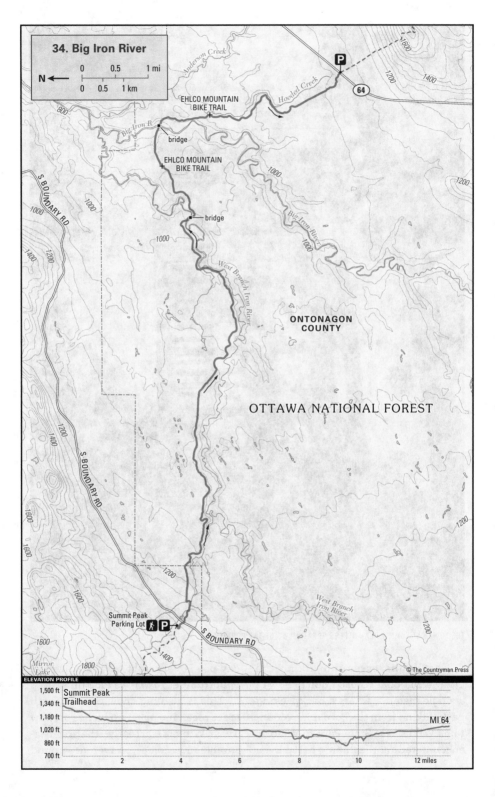

34. Big Iron River

N ←

| 0 | 0.5 | 1 mi |
| 0 | 0.5 | 1 km |

Anderson Creek

Hooded Creek

64

EHLCO MOUNTAIN
BIKE TRAIL

Big Iron R.

bridge

EHLCO MOUNTAIN
BIKE TRAIL

S. BOUNDARY RD

bridge

West Branch Iron River

Big Iron River

ONTONAGON
COUNTY

OTTAWA NATIONAL FOREST

S. BOUNDARY RD

West Branch
Iron River

Summit Peak
Parking Lot

S BOUNDARY RD

Mirror
Lake

© The Countryman Press

ELEVATION PROFILE

1,500 ft	Summit Peak
1,340 ft	Trailhead
1,180 ft	MI 64
1,020 ft	
860 ft	
700 ft	

2   4   6   8   10   12 miles

THE TOWER AT SUMMIT PEAK OFFERS GREAT VIEWS OF THE PORKIES

That is the case with hiking the Ottawa National Forest. I don't know of a single instance where a backpacking party hiking from the Porcupine Mountains Wilderness State Park to Victoria encountered another hiking party. Even day use is very light, as there are few opportunities to make a loop hike.

This is also big snow country, with areas receiving over 200 inches of snow a year. Winters start early—the first measurable snow comes, on average, around

Halloween. Snow frequently lingers well into May.

HOW TO FIND

The west trailhead at Summit Peak can be reached from Wakefield and MI 28, by turning north on CR 519. After about 10.0 miles, a parking lot is on the left at another designated trailhead. Continue north 2.5 miles, and turn east (right) onto South Boundary Road. Summit Peak is about 12.0 miles from this intersection.

The east trailhead can be reached by traveling on MI 64 to a point about 7.0 miles north of Bergland.

FACILITIES AND SERVICES

None, though backcountry camping is permitted.

THE HIKE

South Boundary Road nearly marks the division between the state park and the national forest. Trail to the east is in the Ottawa National Forest, to the west in the state park. The trail between here and the Ottawa National Forest is managed by the local chapter and from then on by the Ottawa National Forest staff all the way to MI 64.

The tread is light as you hike southeast 1.0 mile before officially crossing the Ottawa National Forest boundary. You are now deep in the woods; the tread is light but well-blazed. The trail follows the bluff overlooking the west branch of the Iron River. This heavily wooded hike goes for 8.2 miles past South Boundary Road before you reach your first definitive point of reference, a bridge crossing the river to its south side.

There is a mountain bike trail system that intersects with and uses the North Country Trail at about 3.0 miles past South Boundary Road. It comes in from the right (south) and exits to the north about 1.0 mile later. Pay close attention to the blazes and bike traffic, which is very light.

At 8.2 miles cross the west branch of the Iron River on an old logging road bridge that spans the river. About 0.6 mile past the crossing, the Ehlco Mountain Bike Trail comes in from the left (north), uses the North Country Trail until it crosses the Big Iron River at the 9.4-mile mark, then splits off into the woods.

Under a heavy snow load, the bridge crossing this wide river collapsed in 1997. The river is normally 1 to 2 feet deep, and by taking the usual precautions, you can ford it. The bridge has since been rebuilt. This is a great location to camp for the night. Practice Leave No Trace!

Hike out to MI 64 (12.9 miles) and you'll find the parking lot on the east side of MI 64.

35

Trap Hills–West

START: MI 64/North Country Trail Trailhead	
END: Norwich Road	
APPROXIMATE HIKING TIME: 10–15 hours	
LENGTH OF SECTION: 20.1 miles	

This is a remote area of the Ottawa National Forest and is the beginning of what is considered the most rugged and demanding section of the North Country Trail. The trail switches back and forth considerably, along with ascending and descending hills that are quite steep. Trap Hills is so named because basaltic lava flows are sometimes known as "trap rock." Although the Trap Hills only rise 500 feet above the surrounding landscape, your view is worth the effort—unbroken forest with few signs of humans in every direction.

This hike is a lesson in geology. Just over 1 billion years ago, a great rift opened in the area that now houses the Lake Superior basin. Lava spilled out and, after it cooled, sediment filled the basin. These materials created today's rock formations made of andesite, basalt, conglomerate, rhyolite, sandstone, and more. The rock formations of the Trap Hills are so dense that they mostly survived damage from the numerous advancing and retreating glaciers.

Hiking the Trap Hills allows for many cliff views, mostly on south-facing sides of the formations; the underlying rock slopes toward the north between 10 and 20 degrees. The up-and-down nature of your hikes brings you to cliffs, but also descends into numerous valleys, which are mostly oriented north–south or northwest-southeast and are home to a few streams providing reliable water. It is in the valleys that the glaciers did most of their scouring and sculpting.

Humans have been roaming the area since about six thousand years ago—signs have been found of native people exploring for copper. Prospectors flocked to this area of the Upper Peninsula in the 1840s when the famed 2-ton Ontonagon Boulder, made of solid

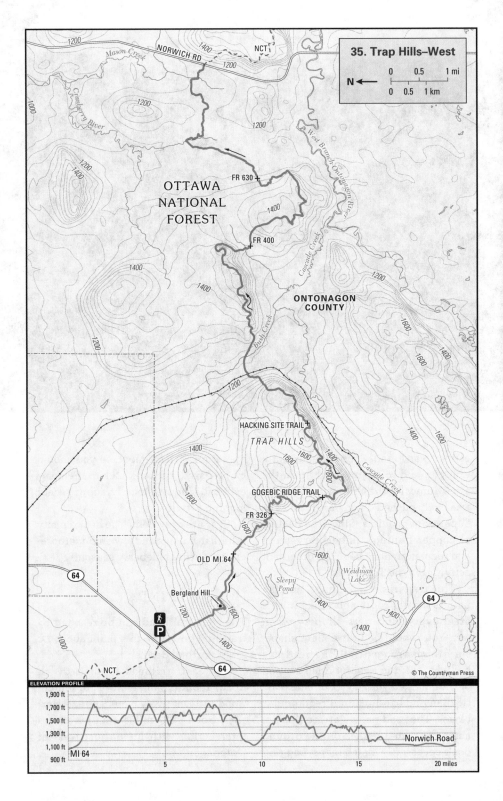

35. Trap Hills–West

N ←
0   0.5   1 mi
0   0.5   1 km

1200
NORWICH RD
NCT
1400
1200
1200
Mason Creek
Cranberry River
1000
1200
1200
1400
FR 630 +
1400
West Branch Ontonagon River
OTTAWA
NATIONAL
FOREST
1400
FR 400 +
Cascade Creek
1400
1200
ONTONAGON
COUNTY
1400
1600
1200
Bush Creek
1600
1400
1200
HACKING SITE TRAIL +
TRAP HILLS
1600
1600
1400
1600
1400
Cascade Creek
1600
GOGEBIC RIDGE TRAIL +
1600
FR 326 +
1600
1600
OLD MI 64 +
1600
Weidman Lake
64
Bergland Hill
Sleepy Pond
1400
64
1200
1600
1400
1400
1000
1400
NCT
64
© The Countryman Press

ELEVATION PROFILE

1,900 ft
1,700 ft
1,500 ft
1,300 ft
1,100 ft   MI 64
900 ft
Norwich Road
5   10   15   20 miles

Thomas Funke

copper, was found. Soon after, exploration pits and mines popped up in the area. Ironically, the Ontonagon Boulder was likely pushed down here from Lake Superior by glaciers. Since the decline of copper mining, timber harvesting and recreation have been the dominant activities in the Trap Hills.

This trail has steep climbs, and the path is mostly roots and rocks in this area; everything gets slippery when wet. You should be in excellent shape, since this is a rugged trail. The tread may be light, but it is a maintained section of trail marked with a mix of blue plastic diamonds and painted rectangular blazes. The road names are confusing, since the actual names on the ground don't necessarily match maps. Logging

operations are frequent, so you should be prepared to bushwhack to the nearest road. Inquire locally about recent logging activity.

Bear are prevalent. The bear density is high in valleys and low on ridgetops—except during blueberry season!

HOW TO FIND

The west trailhead can be reached by traveling on MI 64 to a point about 7.0 miles north of Bergland.

The east trailhead is on Norwich Road, about 9.5 miles north of Matchwood. Alternatively, you can take Norwich Road 14.0 miles south from its intersection with MI 64 just west of Ontonagon.

FACILITIES AND SERVICES

None, though backcountry camping is permitted.

THE HIKE

With your back to MI 64, follow the blue blazes east. Take a deep breath before you climb about 700 feet in elevation to the top of Bergland Hill—a former location of a lookout tower. Just past the site about 3.0 miles is Old MI 64.

You have just climbed your first hill of many in the Trap Hills. The habitat is hardwood forest and is quite dry. From here to Victoria, the trail zigzags, ascends, and descends—with spectacular views. Old MI 64 is a lightly used gravel road.

Hike into the woods and at 3.8 miles, cross Forest Road 326 (FR 326). You'll have climbed in elevation only to drop, walking near an old beaver pond through mucky footing. Intersect the Gogebic Ridge Trail (4.8 miles), which heads southwest for 8.0 miles, crossing Old MI 64. The trail continues to zigzag, ascending and hugging the edge of the Trap Hills for more great views. You should be huffing and puffing your way through this great hike.

The FR 326 Access Trail is at the 7.3-mile point into this segment's hike. Shortly after, look for a spur trail—the

TRAP HILLS

Thomas Funke

Hacking Site Trail, marked with white blazes, intersects the North Country Trail and heads left (northwest) for 1 mile to FR 326. A hiker registration box is located at this intersection.

Shortly before Bush Creek, at the 9.0-mile mark, you will cross the Canadian National Railroad. There is a bridge crossing the creek, which will be replaced as it is in disrepair. You are at the bottom of a river valley, and you will be ascending back into the hills shortly. Good campsites are hard to find near the creek due to wet ground and alder thickets. Get out of the swampy areas and onto drier land for potential backcountry camping opportunities. You'll continue your adventure of climbing up and down across the landscape.

At 13.1 miles, cross FR 400, a lightly used Forest Road. There is possible camping and roadside parking, and the road is marked with a Forest Service sign. There is a nice view in this trail segment, and camping is also possible several hundred feet west of FR 400 along an intermittent rocky stream.

Cross FR 630 (16.4 miles), a gravel road not plowed in the winter. The topography east of FR 630 is flatter and contains mixed forest. In 1.6 miles is an unnamed stream, a reliable water source with potential campsites west of the stream crossing.

A named stream, Mason Creek (19.9 miles), is another reliable stream—with a bridge. This is the last water for about 4.0 miles until after you cross Norwich Road (20.1 miles).

Norwich Road is your last paved road until you reach Victoria. This would be your best place to hitch a ride north and then east on Victoria Road to Rockland (post office, small store, diner, lodging) or Ontonagon (full services) or south to Bergland (camping, restaurant, post office).

36
Ontonagon River Valley

START: Victoria Shelter

END: Forest Road 1100 (FR 1100)

APPROXIMATE HIKING TIME: 15–25 hours

LENGTH OF SECTION: 25.7 miles

Welcome to Victoria, where you'll have the opportunity to experience two pieces of Michigan history. Mining exists in this area due to the discovery of the Ontonagon Boulder, a 2-ton piece of copper. Native Americans used the boulder for ceremonies. In 1677, Claude Dablon confirmed the existence of the boulder. Alexander Henry, and later Henry Schoolcraft, confirmed the boulder was there in later years. However, Julius Eldred, an entrepreneur from Detroit, bought it; he paid the local Native Americans $150. Upon returning to move the boulder, he had to pay ten times that amount as the land underneath the boulder had been purchased. After several tries, the boulder was moved to Detroit—and then the Smithsonian Institution.

The boulder brought mining prospectors, starting in 1771 with the same Alexander Henry. Dubbed the Victoria Mine, the project failed, and the area was abandoned. In 1849, the mining resumed for about eight years, and then various mining companies sporadically ran it until the end of the century. Records show that about 250 tons of copper were removed.

At the turn of the last century, the Victoria Mine was resurrected when a dam was created on the river to provide power for mining operations. This drastically reduced the price of extraction, which allowed the current owners of the Victoria Mine to outlast many of its competitors. Unfortunately, when the price of copper bottomed out right after World War I, the mine closed for good in 1921.

The old dam was converted into today's Victoria Dam, built in 1929 to create electricity for the local area. Today, the Upper Peninsula Power Company uses the water from the river to create hydropower. The river is dry the vast majority of the time and has an interesting view. When the amount of water

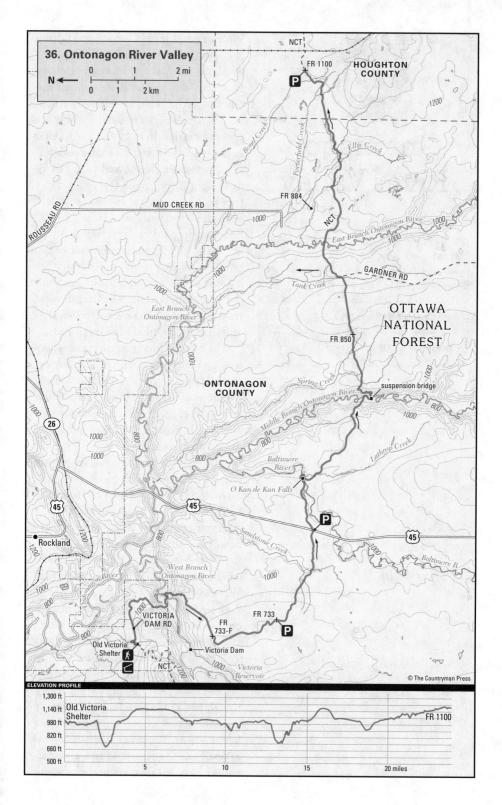

36. Ontonagon River Valley

N ←

| 0 | 1 | 2 mi |
| 0 | 1 | 2 km |

NCT

FR 1100

P

HOUGHTON COUNTY

1200

Bond Creek

Porterfield Creek

Ellis Creek

FR 884

NCT

East Branch Ontonagon River

1000

ROUSSEAU RD

MUD CREEK RD

1000

1000

GARDNER RD

Tank Creek

1000

East Branch Ontonagon River

OTTAWA NATIONAL FOREST

FR 850

1000

800

26

1000

ONTONAGON COUNTY

Spring Creek

Middle Branch Ontonagon River

suspension bridge

800

800

1000

800

Baltimore River

Lathrop Creek

O Kun de Kun Falls

1000

1000

45

P

45

Sandstone Creek

Baltimore R.

45

1000

Rockland

1200

West Branch Ontonagon River

1000

1000

800

FR 733

P

FR 733-F

VICTORIA DAM RD

1000

800

Old Victoria Shelter

Victoria Dam

NCT

1200

Victoria Reservoir

1000

© The Countryman Press

ELEVATION PROFILE

1,300 ft
1,140 ft — Old Victoria Shelter
980 ft
820 ft
660 ft
500 ft

FR 1100

5   10   15   20 miles

running into the reservoir exceeds what can be sent through the turbines, the gates will open and water will flow down into what seems to be a dry river most of the year. This usually occurs in the late spring during snowmelt and heavy summer rains.

The lack of water usually allows for a shallow crossing over sometimes slippery rocks. When the dam is about ready to release water, an alarm sounds. The riverbed is less than 100 yards wide. After crossing the river, you head right back up the elevation you lost into the woods. The hike then becomes a remote section of trail through mature forests. The trail tread is light; however, it is well blazed.

You'll also cross three branches of the Ontonagon River, two of which you'll have to ford to cross. Be aware that bear are prevalent, that there are still some significant elevation gains in and out of the Ontonagon River valleys, and that there are no bridges on the Ontonagon River or its east branch. Logging operations are frequent, so be prepared to bushwhack to the nearest road—although loggers are asked to maintain the integrity of the trail and the blazes. Inquire locally about recent logging activity. In addition, the area is prone to forest fires; inquire locally about risks.

The local trail chapter has recently rolled up their sleeves and resurrected the trail in this segment, allowing even novice hikers to find their way through a very remote area.

HOW TO FIND

The west end of the trail is found by driving from Bruce Crossing and the intersection of MI 28 and US 45. Take US 45 for 16.0 miles north to Rockland. In Rockland, turn south onto Victoria

Dam Road. You'll descend a steep hill, cross the Ontonagon River, ascend to Old Victoria, and park at the Old Victoria townsite.

The east end of this segment is FR 1100. Take FH 16 north from Kenton for about 16.0 miles, and turn left (west) onto Pori Road. Continue for 3.0 miles, turning south on FR 1100 to find roadside parking.

The trail can also be accessed from US 45 about 7.0 miles north of Bruce Crossing, where there is a parking lot. Gardner Road has a parking area as well, which is accessed by taking Gardner Road 13.0 miles north out of Trout Creek.

FACILITIES AND SERVICES

None, though backcountry camping is permitted in the Ottawa National Forest. Rockland has a store, diner, and lodging; it is 4.2 miles north of Old Victoria Shelter on Victoria Dam Road.

THE HIKE

Settled in 1849, Victoria attracted copper and silver speculators. They came because of the Ontonagon Boulder. These speculators left an incredible mess and disappeared as quickly as they appeared. Today, there is a hydropower dam in the vicinity. A shelter, built by North Country Trail volunteers, is a deluxe sleeping experience located about 100 yards east of Old Victoria. If you are hiking west, it is about 50.0 miles until your next maintained camping facilities.

The North Country Trail descends to Victoria Dam Road; at 1.2 miles, turn right to follow along a north–south gravel road, past a closed gate, and then over a water pipe on an old bridge to a gravel road. Bend left on the gravel road, then head, via a sharp right turn, to the

O KUN DE KUN FALLS

powerhouse access road onto the North Country Trail. This will take you to the dry river crossing.

If you need to bypass the river, take the paved Victoria Dam Road 3.0 miles to Rockland, head south on US 45 for 2.0 miles to the intersection with MI 26, turn south on US 45, and go 6.0 miles to the O Kun de Kun Falls North Country Trailhead (the local chapter has this bypass map on their website).

The dry, rock-strewn west branch of the Ontonagon riverbed (2.7 miles) is a mere trickle of water most of the year. The Victoria Dam diverts the Ontonagon River downstream to a power plant for electricity generation. Crossing the river is easy—provided you hear no sirens and take care crossing the slippery rocks. When the water in the reservoir becomes too high, water is released into the riverbed, making it impossible to cross. If the flow is over 750 cubic feet per second, the crossing will likely be too dangerous. The Upper Peninsula Power Company updates the flow rate several times an hour at their website (www.uppco.com).

After the mostly dry riverbed crossing, there is a steep hill to climb—but it is level hiking out of the river valley. At 5.6 miles, cross FR 733-F. Vehicle access to FR 733-F is blocked by a locked gate. In 2.0 miles you'll cross FR 733. The trail between FR 733-F and FR 733 is even in elevation but with a rocky footing. The trail descends slightly to a reliable water crossing (Sandstone Creek) with possible bivouac campsites west of the creek, then heads to US 45 (10.1 miles).

Kun de Kun Falls you should also be able to see the magnificent suspension bridge over the middle branch of the Ontonagon River (17.7 miles). There is a picnic table, a fire ring, and room to camp.

From the west, climb to a 1,000-foot plateau, then descend 220 feet to cross on an impressive, 130-foot-long suspension bridge where there are possible sites to backcountry camp. You'll climb right out of the ravine and the trail will level off until you cross FR 850 at the 19.0-mile mark. The trail is a little-used, gated forest road. It continues through maturing forest, crossing another old road (19.9 miles) that leads to private property, so stay on the trail.

Hike west, thorough forest, towards the East Branch Ontonagon River, which, as of this writing, is a bridgeless crossing, but a bridge is under construction and should be in use in 2016. The water in summer and fall is shallow, less than one foot deep.

Contact the local Peter Wolfe Chapter for information regarding water levels. A bypass route during high water can be found by hiking Gardner Road north and turning right (east) on Mud Creek Road (FR 209), then heading right (southeast) on the defunct FR 884 to pick up the trail again after a 3.8-mile road walk.

Continue hiking through relatively flat terrain to Ellis Creek (23.8 miles), a reliable water source in nondrought years and potential backcountry campsite.

FR 1100 is your easternmost access point and parking area at the 25.7-mile point into the hike.

The US 45 parking lot is accessible by a short spur trail. The trail descends about 100 feet in elevation into the Baltimore River valley. There is another falls along this route that hikers often confuse with the O Kun de Kun Falls—be sure to walk another 800 feet to the see the larger of the two falls. The trail is well-used and is being improved to be handicap accessible from the highway to the falls.

The trail parallels the Baltimore River and affords you the view of O Kun de Kun Falls (14.5 miles). When you see the O

37

Ottawa National Forest Highlands

START: Forest Road 1100 (FR 1100)

END: South Laird Road eastern parking lot

APPROXIMATE HIKING TIME: 7–9 hours

LENGTH OF SECTION: 13.6 miles

You are high and dry, on the dividing line between the Ontonagon River and Sturgeon River watersheds. This is a remote section of trail with several ups and downs, making for a pleasant hike. Heading east, you are nearing the end of the longest remote stretch of the North Country Trail. The habitats become more dry, yielding jack and red pine as the dominant pines, and red maple with poplar as the dominant broadleaf trees. There is a recognizable lane and light tread in this area blazed with blue rectangles.

This is a little-used segment of trail, hiking for those with higher skill and in good shape. Be alert for several small ravine crossings and a few marshy areas. The end of steep climbs is over, for a while anyway. Rolling topography through wetlands and swamps may include crossing beaver dams. The trail can be overgrown with no recognizable tread or lane. Blazes are to be converted from blue plastic diamonds to blue rectangles soon, so take your orienteering skills with you.

HOW TO FIND

The west end of this segment is FR 1100. Take FH 16 north from Kenton for about 16.0 miles and turn left (west) onto Pori Road. Continue for 3.0 miles, turning south on FR 1100 to find roadside parking.

South Laird Road is the east end of the segment. You can access it from the north via MI 38 east of Rockland. Drive south until the road comes to a right turn. You can access it from the south by taking FH 16 north from MI 28 at Kenton and turning right at South Laird Road.

There is a parking area at FH 16 and you can take a spur trail in from Bob Lake

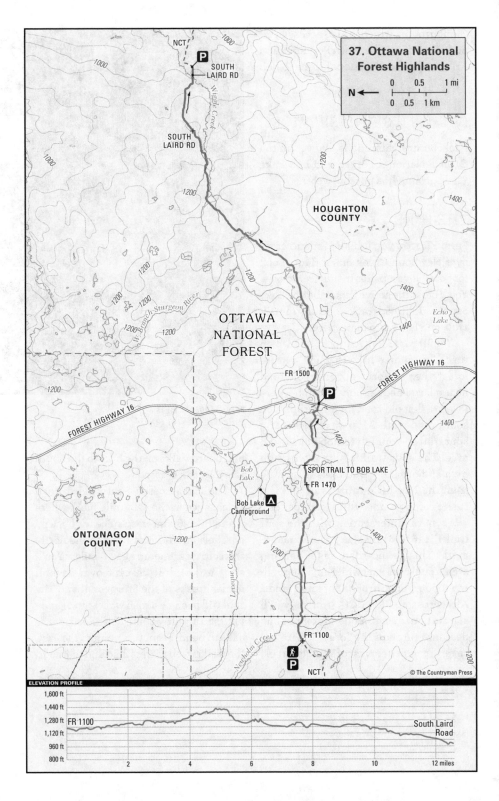

37. Ottawa National Forest Highlands

N ←

0   0.5   1 mi

0   0.5   1 km

NCT

P

SOUTH LAIRD RD

SOUTH LAIRD RD

Wigale Creek

HOUGHTON COUNTY

OTTAWA NATIONAL FOREST

W. Branch Sturgeon River

Echo Lake

FOREST HIGHWAY 16

FR 1500

P

FOREST HIGHWAY 16

SPUR TRAIL TO BOB LAKE

FR 1470

Bob Lake

Bob Lake Campground

ONTONAGON COUNTY

Lexeque Creek

Newholm Creek

FR 1100

NCT

© The Countryman Press

ELEVATION PROFILE

1,600 ft						
1,440 ft						
1,280 ft	FR 1100					
1,120 ft						South Laird Road
960 ft						
800 ft	2	4	6	8	10	12 miles

Campground, which is also accessed off South Laird Road between Pori Road and FH 16. Look for directional signs to Bob Lake.

FACILITIES AND SERVICES

Backcountry camping is allowed in the Ottawa National Forest, and Bob Lake Campground has potable water.

THE HIKE

From FR 1100 you'll hike east and cross over Newholm Creek on a bridge. Look for possible campsites in this scenic area. You'll cross the active Escanaba and Lake Superior Railroad tracks 0.5 mile from FR 1100, and head into mature forest.

You'll cross FR 1470 (3.2 miles), which turns into a nice hike through mature forest, then a short walk on an old road near a large beaver pond. Watch where to leave that old road for an abrupt turn south onto trail. Afterward, look for a spur trail on your left to Bob Lake in 0.4 mile. The spur trail is blazed white on high and dry land. Bob Lake is 1.0 mile from the North Country Trail and is a rustic campground with 17 campsites.

From the intersection with the spur trail, FH 16 (4.6 miles) is your next landmark. This paved road has a parking area. You'll hike east while enjoying rolling topography through forested lands. After crossing FR 1500 (5.9 miles), you'll start to notice some moderate climbs and descents through the forest. There are several campsites west of Wiggle Creek,

Thomas Funke

BEAVER LODGE TRAIL IS A SPUR TO THE NORTH COUNTRY TRAIL

and boardwalks on the hike to the South Laird Road crossing.

The trail crosses South Laird Road twice, once at the 12.4-mile mark where it and FR 1360 intersect. The trail briefly parallels South Laird Road to the north, then crosses it again at 13.6 miles. You'll start a downhill descent over several feeder creeks of the Sturgeon River. The trail will become a road walk for 0.25 mile until shortly after South Laird Road makes a north bend. From this point to the east, the trail is well maintained and marked.

38

Sturgeon River and Baraga Plains

START: Where South Laird Road turns from a N–S road to an E–W road

END: US 41

APPROXIMATE HIKING TIME: 12–22 hours

LENGTH OF SECTION: 31.3 miles

You need to be stocked up on water for this stretch. Although this is another remote and rugged section of trail, it is within short distances of more traveled roads. You will climb to the top of several ridges and follow some well-marked old logging roads as you approach the Sturgeon River Gorge Wilderness. Continue to cross several Forest Roads, some well-used, some barely noticeable. Most roads are traversable by automobile. The tread is light, but lane and blazes keep your confidence high.

The North Country Trail parallels the northern and eastern boundaries of the Sturgeon River Gorge Wilderness for about 8.0 miles. The Sturgeon River is a federally designated Wild and Scenic River. This river comes out of the northern portion of this wilderness, heads over the 20-foot volcanic outcroppings of Sturgeon Falls, and then through a gorge that reaches 350 feet in depth and 1.0 mile in width. The canyon created by the river is noticeable from the nearby road—especially after leaf off in the fall. Throughout this rugged, steep wilderness, the Sturgeon and Silver Rivers and their tributaries have carved falls, rapids, ponds, oxbows, and terraces. Stunning views are possible from the eastern rim of the gorge. Except for a few naturally bare slopes, most of the land is forested with pine, hemlock, aspen, sugar maple, birch, and basswood. There is a spur trail to the waterfall starting at the parking lot on FR 2224. Since this is a wilderness area, there are few established trails in Sturgeon River Gorge.

You'll start to notice a transition from the mature hardwood and pine forests to more young, open-canopy forests. The mature forests have been growing in mostly rugged areas with rugged topography. Along the Sturgeon Gorge,

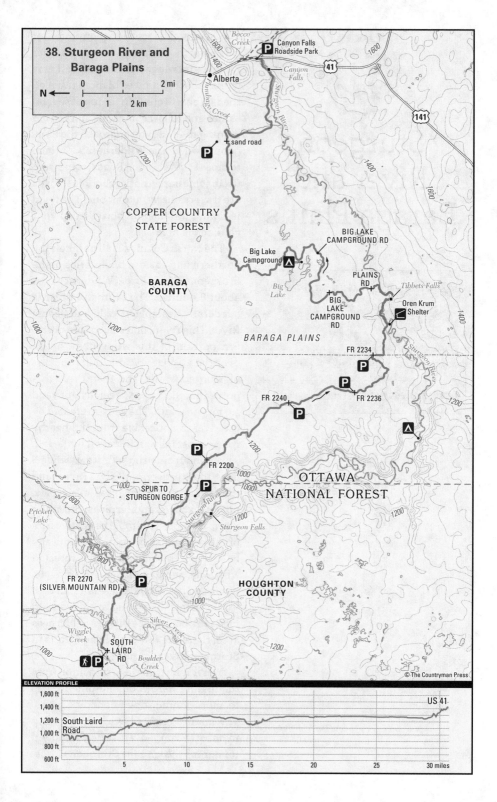

38. Sturgeon River and Baraga Plains

N ←

0 ... 1 ... 2 mi
0 ... 1 ... 2 km

Bocco Creek

P **Canyon Falls Roadside Park**

1600

1400

1600

● Alberta

Canyon Falls

41

141

Plumbago Creek

Sturgeon River

P → sand road

1200

1400

1600

COPPER COUNTRY STATE FOREST

BIG LAKE CAMPGROUND RD

Big Lake Campground △

BARAGA COUNTY

Big Lake

PLAINS RD

Tibbets Falls

BIG LAKE CAMPGROUND RD

Oren Krum Shelter

1200

1400

BARAGA PLAINS

FR 2234 P

1000

FR 2240 P

FR 2236

Sturgeon River

1200

P FR 2200

△

1200

1000

P SPUR TO STURGEON GORGE

Sturgeon River

1000

OTTAWA NATIONAL FOREST

1200

Prickett Lake

800

1000

Sturgeon Falls

1200

1200

FR 2270 (SILVER MOUNTAIN RD)

P

1000

HOUGHTON COUNTY

Silver Creek

1000

Wiggle Creek

1000

SOUTH LAIRD RD

🚶 P

Boulder Creek

1200

© The Countryman Press

ELEVATION PROFILE

1,600 ft
1,400 ft
1,200 ft — South Laird Road
1,000 ft
800 ft
600 ft

US 41

5 ... 10 ... 15 ... 20 ... 25 ... 30 miles

you'll be starting your hike along the known Baraga Plains, where the land management transfers from the US Forest Service to the Michigan Department of Natural Resources.

The Michigan Department of Natural Resources manages over 12,000 acres of barrens and dry northern forests composed of jack pines. The area is very flat and the soils are sandy, supporting a carpet of lichen, blueberry, sweet fern, and many species of grass and sedge; it is a habitat prone to fire. More savannah than forest, this area is also home to a few nesting Kirtland's warblers. The Baraga Plains is a lesson in botany and biology, so be sure to bring a field guide with you.

The trail eventually parallels the Sturgeon River until you reach Plains Road, where there is a side trail to Tibbets Falls. The trail spur to Tibbit's Falls is marked with white rectangular blazes, and there is a parking area.

Continue north, weaving around a mix of land uses and types—swamp, blueberry fields, jack pine forests, and open marshes over mostly flat terrain—until you reach Plumbago Creek. The trail then follows along the Sturgeon River; you will see a number of dramatic falls and rock cliffs along this "Canyon Falls" Trail to US 41.

HOW TO FIND

South Laird Road is the west end of the segment. You can access it from the north via MI 38 east of Rockland. Drive south until the road comes to a right turn. You can access it from the south by taking FH 16 north from MI 28 at Kenton and turning right at South Laird Road.

US 41 is the east end of the segment, at Canyon Falls Roadside Park. The park is 2.5 miles north of the US 141/US 41/MI 28 junction.

FACILITIES AND SERVICES

There is a registration box on the Plumbago Bridge along with a spur trail to US 41 and a paved parking lot, seasonal bathrooms, and picnic areas. Covington is the nearest town, 3.5 miles south of the Plains Road and Sturgeon River crossing. The only services are a post office and convenience store. Backcountry camping is allowed in the national forest.

THE HIKE

From South Laird Road, the elevation decreases toward the Sturgeon River. You will cross several small feeder creeks and you may run into some beaver activity. There is a registration box for comments between Boulder Creek and Silver River on the ridge, in an old-growth hemlock stand where there are several camping options.

At 2.0 miles, cross FR 2270 (Silver Mountain Road) where the trail jogs left (west) on a private road just west of the bridge over the Sturgeon River (2.6 miles). Watch for blazes as this is a little-hiked segment of trail. At the Sturgeon River Bridge, there is a swimming and fishing hole along with a sand beach at the first bend northeast of the bridge. The trail parallels FR 2270 for a beautiful hike through mature forests from the bridge eastbound. To the east, you will be high and dry for about 10.0 miles until the trail brings you back to this same river. Load up on water now! You will cross several sandy roads—some of them used, some of them long abandoned.

At 6.1 miles you'll find a spur trail, blazed white, on your right as you head to the Sturgeon Gorge. Parking is available at FR 2270. The trail continues on high, dry, and sandy soils.

After crossing FR 2200 (7.1 miles),

GORGE FALLS IS ACCESSED VIA A SIDE TRAIL

you are on the west end of the Baraga Plains, which were created by glacial outwash. Jack pine thrives in this sandy soil. Keep a close eye on the trail and the blazes, as many abandoned roads and trails crisscross the area.

At the 10.0-mile mark, cross FR 2240, which has parking available. Be especially alert for blazes, as there are innumerable old trails and roads in this area—and the trail will use some of these unimproved roads. You are high and dry, enjoying the walk through jack pine forests.

You'll cross FR 2236 (11.6 miles), which also has roadside parking. Your hike is pleasant, through open woods in places, with flat to rolling topography.

At 13.7 miles, you'll cross FR 2234, which also affords the hiker roadside parking. Be advised to park completely off the road. The Baraga Bump Fire affected this area in 2007, so blowdown and dead trees are present.

At the 15.2-mile mark you'll come to the Sturgeon River, your first water source in nearly 13 miles. This wild and scenic river is heavily wooded and rugged. Take the time to admire the maturing mixed forest. If it suits you, the Oren Krumm Shelter may be a great place to camp for the night. There is a side trail

Dave Day

trail and into the Big Lake State Forest Campground (21.0 miles), a rustic state forest campground located on a shallow, sandy-bottomed lake, which has 12 sites.

From here, traverse a mix of wetland and upland ridges; the trail keeps to the ridges most of the way. Be prepared for some squishy footing after snowmelt or heavy rains in the low areas.

After crossing Major Sand Road at the 24.0-mile mark, your hike takes you through a variety of current and past forestry practices and open savannas, while skirting wetland areas. The trail will come to the top of the Plumbago Creek valley and follow the escarpment before descending to the creek.

Cross Major Sand Road again (27.7 miles); if you want to enter or exit the trail, 0.2 mile to the north via Sand Road is Baraga Plains Road (aka Prison Camp Road), which is plowed in the winter. The road is gated near Baraga Plains Road. If parking there, do not block the gate. This hike traverses private land along Plumbago Creek to the Sturgeon River, so there is no camping and you should stay on the trail.

At the 28.0-mile mark, there is a bluff overlooking Plumbago Creek valley. The trail will come to the top of the Plumbago Creek valley and follow the escarpment before descending to the creek to cross (29.4 miles). Cross the creek, head east, and eventually you'll follow the Sturgeon River in close proximity. There is a registration box on the Plumbago Bridge. Past here is a beautiful hike along the Sturgeon River, also known as the Canyon Falls Trail. Canyon Falls is at the 30.9-mile mark; the roadside park giving access to motorists from US 41 is another 0.4 mile.

From US 41, it is a 13.5-mile road walk east to North Nestoria Road and onto Long Lake Road, where the North Coun-

to Tibbets Falls 0.1 mile past the shelter, to your right. If you hike down to the river for water, also look for the steeply tilted layers of slate rock that make this an interesting series of shelf waterfalls.

You'll cross Plains Road (16.4 miles) and head into mixed second growth forest and open areas, with some swampy footing in places. Cross Big Lake Campground Road (20.3 miles) and hike into flat terrain dominated by jack pine with a carpet of blueberry, lichen, and sweet fern.

In 0.3 mile the trail comes to Big Lake Campground Road on your right, which you'll need to walk for about 0.75 mile before heading back left onto the

ROAD WALK TO CRAIG LAKE

try Trail starts again and goes east to Craig Lake State Park. Refer to the Peter Wolfe Chapter website for up-to-date trail construction and recommended road routes.

One route is to hike a grassy abandoned road to the Sturgeon River under the US 41 bridge, and head north onto US 41, then turn right (east) onto Old US 41. Walk south, cross over US 41 at 6.8 miles, and the road changes names to King Road. At 8.5 miles the road comes to a T; turn left (which swings back to the northeast) and cross over US 41 a second time; you'll come to another T-intersection, so turn right (east) onto Herman Nestoria Road, which then brings you southeast right back to US 41. Alternatively, you could walk US 41 all the way to the intersection you'll need to get back onto the trail—with North Nestoria Road, the first road east of the railroad track crossing.

Craig Lake and Michigamme Highlands

START: North Nestoria Road and US 41

END: West McCormick Wilderness Trailhead

APPROXIMATE HIKING TIME: 8–12 hours

LENGTH OF SECTION: 16.2 miles

This stretch is the first part of a more than 50.0-mile continuous hike through remote areas, with few paved roads and few regularly traveled gravel roads—many of which are unnamed or unmarked. Although it can be broken up into shorter day hikes, one needs to have a good map, a high-clearance vehicle, and a sense of adventure to find the trailheads.

From MI 28/US 41, you'll hike up North Nestoria Road—a gated, rutted track—into the thick woods. The ground has many places where you will see exposed rocks, as the soil is very thin in this stretch. The road splits, with North Nestoria Road going to the right (west fork) and Loon Lake Road going to the left (east fork). Bear right on North Nestoria Road, which will bring you to a trailhead on Craig Lake, about 3.5 miles from MI 28/US 41.

Plunge into the state forest and cross into Craig Lake State Park, the most remote state park in Michigan. Craig Lake State Park is land originally owned by Fred Miller of the Miller Brewing Company. Acquired in the early 1950s, the land was hunted by the Miller family until his unfortunate demise in 1954. Within 10 years, the area was turned into a state park.

There are two places in the Upper Peninsula where you have a good chance to see a moose, and this is one of the areas. There is a hiking trail that circumnavigates the entire lake, although you won't be able to see much of it. The North Country Trail skirts the south and east sides of the lake. On the south are a primitive launch, 17 campsites, and a day use area. As you continue to the east side of the lake, you'll enter the woods and be out of sight of the lake. If you really want to see a moose, hike

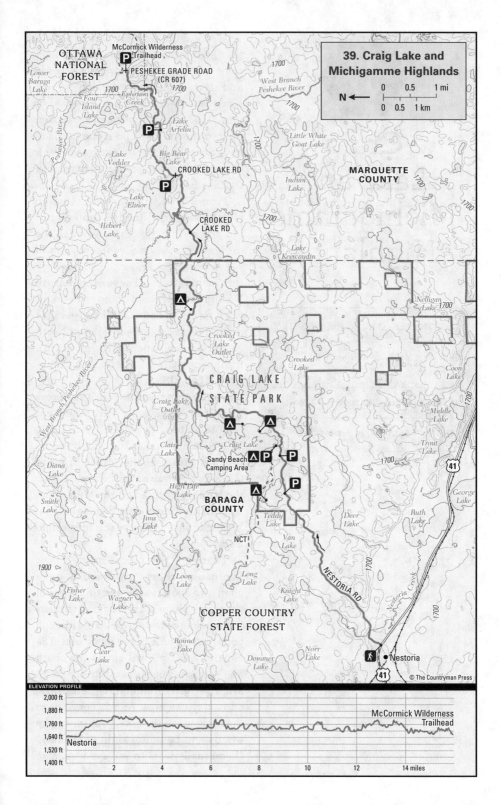

39. Craig Lake and Michigamme Highlands

OTTAWA NATIONAL FOREST

McCormick Wilderness Trailhead

PESHEKEE GRADE ROAD (CR 607)

Lower Baraga Lake

Ephriam Creek

1700

1700

Four Island Lake

West Branch Peshekee River

1700

1700

Lake Arfelin

Little White Goat Lake

Lake Vedder

Big Bear Lake

CROOKED LAKE RD

Indian Lake

MARQUETTE COUNTY

1700

1700

Lake Elinor

CROOKED LAKE RD

1700

Hebert Lake

1700

Lake Keewaydin

Nelligan Lake

1700

Crooked Lake Outlet

Crooked Lake

Coon Lake

1700

CRAIG LAKE STATE PARK

Craig Lake Outlet

Clair Lake

Craig Lake

Middle Lake

Diana Lake

Sandy Beach Camping Area

Trout Lake

1700

High Life Lake

George Lake

Smith Lake

BARAGA COUNTY

Deer Lake

Ruth Lake

Jims Lake

Teddy Lake

1900

NCT

Van Lake

Long Lake

NESTORIA RD

1700

Nestoria Creek

Fisher Lake

Wagner Lake

Loon Lake

Knight Lake

1700

Clear Lake

Round Lake

COPPER COUNTRY STATE FOREST

Dommer Lake

Norr Lake

Nestoria

© The Countryman Press

ELEVATION PROFILE

McCormick Wilderness Trailhead

Nestoria

2,000 ft
1,880 ft
1,760 ft
1,640 ft
1,520 ft
1,400 ft

2   4   6   8   10   12   14 miles

Thomas Funke

CRAIG LAKE IS AN EXCELLENT PLACE TO FIND MOOSE

up the west side of the lake, overnight camp, get up an hour before sunrise, and position yourself with a view of the lake. However, you are more likely to see a "sign" on the trail or possibly a monstrous hoofprint.

After Craig Lake, the trail continues to undulate through the forest and you'll see rock outcroppings of various sizes—some accumulations are larger than a small house. Craig Lake State Park continues to the Baraga and Marquette County line, and then enters the state forest. It continues to be heavily wooded, with several small stream crossings and a couple of road crossings (with parking) until it comes to the western boundary of the McCormick Wilderness.

HOW TO FIND

The westernmost point where you could legitimately park a vehicle is at Craig Lake State Park, at the end of Craig Lake State Park Road (note that this is a high-clearance vehicle road). Craig Lake State Park Road (also called Nelligan Road) is well marked on MI 28/US 41, about 1.5 miles west of Michigamme.

The eastern end of this segment is the western border of the McCormick Wilderness. The western access point to the McCormick Wilderness is accessed by turning north (right) onto County Road 607 (CR 607)/Peshekee Grade from MI 28/US 41 approximately 1.2 miles west of Van Riper State Park. Although blacktopped, it is rough going. You'll drive about 9.1 miles until you reach the entrance drive and parking area on the right side of CR 607.

FACILITIES AND SERVICES

None. You must camp at designated campsites in Craig Lake State Park, all of which require permits which can be obtained either from Van Riper State Park on MI 28/US 41 to the east or the Craig Lake State Park parking lot. Off-trail camping is allowed on state forest and national forest lands. Registration for hiking and camping is done at the west entrance kiosk to the McCormick Wilderness.

THE HIKE

Long distance hikers coming in from the west, who don't need to park a car, will hike up Nestoria Road to Craig Lake State Park. Otherwise, day hikers and those needing to park a car will start at the parking area at Craig Lake State Park. Hike up North Nestoria Road 4.0 miles to the parking area of Craig Lake, on its south shore. About 0.1 mile to the left (north), the shared Craig Lake Trail and North Country Trail start to circumnavigate the lake clockwise. The North Country Trail splits off to the left and will be a dead-end trail to the park's border until the two local trail chapters can work out agreements with private landowners to connect to US 41.

For now, hike to the right (counter-clockwise) around Craig Lake using the shared trail. There are several rustic and bivouac camping opportunities around Craig Lake, the first being the Sandy Beach Camping Area, which has three tent pads. The next camping opportunity is in 1.3 miles.

At the 5.4-mile mark you'll find a small parking lot and campground over-looking Craig Lake. Hike an old road to the west and then into the woods in a northerly direction. There are several portage and spur trails on your left to campsites on the east side of Craig Lake. The topography is rolling and rocky, with no views of the lake until you reach a bridge over an outlet to the lake in about 3.6 miles.

At the 6.0-mile mark you'll find another spur trail on your left to a biv-ouac camp. Hike another 1.3 miles on the old road to encounter another spur trail headed left (west) to another bivouac site. Yet another spur trail is encoun-tered in 0.3 mile. There will be two more spur trails to lakeside bivouac campsites on your left. You'll continue hiking the heavily wooded segment of trail that winds up and around low areas to keep a dry footing.

At the 8.0-mile mark, the North Country Trail will leave the Craig Lake Loop and head east. You'll see a trail intersection where the state park trail comes across a newly constructed and impressive bridge over a Craig Lake out-let, which is a reliable water source. Take a moment and walk onto this bridge, as this will be your last view of Craig Lake, albeit through a narrow bay lined with majestic pine and hemlock. The North Country Trail heads east and stays in the state park for several more miles.

The trail follows an old access road until the Craig Lake bridge just 0.6 mile east of the turn to the Craig Lake parking lot. From that point on it goes on trail and old, unused roads.

At 10.3 miles is another spur trail to a bivouac site. About 0.4 mile to the west you'll negotiate over the downstream segment of the Crooked Lake outlet, which eventually empties into the west branch of the Peshekee River. The trail continues to wind through heavy forest between Craig Lake State Park and Peshekee Grade Road. You'll cross several small streams as you hike through a very wild area. When you cross the west branch of the Peshekee River (12.5 miles), imagine a US Coast Guard helicopter dropping a bridge from overhead. That's how the bridge was placed, a spectacular sight indeed!

You'll cross Crooked Lake Road and hike in an easterly direction. This area is a matrix of lowland swamps and hills. The trail keeps your feet dry by utilizing the higher, dryer ground. At 12.9 miles, endure your second crossing of the west branch of the Peshekee River over and through a rocky, beautiful area.

The trail continues as a heavily wooded walk over rolling topography, past Little Bear Lake and another access on Crooked Lake Road. At 15.4 miles, a bridge crosses Ephraim Creek, which uses the road to cross. The trail takes a northerly turn, following the contour of two large hills to your west, and heading up and over a saddle. Continue clockwise around the bottom of another hill, bending east, then head north and cross CR 607/Huron Bay Road/Peshekee Grade Road. Follow the trail to the McCormick Wilderness parking lot and outhouse at 16.2 miles.

40

McCormick Wilderness and Huron Mountains

START: McCormick Wilderness west access

END: Little Garlic Falls/North Country Trail Trailhead

APPROXIMATE HIKING TIME: 10–16 hours

LENGTH OF SECTION: 24.1 miles

Cyrus McCormick, the inventor of the reaping machine, originally owned the 16,850-acre McCormick Wilderness. Three generations of McCormicks continued ownership until the land was donated in 1967 to the Forest Service; it is now a federally designated wilderness. The McCormicks lived in Chicago and used this land as their getaway and hunting grounds.

You are in the Huron Mountains. These hills are made of dense, igneous rocks have been shaped and formed over billions of years by uplifting and erosion. This area is a classic example of the Canadian Shield, representing some of Earth's oldest rock formations. The area is also representative of boreal forest. Hemlock and hardwood are found in the higher elevations, oak and pine in the valleys. There is quite a bit of topography, and Michigan's first and second high points—Mount Curwood (1,978 feet) and Mount Arvon (1,979 feet)—are found in Baraga County, the next county over. It's hard to believe that some of the original mountains of this geological formation, long since eroded, reached over 30,000 feet in elevation.

The trail heads easterly through mostly forested areas, with some climbs for views; then it heads northerly, then back to the east before exiting at another parking lot. It is very important to note that the trail is not marked with blazes—therefore, it is critical you bring a map, compass, and probably a GPS as well.

To access this parking area, one needs to pass through a private gate, so please do not leave it open. The trail continues easterly toward the Silver Lake Basin and traverses to the north side of the body of water. The basin, although natural, has been dammed to raise the water level several times over the years. Unfortunately, the dam failed in 2003 and

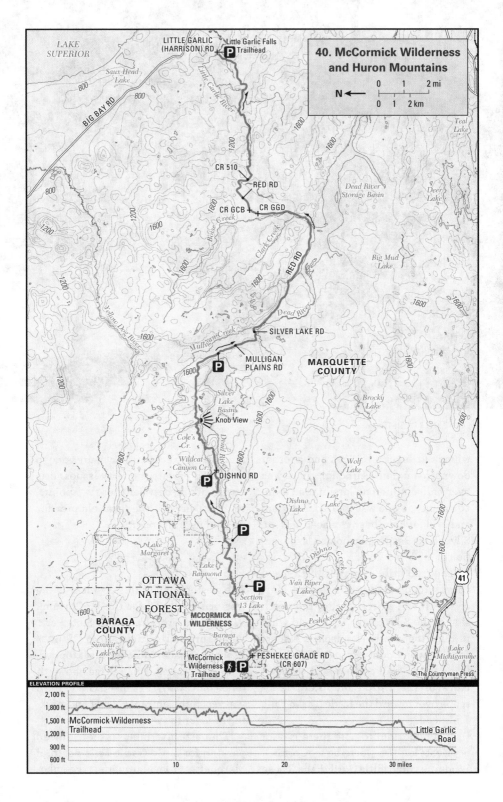

LAKE SUPERIOR

Saux Head Lake

BIG BAY RD

800

800

Little Garlic River

LITTLE GARLIC (HARRISON) RD

Little Garlic Falls Trailhead
P

40. McCormick Wilderness and Huron Mountains

N ←

0   1   2 mi
0   1   2 km

1200

1600

1600

Teal Lake

Dead River Storage Basin

Deer Lake

CR 510

RED RD

1200

Boise Creek

CR GCB   +   + CR GGD

1600

1600

RED RD

Clark Creek

Big Mud Lake

1600

Dead River

1600

1600

1600

Yellow Dog River

1600

Mulligan Creek

SILVER LAKE RD ←

1600

P

MULLIGAN PLAINS RD

MARQUETTE COUNTY

1200

Silver Lake Basin

Brocky Lake

1600

Knob View

Cole's Cr.

1600

Wildcat Canyon Cr.

Dead River

Wolf Lake

P   DISHNO RD

Dishno Lake

Log Lake

Dishno Creek

1600

P

Lake Margaret

Lake Raymond

Van Riper Lakes

P

41

OTTAWA NATIONAL FOREST

MCCORMICK WILDERNESS

Section 13 Lake

Peshekee River

1600

BARAGA COUNTY

1600

Baraga Creek

Summit Lake

McCormick Wilderness Trailhead   P

PESHEKEE GRADE RD (CR 607)

Lake Michigamine

© The Countryman Press

ELEVATION PROFILE

2,100 ft
1,800 ft
1,500 ft   McCormick Wilderness
1,200 ft   Trailhead   Little Garlic Road
900 ft
600 ft
                    10   20   30 miles

GARLIC RIVER IN WINTER

Jacob P. Emerick

wiped out several bridges and another downstream dam. Although there was over half a million dollars in road damage alone, no one was injured. The dam and bridges have been replaced and the Silver Lake Basin again holds a large section of the Dead River.

The trail utilizes several little-used county roads as it heads toward Marquette. It will skirt a part of the north side of the Silver Lake Basin and wind through the forested landscape. A short road walk on County Route 510 (CR 510) leads to the trail cutting east through more of the Huron Mountain landscape over toward the Little Garlic Falls Trailhead.

It is important to note there is a lot of private land between the McCormick Wilderness and Little Garlic Falls. These lands are subject to trail closures due to sales and private property issues. It is best, if hiking between these two points, to check in with the local chapter for up-to-date trail conditions.

HOW TO FIND

The western end of this segment is the western trailhead for the McCormick Wilderness. From Van Riper State Park, you'll turn north (right) onto CR 607/ Peshekee Grade. Although blacktopped, it is rough going. You'll drive about 9.1 miles on CR 607/Peshekee Grade until you reach the entrance drive and parking area for the wilderness area.

The eastern terminus is the trailhead parking for Little Garlic Falls north of Marquette. From Marquette, take Lakeshore Road north and turn west (left) onto Hawley Road. This becomes CR 550/The Big Bay Road following Lake Superior to the north. Turn left onto Harrison (also known as Little Garlic Road) 10.7 miles north of the Sugarloaf Avenue and Hawley Road intersection. Trailhead parking is 1.7 miles down a rugged gravel road that is often impassible in the spring months.

There are several other access points between the east and west terminus, albeit accessed by rugged county roads. Check the North Country Trail Hikers Chapter website for maps and directions. One relatively easy one involves taking CR 607/Peshekee Grade north from MI 28/US 41 for 4.2 miles. Turn right onto Dishno Road. Follow Dishno Road for approximately 1.6 miles east. Turn slightly left, heading in a northeast direction, and follow this unnamed but good gravel road for another 6.1 miles. Turn right and continue to follow this unnamed road for about 3.2 miles. You will cross the Dead River about 0.5 mile before reaching the trail. Parking is just south of the trail off the east side of the unnamed road. Another such access point that is easily found and relatively easy to drive to is where the trail crosses CR 510 north of Negaunee. CR 510 starts between Marquette and Negaunee and heads north, and the trailhead is about 11.5 miles north of MI 28/US 41.

FACILITIES AND SERVICES

None, though backcountry camping is permitted in the national forest and wilderness area (but be aware of private property).

COLES CREEK OUTCROPPING LOOKING WEST

THE HIKE

Enter the McCormick Wilderness by crossing the Peshekee Grade and hiking north into the woods. Within 0.1 mile, your blazeless hike through the McCormick Wilderness will begin, although you should keep your eyes open for cairns and axe marks in trees to guide your way. The hike is a winding one, with several opportunities to take a wrong turn. Cross the Peshekee River Bridge and you'll find your first trail intersection. Take the right turn. Walking through a roadless wilderness area allows one to let one's mind wander. Although there are several vistas, many geological features, and differing habitats, there are only two confirming landmarks—stream crossings at 3.9 miles and 4.7 miles.

It is a 6.7-mile trek across the McCormick Wilderness, and you'll come to the eastern trailhead kiosk and parking lot. At this point, the trail runs through private property, mostly paper company lands. Watch for old Forest Roads and keep your eyes on the blazes, which have reappeared.

Dishno Road is at the 11.3-mile mark; you'll hike east toward the Silver Lake Basin, where you'll be up in the woods

WILDCAT CANYON FALLS

Jacob P. Emerick

looking down on the lake. This is a very scenic area with rocky footing and outcrops. You'll descend into a valley, cross Wildcat Canyon Creek (12.6 miles), and ascend back up to the highlands in a heavily forested and sometimes topographically challenging landscape. You'll reach Cole's Creek at the east end of the Silver Lake Basin (14.2 miles) in a remote, hilly area. Coming up out of Cole's Creek, you'll climb up a spur trail to Knob View (14.6 miles) where you can easily look back toward Cole's Creek or out to the Silver Lake Basin.

Return to the North Country Trail and head east through more ruggedly beautiful forest with hills, cross a cedar swamp, then climb up again. The trail heads almost due east before beginning a steep decline crossing a small stream, passing a rock face, and then descending further to the Mulligan Plains.

At the 16.8-mile mark you'll start hiking south on Mulligan Plains Road. In 2.5 miles you'll turn left (east) onto Silver Lake Road, hike 1.1 miles, and then turn left again onto Red Road. Hike Red Road for 8.4 miles as it goes southeast, parallels the Dead River Storage Basin, turns northeast and squeezes between two large hills on both sides, and crosses Deer Creek. Follow as it goes northerly, passing CR GGD on the east (6.0 miles from the Silver Lake Road/Red Road intersection) then CR GCB (at 6.6 miles).

Then Red Road bends gently to the east, intersecting with CR 510. The total mileage from the Silver Lake Road and Red Road intersection to CR 510 is 8.4 miles. Note that this whole road walk is in the process of being rerouted as new trail is built, so watch carefully for the blue blazes that will take you off Mulligan Plains Road, Silver Lake Road, Red Road and CR 510 and will connect the trail from the west to the trail on the east.

Turn south (right) onto CR 510, and hike approximately 0.5 mile to the trailhead on the left. From CR 510, head east down the old road. At the Y-intersection, stay right, continuing straight for about 0.5 mile total from CR 510. Go past the large boulders and watch for the blue blazes and Carsonite post on the right, where you turn onto recently created trail. Take this segment with great views for 3.1 miles and end by following the Little Garlic River. You will emerge out onto an old road just north of the Little Garlic River. There is a large rock at the corner painted with the number 510 and an arrow pointing to the west. This road walk is on a private road, and some of the landowners do not want maps or directions published but have given us permission to provide a map of this area and more details to thru-hikers or section hikers. It is best to contact the local North Country Trail chapter for up-to-date information on this area.

41

Marquette

START: Little Garlic Falls Trailhead

END: Michigan Department of Transportation Visitors Center

APPROXIMATE HIKING TIME: 17–22 hours

LENGTH OF SECTION: 27.0 miles

Marquette is the largest urban center in the Upper Peninsula. With a population around 21,000 (much greater when Northern Michigan University is in session), Marquette is home to an Olympic Education Center and all the amenities of a medium-sized town. For the long-distance hiker, this will be the first of several places named after Father Jacques Marquette, a Jesuit missionary, who explored the Upper Peninsula in the 1600s.

A mission was set up in the area in 1675, but the area wasn't permanently settled until 1844. The discovery of iron ore deposits led to a mining boom, and iron ore is still mined in the area and loaded into cargo ships at the docks visible from the trail.

Today, Marquette is Michigan's "trail town," as residents and tourists alike utilize the many trails, trail networks, bike trails, and even a water route on Lake Superior designated for sea kayakers. Trail enthusiasts are found year-round, as there are many ski trails as well as bike and hiking trails.

Starting at the Little Garlic Falls Trailhead, you are still under the influence of the Huron Mountains' many ups and downs as you hike south toward town. The trail crosses County Route 550 (CR 550) to take you to the lakeshore, and from there you will use not only certified trails, but also abandoned railroad grade, sidewalks, and bike paths through Marquette.

With such a great trail system, you'll especially notice in the warmer months a high number of trail users. North Country Trail markings and lanes are complete and obvious, with painted blue rectangles being the norm; however, bike trail signage is used on urban bike paths.

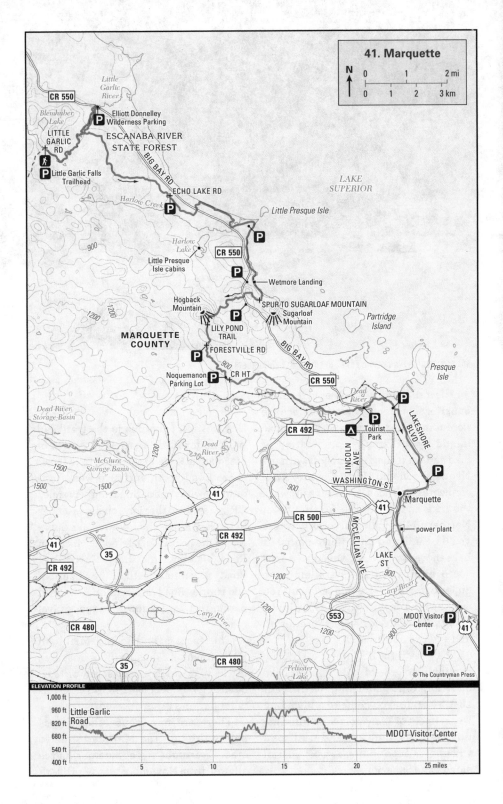

41. Marquette

N

| 0 | 1 | 2 mi |
| 0 | 1 | 2 | 3 km |

Little Garlic River

CR 550

Blemhuber Lake

LITTLE GARLIC RD

Little Garlic Falls Trailhead

Elliott Donnelley Wilderness Parking

ESCANABA RIVER STATE FOREST

BIG BAY RD

ECHO LAKE RD

Harlow Creek

Harlow Lake

CR 550

Little Presque Isle cabins

Little Presque Isle

LAKE SUPERIOR

Wetmore Landing

Hogback Mountain

LILY POND TRAIL

SPUR TO SUGARLOAF MOUNTAIN

Sugarloaf Mountain

MARQUETTE COUNTY

FORESTVILLE RD

CR HT

Noquemanon Parking Lot

Partridge Island

Presque Isle

BIG BAY RD

CR 550

Dead River

LAKESHORE BLVD

CR 492

Tourist Park

LINCOLN AVE

WASHINGTON ST

Marquette

Dead River Storage Basin

Dead River

McClure Storage Basin

900

1500

1500

1500

1200

41

35

CR 492

CR 492

CR 500

MCCLELLAN AVE

power plant

LAKE ST

900

41

553

Carp River

1200

1200

CR 480

CR 480

35

Pelissier Lake

Carp River

MDOT Visitor Center

41

© The Countryman Press

ELEVATION PROFILE

1,000 ft	
960 ft	Little Garlic Road
820 ft	
680 ft	
540 ft	
400 ft	

MDOT Visitor Center

5   10   15   20   25 miles

ROCKY OUTCROPPINGS ALONG LAKE SUPERIOR, NEAR MARQUETTE

Dove Day

The trail eventually comes to the Lake Superior shore for the first time since the Porcupine Mountains, and then turns inland by utilizing a combination of bike and ski trails. It intersects with the Noquamegon and North Country Trail connector trailhead, then turns toward the lake and skirts the north side of Northern Michigan University, where you'll be utilizing paved bike paths. At Lakeshore Boulevard, the trail turns south and essentially parallels Lake Superior for the rest of this segment. You will skirt the downtown district with its many shops, eateries, several breweries, and even an outfitter.

You'll leave the downtown district by continuing on the bike path along Lake Superior, while paralleling the busy MI 28/US 41 until you come to a Michigan Department of Transportation information area. The highway and trail split, with the trail continuing as a paved trail along Lake Superior.

HOW TO FIND

The western terminus is the trailhead parking for Little Garlic Falls north of Marquette. From Marquette, take Lakeshore Road north and turn west (left) onto Hawley Road; Sugarloaf Avenue/ CR 550 splits to the right, changes names to Big Bay Road, and follows Lake Superior to the north. Turn left onto Harrison Road (also known as Little Garlic Falls Road) 10.3 miles north of the Sugarloaf and Hawley Road intersection. Trailhead parking is 1.7 miles down a rugged gravel road.

The eastern end is the Michigan Department of Transportation rest area in Harvey, which is just south of Marquette city proper on MI 28/US 41. Overnight parking is not allowed.

There are numerous other access points through the Marquette metro area. Overnight street-side parking is allowed from November 1st to April 15th where marked. Parking lots and parking meters typically do not allow overnight parking. There are several parks along the trail that allow daytime parking but not overnight parking. Little Presque Isle Natural Area has day use parking.

FACILITIES AND SERVICES

Marquette is a full-service and official North Country Trail town. Nearly all services can be found on or within 0.5 mile of the trail.

THE HIKE

Currently, the trail comes in from the west on an unimproved road to the trailhead, and then heads south. A spur trail takes hikers to the north side of the road to the Little Garlic Falls, with a tent site about 0.9 mile in and the trail ending shortly after the falls. Hike south, parallel the scenic river through the woods, then bend northeasterly and come to a parking lot at CR 550.

At 2.7 miles, you'll enter the Elliott Donnelley Wilderness, a 1,450-acre Michigan Department of Natural Resources wilderness in the Escanaba River State Forest. This tract was gifted to protect the trout fishery in the Little Garlic River. Experience your first of several climbs in the Marquette area to the top of an 850-foot-tall hill. Catch your breath, take in a view, and hike downhill to Echo Lake Road.

From the Elliott Donnelley Wilderness parking lot, walk out to CR 550, turn right, cross the Little Garlic River on the bridge, and then reenter the trail south of the bridge. Follow the Little Garlic River west for about 0.8 mile before turning left and walking through a mix of trail and old logging roads. About 1.6 miles farther on you'll pass a high point. Take a couple of minutes to climb to the summit, catch your breath, take in the view, and then return to continue hiking downhill to Echo Lake Road.

The trail enters the woods on an old road, crosses an old railroad right-of-way, and then bends north to cross CR 550.

Enter the Little Presque Isle Natural Area and head right for Lake Superior to parallel its shoreline. This natural area is managed by the Michigan Department of Natural Resources, so you will need your recreation passport. Wooded dune and swale, a very rare habitat, persists here. There is a cabin for rent by advance reservations.

The trail hugs the lakeshore, turns inland, follows a swampy area, and crosses Harlow Creek 1.5 miles from crossing CR 550. The Songbird Trail, an interpretive trail, intersects with the North Country Trail for a short distance. Enjoy the white and red pine growing in the sandy soils. The trail then comes back to the shore through a stand of red pine. You'll see and hear traffic as the trail parallels the entry drive to the Little Presque Isle Natural Area. At the tip of the peninsula, Little Presque Isle is just hundreds of feet from shore.

At 9.9 miles, Wetmore Landing/the Little Presque Isle parking area and beach is 2.1 miles from crossing CR 550; the trail continues along the beach and then turns east uphill towards CR 550 but does not cross it yet. In 1.6 miles you'll reach the parking area at Wetmore Landing. The trail continues along the lakeshore for about 0.5 mile, and turns inland. A side trail to the top of Sugarloaf Mountain is on the south side of the trail. Enjoy a steep climb to the top of Sugarloaf Mountain for a spectacular view of the city of Marquette from the north. Upon your return to the North Country Trail via the same spur, you'll hike another 0.5 mile and come to CR 550.

The segment between the two CR 550 crossings is about 4.5 miles, and after crossing back over to the west side of the road the trail heads inland, merging with the Sugarloaf Mountain trail system, which is open to bikes. There are two parking areas, one to the north and one to the south of the trail crossing, each under 0.5 mile away. The south parking area links to the North Country Trail through hiking by Wetmore Pond. The trail climbs up the side of Hogback Mountain, where it intersects with a bike trail. For a great view, take the bike trail around to the vista as a short side trip.

You'll descend back down the mountain to the North Country Trail, and about 0.2 mile south another side trail (the Lily Pond Trail, on the left) can be used to take you back to the Wetmore Pond area. When you emerge from the woods, continue straight across the intersecting road and take a walk on the unmarked road until you reach Forestville Road in 0.5 mile. Parking is allowed along either of these roads. The forest continues to envelop you as you wind around the many hills and knobs, making your way to the south. Walk under a power line and across a wide right-of-way.

The North Country Trail connector and Noquemenon Blue Trail intersect 1.6 miles from the top of Sugarloaf Mountain. The North Country Trail connector comes in from the west. This is where the temporary connector trail and the current North Country Trail intersect. The Noquemenon is a popular ski trail system, open to bikes and hikers in the snowless months.

The Noquemenon parking lot (15.8 miles) is a large parking lot. Head into the woods, and cross CR HT and Forestville Road. You'll wind easterly up and down rocky hills and through the forest. The trail is not far off CR HK, as it parallels it for about 0.8 mile. You'll enter a power line right-of-way just before crossing some railroad tracks. Note that there are no blazes across the power line right-of-way but the trail is very visible due to the high usage it receives, being so close to Marquette.

Cross some railroad tracks (18.6 miles) and walk through an open area along the Dead River. Pay attention to trail markers in this segment as it continues to utilize parts of the Noquemanon Trail Network. In 1.3 miles, after crossing the tracks, you'll come to Sugarloaf Avenue and the Tourist Park Trailhead at the Dead River. Cross the Dead River by following the trail under the bridge on CR 550. Tourist Park is on the south side of the road after you cross the Dead River and is a modern campground with 100 campsites.

Through Marquette, you'll mostly be using paved bike trails, surface streets, and sidewalks. Hike over a camelback bridge and then a wooded walk along the Dead River. Hike past the power plant and the River Park Sports Complex by following the old railroad bed, then heading east on Hawley Road, which ends at Lakeshore Boulevard. For the long-distance hiker, your rocky and hilly trail hiking will come to an end at Marquette's multiuse pathway.

Using Lakeshore Boulevard (21.0 miles) and through Marquette city proper, you'll be on the paved multiuse pathway following the Lake Superior shoreline. You will pass Shiras Hills Park, McCarty's Cove, the Ellwood A. Mattson Lower Harbor Park, and Founder's Landing; all have public restrooms.

Take some time to enjoy the beach and views of Marquette's historic lighthouse. At the intersection of Main Street and Lakeshore Boulevard, the Iron Ore Heritage Trail connects to the Marquette multiuse pathway and follows it and the North Country Trail all the way to Kawbawgam Pocket Park east of Harvey. If you take the Iron Ore Heritage Trail west, you can eventually reach Republic on the west side of Marquette County.

Skirt by the power plant (24.7 miles) and follow the trail out of the downtown area along Lake Street, passing South Beach Park on your way to the Carp River Bridge. The Marquette multiuse pathway crosses the Carp River Bridge (25.6 miles) as it parallels MI 28/US 41 and the Lake Superior shore. At the Carp River Bridge, a connection is made with the south of the Noquemanon Trail Network by taking the trail that goes under the MI 28/US 41 highway bridge alongside the river to the Noquemanon Trailhead at the base of Mount Marquette. Upon returning to the North Country Trail on the Marquette multiuse pathway, you should continue along Lake Superior to the Michigan Department of Transportation Visitors Center (27.0 miles).

Overnight parking is not allowed, though bathrooms, water, and information are available. The Marquette multiuse pathway ends here but turns into an old railroad bed that becomes the North Country Trail going east, paralleling the shoreline for a while. Note that during the snow season from the Carp River Bridge to Kawbawgam Pocket Park farther east, this portion of trail is a snowmobile trail. Hike with extreme caution during snow season.

Jacob P. Emerick

LITTLE PRESQUE ISLE ISLAND

Hiawatha National Forest– Whitefish River

START: Michigan Department of Transportation Visitors Center

END: Rumley Road Trailhead

APPROXIMATE HIKING TIME: 9–18 hours

LENGTH OF SECTION: 24.7 miles

Your urban hike through Marquette, albeit a trail town with pathways conducive to the hiker, is coming to an end as you move east toward the Hiawatha National Forest. You'll use paved and improved multiuse trails, little-used county roads, and bonafide trail from the Lake Superior shore inland to the Laughing Whitefish River.

From the visitors' center, the trail continues to use a multiuse crushed limestone bike trail until the Kawbawgam Pocket Park Trailhead, where it moves off the old railroad bed and becomes a hiking trail again. You'll start in unincorporated Harvey, which is a residential area on the outskirts of Marquette.

Cross the Chocolay River, a trout stream, and head east—passing the Northern Michigan University golf course—until the Kawbawgam Pocket Park trailhead. At this point, you leave the old railroad bed and begin hiking through lands both privately held and owned by the Michigan Department of Natural Resources.

You'll notice that the habitats are quite sandy, being in close proximity to Lake Superior. You'll come to Lake LeVasseur, and then utilize parts of an unimproved multiuse trail system as well as the old railroad right-of-way. You will pass a hiker's shelter at Lakenenland Sculpture Park; continue on an old abandoned county road, and then cross the Sand River. At this point, the trail leaves the proximity of Lake Superior and heads south into the woods.

You will pass through the parking area at Jeske Flooding. After crossing Magnum Road, you'll climb up a steep hill, follow its north side (with overlooks), descend, cross Peter White Road, and then cross a bridgeless stream. Continue south, and at the intersection with the spur trail to Laughing Whitefish Falls,

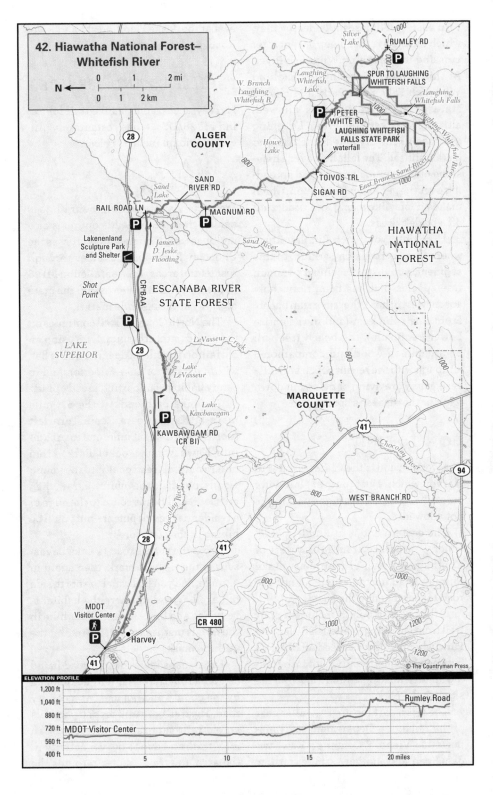

42. Hiawatha National Forest– Whitefish River

N ←

0   1   2 mi
0   1   2 km

Silver Lake

RUMLEY RD

P

SPUR TO LAUGHING WHITEFISH FALLS

1000

Laughing Whitefish Lake

W. Branch Laughing Whitefish R.

Laughing Whitefish Falls

Laughing Whitefish River

P

PETER WHITE RD

LAUGHING WHITEFISH FALLS STATE PARK

waterfall

ALGER COUNTY

Howe Lake

28

800

East Branch Sand River

1000

SAND RIVER RD

Sand Lake

TOIVOS TRL

SIGAN RD

HIAWATHA NATIONAL FOREST

RAIL ROAD LN

P

MAGNUM RD

P

Sand River

Lakenenland Sculpture Park and Shelter

James D. Jeske Flooding

ESCANABA RIVER STATE FOREST

CR BAA

Shot Point

P

LeVasseur Creek

800

1000

28

Lake LeVasseur

LAKE SUPERIOR

Lake Kawbawgam

MARQUETTE COUNTY

P

41

KAWBAWGAM RD (CR BI)

Chocolay River

94

Chocolay River

800

WEST BRANCH RD

28

800

41

1000

1000

1200

MDOT Visitor Center

CR 480

1000

P

Harvey

1200

© The Countryman Press

41

800

ELEVATION PROFILE

1,200 ft				Rumley Road
1,040 ft				
880 ft				
720 ft	MDOT Visitor Center			
560 ft				
400 ft				
	5	10	15	20 miles

turn east; you'll descend a deep valley, which means a rather steep ascent after crossing the Laughing Whitefish River. At this point, you are in the Laughing Whitefish Falls State Park, a Michigan state park. No camping is allowed, although it is very tempting. Laughing Whitefish Falls is a good side trip and has a trailhead. The falls flow over a limestone outcropping, fanning and spreading over the geological formation, which makes it look like a long and wide train off a bride's dress.

Hike until you reach Rumley Road, where there is roadside parking. In this segment, you'll start seeing a common tree species that has been noticeably absent west of here, the American beech. From this point east (and in the entire Lower Peninsula), the beech tree will be a common woodland companion— although with the recent beech bark disease, many are dying or being cut down to deter the disease's spread.

HOW TO FIND

The western end is the visitors center in Harvey, which is just south of Marquette on MI 28/US 41. Overnight parking is not allowed.

The eastern end is at Rumley Road, which is accessed from MI 94 west of Chatham and east of Marquette. Take Rumley Road north 3.0 miles until the road takes a bend to the east.

Other access points include a spur trail from Laughing Whitefish Falls State Park, which is also accessed off of MI 94 between Marquette and Chatham by taking Sundell Road north and following the signs to the park.

There is a parking area 7.5 miles east of the Michigan Department of Transportation Visitors' Center on Kawbawgam Road, and another 5.0 miles farther east at the Jeske Flooding at Sand River Road. Both are accessed off MI 28.

FACILITIES AND SERVICES

Harvey, accessed by a bike trail following MI 28/US 41, has restaurants, groceries, and financial services.

THE HIKE

From the visitors center, the trail goes behind the building and continues as a multiuse trail; it immediately crosses the Chocolay River, and traverses through residential areas while paralleling MI 28 in the near distance—crossing the state highway at the 2.5-mile mark.

The North Country Trail continues on the paved path, crossing MI 28 using an old railroad trestle bridge. The trail is flat, within earshot of Lake Superior, and in sandy habitats supporting mostly pine.

The bike path ends at the 6.2-mile mark at Kawbawgam Road. Turn left (north), less than 0.1 mile, and turn right into Kawbawgam Pocket Park. From here, a natural tread goes into the young woods, parallels the multiuse trail, then crosses it and heads south to the edge of a residential development—but you'll be hiking in the state forest.

Cross the access road to Lake LeVasseur at the 7.5-mile mark, then again in 0.3 mile, and you'll parallel the north side of Lake LeVasseur, where the habitat is jack pine and bracken fern. Your hike in the woods merges with an old road at the 9.1-mile mark.

Local maps have this old road listed as CR Baa but it is essentially abandoned by the county and not used as a county road. The trail both utilizes and parallels an old railroad grade which is now an ATV trail; and due to beaver activity in the area, the trail chapter reroutes the

NORTH COUNTRY TRAIL

↑	LAKE LAVASSEUR	1.5
↑	LAKENENLAND	5.0
↑	JESKE FLOODING	6.6
↓	WELCOME CENTER	6.2
↓	DOWNTOWN MQT	9.4

TRAIL SIGNAGE IN THE MARQUETTE AREA

trail, utilizing the old rail grade as conditions warrant. You'll hike though mostly young jack and red pine habitats, along a swamp to your south.

Lakenenland Sculpture Park hiker's shelter (11.0 miles) is the only trail shelter for hundreds of miles in either direction. It is rather deluxe, with sliding patio doors and a very nice open-air latrine. Take a break here and follow the drive north to the sculpture park. You will not regret it. Tom Lakenen has artfully crafted about 80 unique sculptures from junk. If Tom is there, stop and chat with him; he built the hiker's shelter as a gesture of his support for the North Country Trail. Be sure to drop a donation in one of his donation pipes (he provides the park and many activities on his own dime), and then head back to the shelter and continue hiking east on the abandoned CR Baa. You'll come out next to a private residence; hike past it and easterly up the road, over the Sand River, and in 0.1 mile turn right (south) onto the North Country Trail.

Rail Road Lane (12.6 miles) is accessed via a parking lot by turning south onto Sand River Road from MI 28, then right (west) onto Rail Road Lane. The trail continues to the south into the woods, comes out to a clearing at the Jeske Flooding old boat launch site, travels along some swampy areas, and comes out to Sand River Road. Hike Sand River Road 0.7 mile until the trail goes back into the woods on the west side of the road. Note that hikers frequently miss the two-entry/exit points off Sand River Road where the trail comes out for this 0.7-mile road walk. To resolve that issue the North Country Trail chapter has installed tall white pipes with red tape and blue blazes. The trail merges with Sigan/Segan Road at the 17.0-mile mark. Continue south on Sigan/Segan Road for 0.7 mile and it will come to an intersection with Toivos Trail, which comes in from the north. Turn south on Sigan/Segan Road for 0.1 mile, where it will turn into the woods on the east side of the road.

Cross Magnum Road at 14.5 miles,

where there is roadside parking. The trail goes south into the woods over rocky terrain while following an intermittent stream for the beginning of the hike. Come to an old road, turn left, follow it for 2.3 miles, and you'll come to an old, unused road. Follow it for a short distance before turning back into the woods on the right, and you'll come to another old road for another 0.7 mile to Sigan/Segan Road.

The trail leaves Sigan/Segan Road (18.8 miles) and traverses up a rather steep slope, with a stream valley on your north side. Near the summit you'll find a small waterfall during wet years. Follow the north side contour of the hill and then head down to Peter White Road (20.9 miles).

There is a small roadside parking area on the west side of Peter White Road. Descend into the Laughing Whitefish River valley second-growth hardwood forest. A bridgeless water crossing of the west branch of the Laughing Whitefish River in 0.4 mile is negotiated by rock hopping. Continue on about 1.0 mile to find a sign pointing you south on a spur trail for 1.9 miles to the Laughing Whitefish Falls, including access to parking. You'll descend downhill via steps and switchbacks to the Laughing Whitefish River.

A small footbridge crosses the wide but shallow Laughing Whitefish River (22.5 miles) in an area with no camping permitted. Climb up out of the valley and onto flat highlands to the southeast. Listen for a waterfall just to your northeast, about 1.9 miles from where you crossed the Laughing Whitefish River. Within a few hundred feet, the trail comes to an old road that heads southeast for 0.3 mile to Rumley Road (24.7 miles).

Hiawatha National Forest–Rock and Au Train Rivers

START: Rumley Road

END: Munising Falls, Pictured Rocks National Lakeshore

APPROXIMATE HIKING TIME: 10–16 hours

LENGTH OF SECTION: 30.0 miles

Following unimproved roads and trails, you'll come to the edge of the 4,687-acre Rock River Canyon Wilderness, established in 1987. The trail follows the boundary—therefore, it is marked as it descends over the Rock River and then ascends to some unimproved, though passable, Forest Service roads. You'll be in the Hiawatha National Forest at this point and you'll essentially have public lands to traverse from this point to St. Ignace. You'll continue your road walk, crossing a few more Forest Service roads until you come to the paved Rock River Road.

Established in 1931, the 894,000-acre Hiawatha National Forest is divided into two major blocks of land (east and west units) and five districts. The national forest also contains Grand Island National Recreation Area, the Whitefish Scenic Byway, six lighthouses, five designated wildernesses, and Clear Lake Education Center. In addition to recreational opportunities, you'll find a wide array of habitats, including northern hardwoods, jack pine and other conifers, and a variety of inland wetland habitats.

A spur trail to the Au Train Lake National Forest Campground allows for your first developed campground in quite some time. Continue through the mixed forest to MI 94. At Valley Spur, the trail goes through the woods for a bit and comes back to MI 94 for a road walk. Stop by Wagner Falls on MI 94; at the intersection with MI 28, Alger Falls is about 100 yards to the east. The road walk continues into Munising, a full-service town home to the western access to the Pictured Rocks National Lakeshore.

HOW TO FIND

The western end is at Rumley Road, which is accessed from MI 94 west of

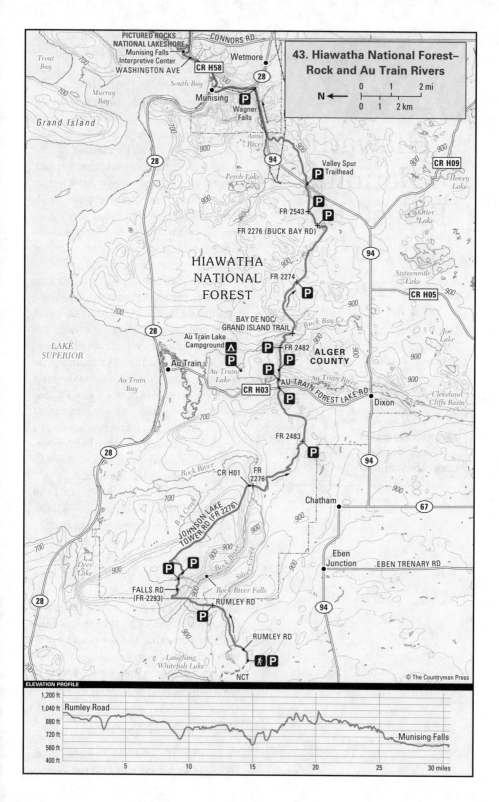

43. Hiawatha National Forest–Rock and Au Train Rivers

PICTURED ROCKS NATIONAL LAKESHORE
Munising Falls Interpretive Center
WASHINGTON AVE
CR H58
CONNORS RD
Wetmore
28
South Bay
Munising
Wagner Falls
Anna River
Trout Bay
Murray Bay
Grand Island

N ◄
0   1   2 mi
0   1   2 km

94
Valley Spur Trailhead
Perch Lake
FR 2543
FR 2276 (BUCK BAY RD)
CR H09
Hovey Lake
Otter Lake
94
Sixteenmile Lake
CR H05

HIAWATHA NATIONAL FOREST

FR 2274
BAY DE NOC/ GRAND ISLAND TRAIL
Buck Bay Cr.
ALGER COUNTY
Joe Lake
Cleveland Cliffs Basin

LAKE SUPERIOR

Au Train Lake Campground
Au Train
FR 2482
Au Train Lake
Au Train River
CR H03
AU-TRAIN FOREST LAKE RD
Dixon

Au Train Bay

FR 2483

28

Rock River
CR H01
FR 2276
Chatham
67
JOHNSON LAKE TOWER RD (FR 2276)
B A Creek
Deer Lake
Eben Junction
EBEN TRENARY RD
94
Rock River
Silver Creek
FALLS RD (FR-2293)
Rock River Falls
RUMLEY RD
28
RUMLEY RD
Laughing Whitefish Lake
NCT

© The Countryman Press

ELEVATION PROFILE

1,200 ft
1,040 ft Rumley Road
880 ft
720 ft
560 ft
400 ft   Munising Falls

5   10   15   20   25   30 miles

Chatham and east of Marquette. Take Rumley Road north 3.0 miles until the road takes a bend to the east.

The Munising Falls Interpretive Center is east of Munising; take H58 2.0 miles, then turn north on Sand Point Road and drive another 1.0 mile to the center. The center is on the east (right) side of the road.

The easternmost trailhead is at Valley Spur, 4.0 miles south of the MI 28 and MI 94 intersection.

Other access points include a spur trail from the Au Train Lake National Forest Campground. Take MI 28 west from Munising to Au Train, turn south on H03, turn east onto Buck Bay Road, and then turn north (left) onto the campground entrance road. Take the Songbird Trail to the spur trail junction, then head south to the North Country Trail.

Other access points include the Rock River Falls Trailhead on Forest Road 2293 (FR 2293). From Chatham, take Rock River Road north, then head west onto FR 2276, and then left (west) onto FR 2293 to the parking lot.

FACILITIES AND SERVICES

Munising is a full-service town. Grocery stores, lodging, food, and supplies are all found on your road walk on MI 28 into town. The Interagency Visitors Center is on the southeast corner at the intersection of H58 and MI 28, and the Fuzzy Boyak Welcome Center is located to the northwest. The hospital is across the street from the Munising Falls Interpretive Center on Sand Point Road. The post office is located at 220 Elm Avenue.

THE HIKE

From the Rumley Road trailhead, the trail uses the unimproved road for 0.8 mile, on mostly rolling topography through private land before entering deep woods in 0.8 mile as it leaves the unimproved road and heads east.

Cross Silver Creek (2.4 miles), which is accented by the Silver Creek Falls. The trail is on an old logging road and used by waterfall hunters on the north side of the creek. Hike north to the parking lot on Rumley Road, cross the road, and continue north into mature forest; you'll descend into the Rock River valley, crossing the Rock River in about 1.0 mile.

At 3.9 miles, you'll start to hike along the Rock River Canyon Wilderness boundary, which welcomes you to the Hiawatha National Forest. The trail will skirt the boundary of the Rock River Canyon Wilderness using FR 2293, a little-used road. Beaver activity is very high in this area, and the trail is frequently flooded and rerouted. It would be in your best interest to contact the local trail chapter for recent updates. Other than the river crossing, the terrain is rather flat and heavily wooded.

You'll pass a parking lot for a waterfall (on a spur trail of about 1.0 mile) on your right. Hike out to FR 2276/Falls Road (5.6 miles) to the east of the parking lot. Ramble on the unimproved road, turning right at the first intersection and heading east. Although passable by car, you'll probably have the forest all to yourself while walking the cobblestoned surface. Many of these local Forest Roads have interchangeable names, one of which is Johnson Lake Tower Road.

Turn right (south) on the gravel H03 (Au Train Forest Lake Road, 9.3 miles), using the bridge to cross Rock River before reentering the woods at the 10.0-mile mark of your journey.

Reenter the woods with a left turn (east) off of H03 after you've passed the intersection of FR 2276, which is now

AU TRAIN RIVER

on the south side of the Rock River. The rolling trail is well used and marked with blue plastic diamonds throughout the heavy woods.

At 11.1 miles, cross FR 2483, a gravel road with parking for two vehicles. The trail goes slightly downhill and crosses Forest Highway 03 (14.3 miles), which has parking for four vehicles. Other parking opportunities are located 150 yards east of FH 03 on the north side of FR 2276, 0.5 mile further east at FR 2596/Campground Road for two vehicles, and at Au Train Lake National Forest Campground (rustic, 36 campsites) 1.0 mile north on FR 2596/Campground Road. Keep hiking easterly as the trail takes you into mixed forest and parallels FR 2276.

At 15.5 miles, cross FR 2482, another unimproved road with roadside parking. The trail splits away from FR 2276 and continues east through rolling ground. The trail will blend with the abandoned FR 2564.

A connector hiking trail, the Bay De Noc/Grand Island Trail, intersects on your right (16.4 miles) as it comes in from the south from MI 94 at Ackerman Lake (where there is parking for multiple vehicles). It is popular with horseback riders and mountain bikes; beware of these trail users and the trail conditions they may cause.

Cross FR 2274 (18.5 miles), a gravel forest road with parking available for two vehicles. Another parking area is 0.2 mile west of FR 2274 as the trail turns down an old Forest Service road. You'll continue through hardwood forests.

resumes behind and to the left of the warming lodge and treks uphill along a right-of-way that can be choked with tall grass (especially fun to hike if it hasn't been mowed recently). Pay attention to your blazes, as the Valley Spur uses blue diamonds to mark mountain-bike difficulty and can be easily confused with North Country Trail markings.

On the outskirts of Munising but still in the hill woods, you'll cross a set of active railroad tracks at the 24.3-mile mark. You'll come back to MI 94, on your left, at the 25.3-mile mark as a road walk into Munising. This is the boundary of the Hiawatha National Forest—and the end of hiking in the national forest until after Tahquamenon Falls State Park. From here into Munising and toward Pictured Rocks National Lakeshore will be a road walk. Wagner Falls will be on your right and is a designated scenic area. The falls are a short walk from the road.

Your road walk is uphill to the 26.9-mile mark at the intersection of MI 94 and MI 28. Continue straight on your road walk into Munising. Shopping, lodging, and dining are found on this stretch of road.

At the 21.0-mile mark, cross FR 2276, a gravel forest road, and hike to the north. Parking for two vehicles is available along FR 2276/Buck Bay Road. In 1.4 miles you'll cross FR 2543, which has parking for two vehicles. Cross the old dirt road and ascend for about 0.5 mile, then hike downhill to cross MI 94 (22.5 miles).

Across the highway is Valley Spur, a warming lodge that is mostly closed for the summer (so no phone is available); however, outhouses and a large parking area are available year-round. The trail

At the blinker light, the Interagency Visitor Center (26.3 miles) will be on your right. Permits are required for overnight backcountry stays in the Pictured Rocks National Lakeshore. Downtown Munising is to your left.

Hike H58 east, then turn north onto Sand Point Road and end your hike at the Munising Falls Interpretive Center (30.0 miles). This is the trailhead for the North Country Trail in the Pictured Rocks National Lakeshore.

44

The Quiet Coast

START: Sable Falls

END: Deer Park Trailhead

APPROXIMATE HIKING TIME: 12–20 hours

LENGTH OF SECTION: 27.2 miles

Tens of thousands of hikers who experience the Pictured Rocks National Lakeshore don't know what they're missing just to the east of the park. This stretch of trail parallels Lake Superior and is great if you want to get away from the sea of humanity that can be found just to the west.

From Sable Falls parking lot, the trail goes down a set of stairs to the falls, out to the lake, then back up and into Grand Marais, an unincorporated town. Grand Marais is the eastern end of the Pictured Rocks National Lakeshore.

Grand Marais means "marsh" and "harbor of refuge" in French. The harbor is home to the Grand Marais Outer Range Light, and has 1 of only 70 operational Fresnel lenses still in operation in the United States—and only 16 on the Great Lakes. Grand Marais has 300 year-round residents, but the town balloons to an average of 1,500 residents in the summer, mostly staying at the Woodland Park Campground. Grand Marais hosts many community events, attracting even more day-trippers. If you are planning on staying in a motel in the summer on a thru-hike, it's best to make plans well in advance. Woodland Park does not accept reservations.

Leave Grand Marais on a road walk and the trail starts again in earnest as it takes you south of H58, then crosses over the Grand Marais Creek and northward toward Lake Superior. The Lake Superior State Forest is nearly contiguous between here and Whitefish Point, offering many opportunities for off-trail camping. Along the way, you can stay at Lake Superior State Forest Campground or Muskallonge Lake State Park.

Lake Superior has a profound impact on the habitats that parallel its shore. The habitats are sandy, dominated mostly by

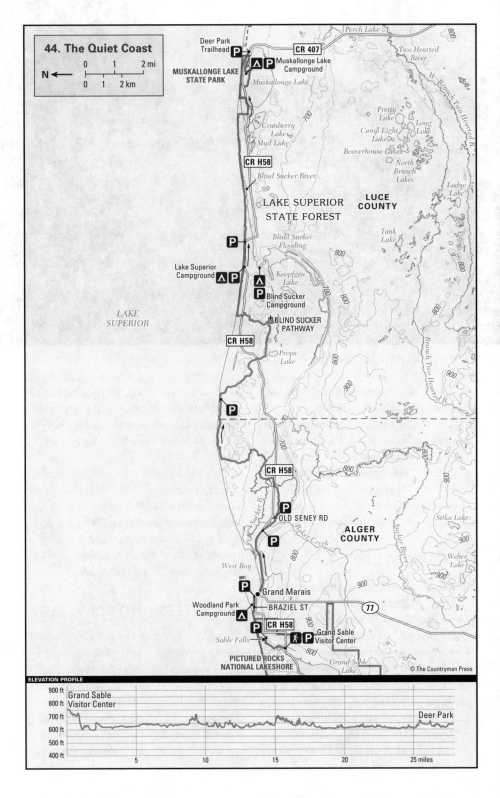

44. The Quiet Coast

N ←

0   1   2 mi
0   1   2 km

Deer Park Trailhead

🅿

CR 407

🅿 Muskallonge Lake Campground

MUSKALLONGE LAKE STATE PARK

Muskallonge Lake

Perch Lake

Two Hearted River

W. Branch Two Hearted R.

Cranberry Lake

Mud Lake

Pretty Lake

Camp Eight Lake

Long Lake

Beaverhouse Lakes

North Branch Lakes

Ladue Lake

CR H58

Blind Sucker River

LAKE SUPERIOR STATE FOREST

LUCE COUNTY

Tank Lake

🅿

Lake Superior Campground 🅿

Blind Sucker Flooding

Keopfgen Lake

🅿 Blind Sucker Campground

BLIND SUCKER PATHWAY

LAKE SUPERIOR

CR H58

Props Lake

🅿

Branch Two Hearted R.

Sucker R.

CR H58

🅿

OLD SENEY RD

Baker Creek

ALGER COUNTY

Sitka Lake

🅿

Weber Lake

West Bay

Sucker River

🅿 Grand Marais

Woodland Park Campground

BRAZIEL ST

77

🅿 CR H58

Grand Sable Visitor Center

Sable Falls

PICTURED ROCKS NATIONAL LAKESHORE

Grand Sable Lake

© The Countryman Press

ELEVATION PROFILE

900 ft
800 ft — Grand Sable Visitor Center
700 ft
600 ft
500 ft
400 ft

Deer Park

5   10   15   20   25 miles

VIEW OF THE DEAD SUCKER RIVER VALLEY

Thomas Funke

jack and red pine—and you'll find that blueberries thrive in this area.

You'll wind through the wooded landscape paralleling Lake Superior. There are several places where the North Country Trail intermingles with ski trails, social trails, abandoned trails, and game trails. When in doubt, find Lake Superior and walk the beach.

HOW TO FIND

The western end of this segment starts in Pictured Rocks National Lakeshore at Sable Falls. From Grand Marais, go west on H58 for 1.0 mile to paved parking. Overnight parking is allowed.

The eastern end is at Deer Park near Muskallonge Lake State Park. Overnight parking is permitted at Muskallonge Lake State Park with prior arrangement with park staff. The trailhead is about 1.0 mile to the east on H58/CR 407. From

Newberry, take MI 123 north to H37 and turn west (left). The road will eventually turn north. From downtown Newberry to Muskallonge Lake State Park is 28.0 miles.

There is a North Country Trail parking lot just east of Grand Marais about 3.0 miles on H58. You can also park at Lake Superior State Forest Campground or Blind Sucker State Forest Campground, both of which are also on H58 between Grand Marais and Deer Park.

FACILITIES AND SERVICES

Grand Marais has restaurants, lodging, groceries, a retail outfitter, and a small medical clinic. Woodland Park Campground is modern, with all the amenities. Lake Superior State Forest Campground has pit toilets and potable water. Dispersed camping is allowed in the Lake Superior State Forest. Permits are free, and downloadable off the Michigan Department of Natural Resources website. The post office is just east of downtown on H58, as is the medical clinic. The town of Deer Park has a small grocery store, cabins, and a laundromat.

THE HIKE

The Grand Sable Visitors Center is at the east end of Pictured Rocks National Lakeshore. If day hiking, you can park either at the visitors center or at Sable Falls. If overnight hiking into the park, you'll be able to park there. Hiking to the east, you'll be best off if you go into Grand Marais and coordinate where to park in town by visiting Grand Marais Outfitters. Otherwise, there is a North Country Trail Trailhead just east of town.

Hike north through some woods, along the backside of some wooded dunes, to the top of a staircase at the Sable Falls parking lot at the 1.0-mile mark.

The trail follows the stairway to the bottom of the falls and takes the river and yourself onto the shore of Lake Superior. Walk the beach west for about 1.0 mile and look for a staircase going up to Woodland Park to your right, a municipal campground with 110 modern and 15 rustic campsites.

At 2.1 miles is the unincorporated community of Grand Marais. Although small and quaint, Grand Marais has most services—including a grocery, bank, restaurants (including a brewery), an outfitter store, a medical clinic, and a post office. Grand Marais is French for "marsh," although you're hard-pressed to find one here today. Walk the surface streets to H58 by turning right as a road walk on Braziel Street to the east and turning right onto Grand Marais Avenue—which immediately turns into

H58. Take H58 east of town and look for a trailhead on your right entering the woods on the south at the 4.8-mile mark.

Leave H58 and take an old road that winds around a swampy area with several ponds. Thick with balsam fir, this section is well-used and well-blazed. Cross Baker Creek and continue east.

Use H58 to cross Grand Marais Creek (6.5 miles), which hosts an ample trout population. North of H58, the North Country Trail is well marked and intermingles with a network of cross-country ski trails hosted by the Burt Township School Forest. After leaving the ski trails, keep a close eye on your blazes as you head north to the lake. Many old roads and social trials intersect in the area. If in doubt, bear north.

Follow the Sucker River (7.4 miles) east through the woods for about 0.6 mile until it turns north. Your footing is sandy and the forest is mostly red and jack pine and quite open.

At the 10.0-mile mark, the view opens up as you reach the Lake Superior shoreline. Turn right, and keep in mind that the trail in this area has experienced some difficulties as the lake is trying its hardest to erode away the shore. The walk is through sandy forests—but if you lose the trail do a beach walk, keeping Lake Superior on your left.

At 12.6 miles, the trail turns south, and it is easy to miss. The sandy footing through second-growth forest takes you on tread that is sparse but well-blazed, crossing H58 (14.4 miles) and taking an easterly direction while undulating up and down some sandy hills. The trail lane eventually disappears but is well-blazed through this dry, sandy habitat of jack pines.

At 16.2 miles, the North Country Trail

SABLE FALLS IS MERELY A TRICKLE IN SUMMER

intersects with the Blind Sucker Pathway. The Blind Sucker Pathway is a 6.7-mile loop that starts at the Blind Sucker State Forest Campground, accessible from H58. You can either take the pathway to the right (east), and it will take you to the rustic Blind Sucker State Forest Campground (bypassing the Lake Superior State Forest Campground), or turn left (north) and continue on the North Country Trail to the Lake Superior shoreline (17.9 miles).

Once you reach Lake Superior, turn right and head in an easterly direction along the Lake Superior shore on a sandy trail through second growth for 2.0 miles to Lake Superior State Forest Campground (rustic with 18 campsites).

The trail abruptly ends where the Blind Sucker River (23.4 miles) occupies a gully about 20 feet down in elevation. Traverse to a safe crossing place where the river is knee deep with a solid bottom. After this bridgeless crossing, follow the river until you see a trail marker up on a hill, directly across from where you arrived.

To avoid some private property, the trail makes a short jog right (south) and then onto H58 (24.1 miles) for another short road walk to your left; all told this is less than 1.0 mile before you enter Muskallonge Lake State Park (25.0 miles), a modern campground with 159 campsites.

CR 407 splits this state park; the Lake Superior beach is to the north and the modern campground to the south, on

A NICE PLACE TO TAKE LUNCH ON THE BLIND SUCKER PATHWAY

Muskallonge Lake, with hot showers, running water, and protection from Lake Superior's howling wind. Turn left (north) to hike into the woods, and you are separated from Lake Superior by a small, wooded dune. The trail bends back to the right, crosses H58, and skirts the campground—then comes out at a day-use parking lot, parallels the road in the right-of-way, and ends as a roadwalk for 0.3 mile to the Deer Park Trailhead (26.6 miles).

There is no parking, but you can park at Muskallonge Lake State Park. There is a small country store to the east, which also has rental cabins.

Two Hearted River and Tahquamenon Country

Starting at the mouth of the Two Hearted River, you'll cut a traverse between the Two Hearted River and Tahquamenon River watersheds as you cut across the Whitefish Peninsula toward Upper Tahquamenon Falls.

Ernest Hemingway made the Two Hearted River famous. Ironically, he wrote about the Two Hearted but really fished the nearby Fox River. Today's Two Hearted River is an excellent fishery and popular with canoeists.

The Duck Lake Fire of 2012 changed the character of the area for years to come. The landscape is mostly jack pine forest, which is a habitat that relies on fire to regenerate. The Thursday night before Memorial Day weekend, after one of the warmest and driest springs on record, a lightning strike caused over 20,000 acres to burn, mostly overnight. The canopy fire raced north to Lake Superior, where most of the fire was extinguished, though lateral fires remained in some places. Although no one was hurt, many buildings were casualties—including the very popular Rainbow Lodge. The only outfitter, store, and source of gasoline for 40 miles in every direction burnt to the ground. They are currently being rebuilt.

Another casualty was the North Country Trail, as the trail had to be closed until the fire was extinguished. Trail crews immediately went out to assess the damage, which was quickly restored, rerouted in places, and had blazes reinstalled. Today, the forest is growing back. Although you will see some scarred trees, the area is rebounding nicely—as a habitat that relies on fire should.

The trail continues south through maturing mixed forest, crosses the Two Hearted River on a short road walk, and then takes a private road to access Tahquamenon Falls State Park.

Tahquamenon Falls State Park is

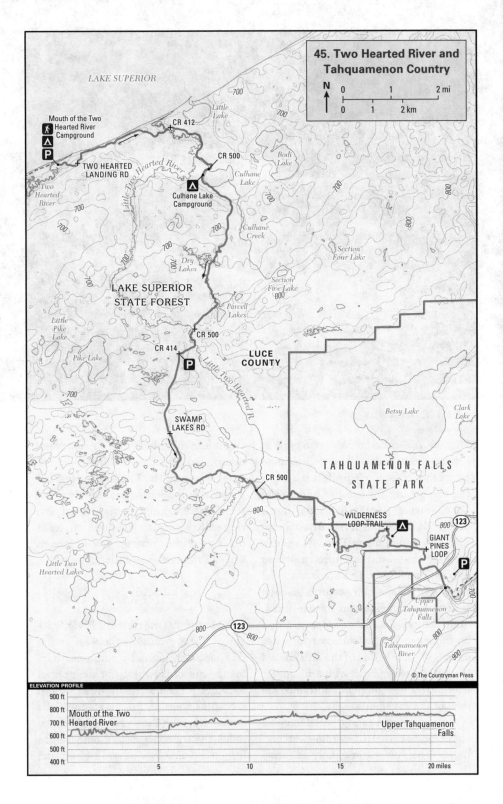

45. Two Hearted River and Tahquamenon Country

N

0   1   2 mi

0   1   2 km

LAKE SUPERIOR

700

700

700

Little Lake

CR 412

CR 500

Bodi Lake

Mouth of the Two Hearted River Campground

TWO HEARTED LANDING RD

Little Two Hearted River

Culhane Lake

Culhane Lake Campground

Two Hearted River

700

700

700

700

700

Culhane Creek

Dry Lakes

800

800

LAKE SUPERIOR STATE FOREST

Section Four Lake

Parcell Lakes

Section Five Lake

800

Little Pike Lake

CR 500

CR 414

P

LUCE COUNTY

Pike Lake

Little Two Hearted R.

Betsy Lake

Clark Lake

700

SWAMP LAKES RD

TAHQUAMENON FALLS STATE PARK

CR 500

800

WILDERNESS LOOP TRAIL

800

123

Little Two Hearted Lakes

GIANT PINES LOOP

P

Upper Tahquamenon Falls

700

123

800

800

900

Tahquamenon River

© The Countryman Press

ELEVATION PROFILE

900 ft			
800 ft	Mouth of the Two		
700 ft	Hearted River		Upper Tahquamenon
600 ft			Falls
500 ft			
400 ft	5	10	15	20 miles

UPPER TAHQUAMENON FALLS

Michigan's second largest state park, at just over 46,000 acres. This park is home to another tract of virgin forest spared the axe during the lumber boom. The Tahquamenon rises from springs north of McMillan and drains an area of more than 820 square miles. From its source, it meanders 94 miles before emptying into Whitefish Bay. The amber color of the water is caused by tannin leached from the tamarack, cedar, spruce, moss, and hemlock in the swamps drained by the river. The extremely soft water churned by the action of the falls causes the extensive amounts of foam, a characteristic of the Tahquamenon since the days of the voyageurs.

Rather flat and sandy, you'll have an opportunity or two to see some wet footing. The habitat starts mostly as sandy sweet fern and blueberries at your feet, dominated by jack pine and red pine. After crossing the Little Two Hearted River, it will become more boggy and swampy, hiking along pine and red pine ridges. Keep your eyes open for some massive white pine as you approach Upper Tahquamenon Falls.

HOW TO FIND

The Mouth of Two Hearted River State Forest Campground is the west end of this segment, found by going north on MI 123 out of Newberry or west out of Paradise on the same highway. About 5.0 miles west of Tahquamenon Falls State Park, take CR 500 north about 6.0 miles, then head west (left) onto CR 414 for 5.0 miles before a hard right to the

THE TRAIL SKIRTS BY AND CUTS THROUGH SOME BOGGY AREAS
IN TAHQUAMENON COUNTRY

northeast onto CR 412. Take this dusty road to its end at the mouth of the Two Hearted River.

The eastern end is Upper Tahquamenon Falls at Tahquamenon Falls State Park. Located on MI 123, it is the only paved road between Paradise and Newberry.

FACILITIES AND SERVICES

Rainbow Lodge, lost in the Duck Lake Fire, is being rebuilt and should have lodging and a camp store in 2016.

THE HIKE

From the bridge crossing the Two Hearted River, turn left and hike along the shore of Lake Superior. Parallel the lake for about 1.2 miles until the trail turns inland to your right. The campground is rustic, with 40 campsites, and was partially burnt in the 2012 Duck Lake Fire.

The trail comes back out to the lake shortly after it turns inland for the campground; at 2.2 miles, the trail turns inland again, crosses CR 412 and parallels it for about 0.2 mile, heads south, and then turns right on CR 500 to gain access to the state forest campground at Culhane Lake. Turn left into Culhane Lake State Forest Campground (4.5 miles), which is on Culhane Lake, a small lake fed by a stream of the same name. It is a rustic campground with 22 campsites. The trail uses the campground road and exits to the south.

The North Country Trail skirts the west side of the Parcell Lakes (7.7 miles) before taking a southwest path toward CR 500; the trail comes close enough for you to collect water. Cross CR 500 at 8.7

miles, then CR 414 at 9.2 miles, where there is a parking area. You can turn right on CR 414 and hike to the west about 2.5 miles to the Pike Lake State Forest Campground–Luce. Otherwise, keep heading south to cross Swamp Lakes Road at 10.8 miles into the hike. From here, it is rather flat walking through second-growth pine forest to CR 500.

Turn right and use CR 500's bridge to cross the Little Two Hearted River (14.0 miles). The river appears sluggish and rather open, making you wonder if you could catch a coldwater fish like a trout.

In 0.5 mile, turn left (east) onto a dirt road and follow blue blazes while looking for an old road that heads east toward the state park. The old road has been improved to allow for forestry equipment and is easy to follow and blazed. The trail chapter will be rerouting the trail off this old road in 2015 partly because of beaver issues in the state park.

You'll enter Tahquamenon Falls State Park at the 15.0-mile mark. A sign on your left will indicate the trail entering Tahquamenon Falls State Park, a level walk through a pristine northern forest. Only second in size to the Porcupine Mountains Wilderness State Park, it is

Thomas Funke

THE UPPER TAHQUAMENON FALLS IS THE SECOND TALLEST WATERFALL EAST OF THE MISSISSIPPI RIVER

35,000 acres in the heart of the Great Manistique Swamp. The Tahquamenon River empties this mosquito-infested swamp of its tannic-stained waters as it flows to Lake Superior.

At the 18.0-mile mark is a trail intersection. Take a right turn to continue on the North Country Trail. Taking the park trail to the left is a longer alternative that will lead you to the Lower Tahquamenon Falls Campground—but you'll miss a great walk along the shores of "Dark Waters," as the Hiawatha called it.

A few hundred feet past the trail intersection is a backcountry campsite, which requires advance reservations from the state park. There is no nearby water source, so plan accordingly.

Another trail intersection (19.3 miles) occurs soon after; take a right turn at this intersection as well. By going straight, you'll end up at a trailhead on MI 123 or continue to the lower falls. This is part of the Giant Pines Loop and you'll walk by some massive white pine reaching 4 feet in diameter.

Cross MI 123 at the 21.0-mile mark. The trail leaves the woods, passes by a large gate, and becomes quite wide before intersecting with the paved path in the park.

Enjoy a 96-step descent to view the second-largest waterfall east of the

Thomas Funke

COTTON PLANT IS REALLY A SEDGE

Mississippi, Upper Tahquamenon Falls (21.3 miles). The trail is paved as it parallels the river for about 0.3 mile. Turning left at the intersection will bring you to a brewery and concessions. You may inquire with park staff about leaving your vehicle in the lot overnight.

46

Hiawatha National Forest–Lake Superior Shore

START: Tahquamenon Falls State Park, Rivermouth Campground Entrance

END: Spur Trail, Soldier Lake National Forest Campground

APPROXIMATE HIKING TIME: 10–15 hours

LENGTH OF SECTION: 22.5 miles

After a 4.0-mile walk along MI 123, you'll be more than ready to head into the woods on a trail. The trailhead is marked with signage on the east side of the road. The trail shares an old road with a snowmobile trail toward Whitefish Bay. You'll reach a gate that is the boundary with the eastern unit of the Hiawatha National Forest, and you'll be on a foot trail only.

The trail will come out to the Whitefish Bay Scenic Byway. Amazingly, this is a little-traveled road even though it provides several access points to Lake Superior. The trail will be within a stone's throw for most of your hike but you'll use the scenic drive to negotiate around low spots and some of the river crossings. You might need to get around low spots, because on a windy day, the waters of Lake Superior may experience a seiche, where water piles up on the south shore of Whitefish Bay and spills into the woods.

After making your southerly turn into the national forest, the terrain passes through rolling topography created by glacial action. The habitats will run the gamut from open fields left from past logging to pine plantations, wetlands, and jack pine and red pine forests.

Timber cutting was more of a concern in the past; however, it may still behoove you to contact the Hiawatha National Forest and the local chapter about upcoming or current logging operations near the trail.

Just before the trail crosses MI 28 you'll pass Stump Lake, which may be the only water source you've seen for a while if you are headed north. Cross MI 28 and look for a side trail to Soldier Lake National Forest Campground.

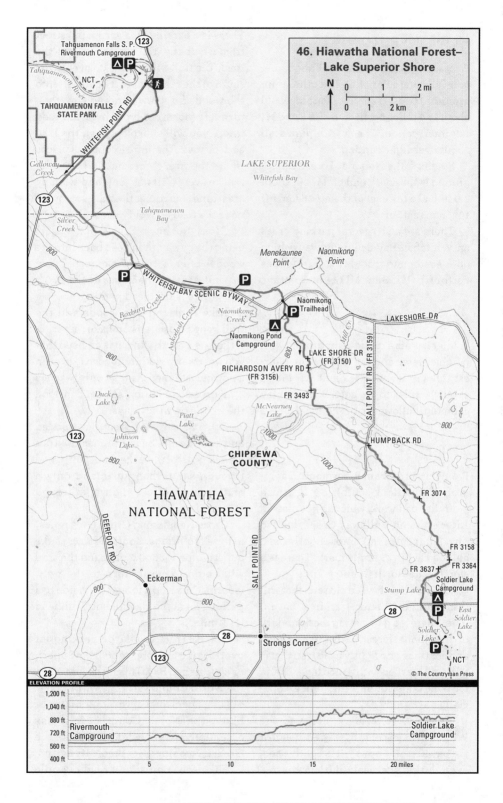

46. Hiawatha National Forest–
Lake Superior Shore

N   0   1   2 mi

0   1   2 km

Tahquamenon Falls S. P.   123
Rivermouth Campground
△ P

Tahquamenon River   NCT

TAHQUAMENON FALLS
STATE PARK

WHITEFISH POINT RD

Galloway
Creek

123

Silver
Creek

800

LAKE SUPERIOR

Whitefish Bay

Tahquamenon
Bay

Menekaunee   Naomikong
Point   Point

P

WHITEFISH BAY SCENIC BYWAY   P

Roxbury Creek   Ankadosh Creek   Naomikong
Creek

Naomikong
Trailhead
P

LAKESHORE DR

Mill Ct.

△

Naomikong Pond
Campground   LAKE SHORE DR
                   (FR 3150)

RICHARDSON AVERY RD
(FR 3156)

FR 3493

SALT POINT RD (FR 3159)

800

Duck
Lake

Piatt
Lake

McNearney
Lake

1000

HUMPBACK RD

800

Johnson
Lake   123

800

CHIPPEWA
COUNTY

1000

FR 3074

HIAWATHA
NATIONAL FOREST

FR 3158

FR 3364

FR 3637

DEERFOOT RD

SALT POINT RD

Soldier Lake
Campground

Eckerman

800

Stump Lake

△
P

East
Soldier
Lake

28

Soldier
Lake

28

P

123   Strongs Corner

NCT

© The Countryman Press

28

ELEVATION PROFILE

1,200 ft

1,040 ft

880 ft
                 Rivermouth   Soldier Lake
720 ft   Campground   Campground

560 ft

400 ft

5   10   15   20 miles

HOW TO FIND

Access the north end at the Tahquamenon Falls State Park Rivermouth Campground, 7.0 miles south of Paradise and about 11.0 miles north of the US 8 and MI 123 intersection. Check with park staff about overnight parking.

Soldier Lake National Forest Campground is the south end off MI 28, about 8.0 miles to the east of the MI 28 and MI 123 intersection.

There are also several parking areas on Whitefish Bay Scenic Byway, which goes eastbound from MI 123 11.0 miles north of the MI 28 and MI 123 intersection.

FACILITIES AND SERVICES

Soldier Lake is a rustic campground with potable water and pit toilets. The nearest full-service town is Sault Ste. Marie about 55 miles to the east. Backcountry camping is allowed in the national forest.

THE HIKE

From the entrance of Rivermouth Campground, turn right (south) on MI 123 for a 5.0-mile road walk, which is not blazed. After crossing Galloway Creek, look to turn left (southeast) onto a lightly used old road at the 4.0-mile mark. There is a sign for the North Country Trail.

Hike the lightly used old road that will thin out into a hiking trail in about 1.0 mile. There is a gate noting the boundary of the national forest. Cross Silver Creek and continue on a lightly used trail that is still well marked with a nice lane. Listen for Lake Superior in the distance, especially on a windy day.

At the 7.1-mile mark, come to the Whitefish Bay Scenic Byway. Although it is a paved scenic byway, it is lightly used, even during the peak tourism season.

There is a parking area across the street from where the trail comes out onto the road. The trail will quickly go over to the south of the road, where it bears left into the woods for a few hundred feet, then turn left (north) to cross over the road where you will snake between the lake and the road. There are a couple of places where the trail comes out and uses the road to avoid trail washouts and swampy areas, and sometimes the trail is rerouted up to the road to avoid wet areas.

Cross Roxbury Creek (8.2 miles) using the byway, then head back into the woods—only to cross Ankodosh Creek (8.9 miles) using the byway again. In 0.3 mile, there is trailhead parking.

Hike back into the woods and the trail keeps close tabs on Lake Superior. If there is a north wind, it is advised that you wear warm clothing, because even in a normal summer the lake only reaches 45 degrees. In addition, seiches can flood the woods on windy days.

Otherwise this is a great, flat, wooded and beach walk. Several times the trail comes out to the lake and you tread through sand, then jut inland only a matter of a few feet and walk through stately pines.

Cross Naomikong Creek (10.3 miles) using a footbridge. Continue along Lake Superior for about 0.2 mile and the trail will begin to slowly turn to the right (south). Climb up a forested hillside to a parking lot at the Naomikong Trailhead (11.3 miles).

You'll arrive at a large parking lot overlooking the forest and Lake Superior's Whitefish Bay. This is the last place the North Country Trail is within view of Lake Superior. For the long-distance hiker, the North Country Trail has essentially paralleled the largest of the Great Lakes since Hovland, Minnesota.

Hike south on an old road 0.3 mile

THE TRAIL UTILIZES SOME OLD TWO TRACKS BETWEEN M-123 AND CURLEY LEWIS ROAD

to the abandoned Naomikong Pond National Forest Campground. This is an abandoned campground that is useable by backpackers, as a trail shelter was built in 2013 by local scouts.

Continue to hike south through rolling terrain and second-growth forest, cross Lake Shore Drive (13.4 miles), and then arrive at Richardson Avery Road (13.6 miles). After passing this gravel road, you'll jog left over Forest Road 3493 (FR 3493) and head southeast over terrain that continues to have many small ups and downs. Cross the paved Salt Point Road/FR 3159 (16.4 miles) and Humpback Roads. You'll continue southeast over similar terrain, enjoying mature hardwoods while following the well-placed tread and hiking lane.

Cross FR 3074 (18.5 miles); 1.6 miles later you'll jog through the intersection of FR 3364 and FR 3158. The trail crosses FR 3364 and then uses FR 3158 for about 0.2 mile before heading southwest, crossing FR 3637, and bending to the west of Stump Lake. You'll walk through old clear-cuts and keep your eyes open for the scant blazes! If in doubt, take a bearing due south to MI 28 (22.3 miles).

Cross the relatively busy state highway and then cross an abandoned railroad bed. There is no parking at MI 28, but there is at Soldier Lake. Cross over and back into a mostly open forest landscape.

On your left, the Soldier Lake National Forest Campground Spur Trail (22.5 miles) is an abandoned old road that leads to the campground (rustic, with 44 sites). If you wish, you can take MI 28 and walk east 0.75 mile to a road leading to the campground.

Hiawatha National Forest– Headwaters and Lakes

START: Soldier Lake National Forest Campground

END: Trout Brook Pond/H40

APPROXIMATE HIKING TIME: 7–15 hours

LENGTH OF SECTION: 19.8 miles

This part of the Hiawatha National Forest will show you a wide variety of artificially managed landscapes and some natural areas as well. As a national forest, it is managed for many uses, and should not be thought of as strictly a wilderness to be preserved.

Between Soldier Lake and Dick Road, the word of the day is patchwork—as in a patchwork of forest blocks, open fields, forestry operations, and forest types. Take the opportunity to learn ahead of time the different forestry practices utilized in managing this area, and what these practices are trying to accomplish.

Cross over to the west side of Dick Road and follow the edge of a massive marsh, known as the Betchler Marsh. If you are a birdwatcher, this section of trail—especially around Betchler Lakes—holds a wide diversity of species. After leaving the marsh, your patchwork of land use types continues until you cross West Lone Pine Road and begin to follow the banks of the forested Pine River.

After a healthy trek along the Pine River, you'll cross over it to the south to another patchwork of forest types, though you'll mostly hike though plantations on sandy fire lanes. When you reach Biscuit Creek, you'll head east along its banks after crossing it to the south. You will skirt along pine plantations while hiking east; the trail will turn south but you'll continue to hike along the edge of more plantations to Trout Brook Pond.

HOW TO FIND

Soldier Lake National Forest Campground is the north end off MI 28, about 8.0 miles to the east of the MI 28 and MI 123 intersection.

Trout Brook Pond is the southern trailhead of this segment, 10.6 miles west

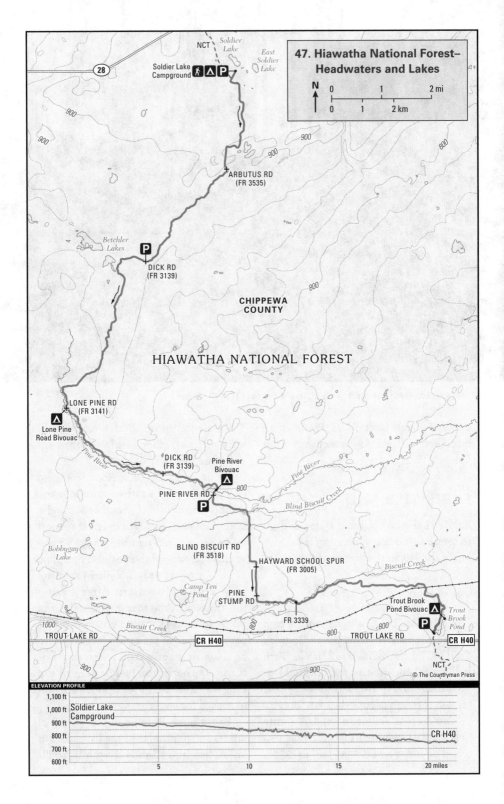

47. Hiawatha National Forest–Headwaters and Lakes

N

0   1   2 mi
0   1   2 km

NCT

Soldier Lake

East Soldier Lake

Soldier Lake Campground

ARBUTUS RD
(FR 3535)

Betchler Lakes

DICK RD
(FR 3139)

CHIPPEWA COUNTY

800

HIAWATHA NATIONAL FOREST

900

LONE PINE RD
(FR 3141)

Lone Pine Road Bivouac

Pine River

DICK RD
(FR 3139)

Pine River Bivouac

Pine River

PINE RIVER RD

Blind Biscuit Creek

Bobbygay Lake

BLIND BISCUIT RD
(FR 3518)

HAYWARD SCHOOL SPUR
(FR 3005)

Biscuit Creek

Camp Ten Pond

PINE STUMP RD

FR 3339

Trout Brook Pond Bivouac

Trout Brook Pond

1000

Biscuit Creek

800

800

800

TROUT LAKE RD

TROUT LAKE RD

TROUT LAKE RD

CR H40

CR H40

CR H40

NCT

900

900

© The Countryman Press

ELEVATION PROFILE

1,100 ft
1,000 ft   Soldier Lake Campground
900 ft
800 ft
700 ft
600 ft   5   10   15   20 miles

CR H40

OPEN PINE AND SPRUCE COUNTRY IN THE HIAWATHA NATIONAL FOREST

Marlene Mullet

on West Trout Lake Road/H40, which intersects with MI 123 just south of Trout Lake.

FACILITIES AND SERVICES

Soldier Lake has potable water and pit toilets. Backcountry camping is permitted in the Hiawatha National Forest.

THE HIKE

From Soldier Lake, it is a 0.7-mile trek to connect back with the North Country Trail via an abandoned rail grade. Turn left (south) and continue to hike old logging roads and railroad grades over flat terrain through second-growth forest.

You'll cross Arbutus Road/Arbutus Truck Trail (1.7 miles), a gravel road also listed on maps as FR 3535 and FR 3536.

The trail continues south along the old railroad grade, then southwest through jack pine forest.

After crossing Dick Road/FR 3139 (4.3 miles), head southwest over to the right (west) side of the road and into the Betchler Lakes area. For the next several miles, your footing can be boggy as it traverses the edge of the wetland complex. This is a great area for birdwatching, so bring the binoculars. After leaving the vicinity of the marsh, the soil turns sandy and gives way to a patchwork of varying ages of jack pine forest due to past logging activities. When the trail turns southerly, the headwaters of the Pine River are to the west, close enough to access for water.

Cross Lone Pine Road/FR 3141 (8.2 miles) and parallel the Pine River for 4.0 miles, heading slightly downhill. You'll start out by using an old road, then a trail, and there are bivouac opportunities along the river.

Cross Dick Road/FR 3139 (10.8 miles) and continue to follow the Pine River, then turn right to cross the river (12.0 miles) before you reach Pine River Road, walking through mixed forest. There is a bivouac campsite at the crossing. Continue hiking through jack pine forest until you arrive at the Biscuit Creek watershed.

After crossing Pine River Road (12.2 miles) turn left (east) and then right (south) on FR 3518; this road will bend east less than 1.0 mile from the next road while staying unmaintained. Cross Blind Biscuit Creek (13.1 miles) on a footbridge and then head due south using a firebreak.

In 0.9 mile you'll cross Hayward School Spur/FR 3005 and then a fire-break in mixed pine forest. At 14.9 miles you'll cross Pine Stump Road, a lightly used dirt and gravel road. Walk along the top of the Biscuit Creek valley with the river to your south.

FR 3339 (15.7 miles), a gravel road, shares its bridge with the North Country Trail to cross Biscuit Creek, which you will parallel for a short stretch before veering away, turning south just before Trout Brook Pond and crossing a railroad grade (17.2 miles) as the trail hugs the edge of managed pine plantations. Pass a couple of firebreaks on your south and west. To the east are lowlands and wetlands, and then you'll come to a spur trail to Trout Brook Pond (18.1 miles), which has bivouac camping opportunities. The trail continues to wind through maturing pine forests mostly in a southerly direction to H40 (19.8 miles).

CONIFERS DOMINATE NEAR LONE PINE ROAD IN THE HIAWATHA

48

Hiawatha National Forest– Mackinac Wilderness

START: H40/Trout Brook Pond

END: Brevoort Lake National Forest Campground Road

APPROXIMATE HIKING TIME: 12–16 hours

LENGTH OF SECTION: 22.3 miles

You'll begin to see some topography again, along with some stream crossings. This area has considerably fewer managed woodlands, especially the nearby Mackinac Wilderness. Although the trail does not go through the wilderness area, it skirts just to the north of its boundary, which is delineated by a utility right-of-way.

The 11,000-acre Mackinac Wilderness was designated in 1987. As with most of Michigan's forest, the area now comprising the wilderness was logged off by 1920. Since then, regeneration has allowed second-growth forest to reclaim the land, and some trees have been standing for nearly one hundred years.

Most visitors come for Mackinac's most notable feature, the Carp River. Flowing through the heart of the wilderness, the sandy-bottomed Carp features water-carved riverbanks and numerous oxbows. Brook, rainbow, and brown trout spawn in the Carp and its tributaries, luring anglers.

After leaving the area around the Mackinac Wilderness, you'll head through some cedar swamp on an impressive boardwalk before crossing the Carp River on an even more impressive bridge. Continue to hike through more forest that starts to give way to less managed and more natural terrain, especially since you'll notice more aspen and younger forest as you trek southwest. You'll end at Brevoort Lake National Forest Campground, which is a popular and heavily used campground.

HOW TO FIND

Trout Brook Pond is the northern trailhead of this segment, 10.6 miles west on H40/West Trout Lake Road, which intersects with MI 123 just south of Trout Lake.

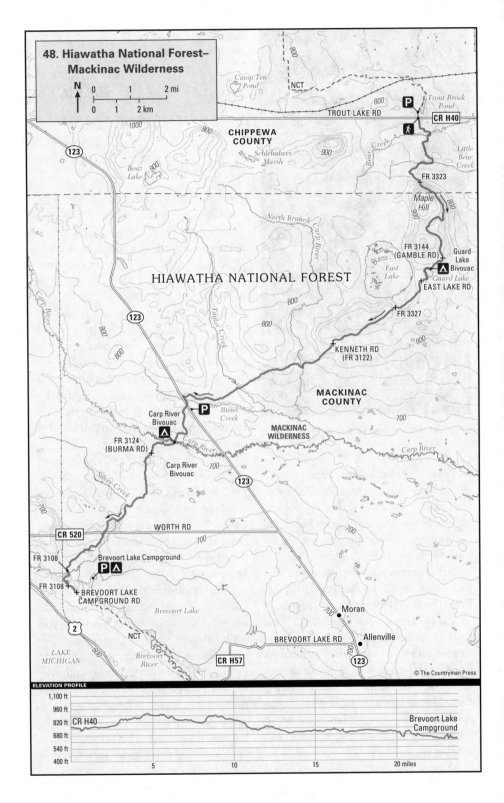

48. Hiawatha National Forest–Mackinac Wilderness

N

0   1   2 mi

0   1   2 km

Camp Ten Pond

NCT

Trout Brook Pond

P

TROUT LAKE RD

CR H40

CHIPPEWA COUNTY

Schlehubers Marsh

Little Bear Creek

Bear Creek

1000

900

900

900

123

Boaz Lake

FR 3323

Maple Hill

900

North Branch Carp River

HIAWATHA NATIONAL FOREST

FR 3144 (GAMBLE RD)

East Lake

Guard Lake Bivouac

Guard Lake

EAST LAKE RD

Carp River

123

Taylor Creek

800

800

800

FR 3327

800

KENNETH RD (FR 3122)

MACKINAC COUNTY

700

Carp River Bivouac

P

Bissel Creek

MACKINAC WILDERNESS

Carp River

FR 3124 (BURMA RD)

Carp River

Carp River Bivouac

700

123

Silver Creek

700

CR 520

WORTH RD

700

700

FR 3108

Brevoort Lake Campground

P

FR 3108

BREVOORT LAKE CAMPGROUND RD

Brevoort Lake

Moran

700

2

NCT

Brevoort River

BREVOORT LAKE RD

Allenville

LAKE MICHIGAN

600

CR H57

123

© The Countryman Press

ELEVATION PROFILE

1,100 ft

960 ft

820 ft CR H40

680 ft

540 ft

400 ft

Brevoort Lake Campground

5   10   15   20 miles

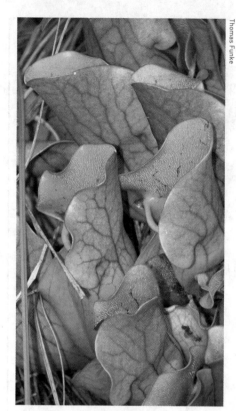

PITCHER PLANTS ARE COMMON IN BOGS

Brevoort Lake National Forest Campground is the southern trailhead, located west of St. Ignace by taking US 2 for 17.0 miles west to Brevoort Camp Road and turning north; the campground is 1.0 mile north on the right.

Other access points include roadside parking at East Lake Road and FR 3122. From the intersection of East Lake Road and H40/Trout Lake Road, take East Lake Road south 5.0 miles. East Lake Road is 1.3 miles east of the Trout Brook Pond parking lot. You can also access East Lake Road from the south starting from Moran by taking Charles Moran Road east about 0.3 mile, then north onto East Lake Road 10.0 miles to the trailhead.

Where the North Country Trail crosses MI 123, there is a parking lot 7.2 miles northwest of Moran.

FACILITIES AND SERVICES

Backcountry camping is allowed in the national forest.

THE HIKE

From H40, hike south, cross Bear Creek, and turn right after crossing Little Bear Creek; both are reliable water sources. Blazes are all painted blue rectangles.

At 2.5 miles, the trail crosses over to the left and skirts FR 3323, an unimproved forest road. Hike along this corridor for about 1.0 mile and then bear right to the south. Maple Hill sprouts up in front of you, but you'll mostly walk around it and another smaller hill as you progress south. Look for rock outcroppings of Niagaran origin—the same formations that make up the Pictured Rocks, Tahquamenon Falls, and of course Niagara Falls.

You'll cross FR 3144/Gamble Road (4.7 miles), a gravel road. Just past the road is Guard Lake. The trail squeezes between two forest roads and Guard Lake. Trail markers are mostly blue painted rectangles and some Carsonite posts. Guard Lake has bivouac camping opportunities.

At 5.6 miles, cross East Lake Road/ FR 3119. Your footing can be a little squishy here during wet years as you walk through maturing hardwood forests. Cross the unimproved FR 3327 (6.7 miles), and then climb up and over a small hill as you make your way to Kenneth Road/FR 3122 (8.9 miles).

The trail generally parallels closely, but does not enter, the Mackinac Wilderness. Cross several small streams, and you'll be generally heading downhill. Be wary that there are several abandoned roads that are not marked in this area (you cross one at the 9.3-mile mark) just before crossing the north fork of the Carp River (9.5 miles). This is a swampy area full of cedars and, in early spring, mosquitoes.

Cross Taylor Creek (11.6 miles), a reliable water source also in a swampy setting. Hike out towards MI 123 (14.1 miles), where the trail takes a hard left to use an abandoned rail grade to cross Bissel Creek. The trail will turn right (west) to cross MI 123. Continue south 0.2 mile to a parking lot. Enter a cedar swamp and you'll utilize several corduroy boardwalks that elevate you above the mire. Be prepared to duck, as the cedars do encroach, making for a small lane in places.

Carp River's (15.5 miles) name is a misnomer. This is actually a trout stream with decent fishing! A massive, well-constructed bridge will take you across. There is a bivouac campsite.

Continue through the cedar swamp and head upwards in elevation back to dry pine forest. The trail will cut through an open area and bend southwest, back into the forest, crossing FR 3124/Burma Road (16.4 miles).

After crossing a gas pipeline right-of-way, the trail utilizes an abandoned Forest Road through pine plantations planted by the Civilian Conservation Corps during the Great Depression. The trail heads southerly until it dips into an unnamed stream valley, then comes back to the uplands and bends south-west. Dip into the Silver Creek valley and the trail turns into boardwalk to cross Silver Creek (18.7 miles). The boardwalk continues through the swamp, and the trail then leads up and out of the valley, bends south, and hugs a pine forest on your west.

After crossing Worth Road/CR 520 (19.4 miles), you'll need to circumnavigate a ravine, cross a little-used dirt road, hike through a pine plantation, and then cross FR 3108 (21.6 miles).

The trail will utilize the paved road to cross the Little Brevoort River; it then heads back into the woods on the west side of the road, crosses FR 3108 in 0.2 mile, and comes to Brevoort Lake National Forest Campground Road (22.3 miles).

Hiawatha National Forest– Brevoort Lake and St. Ignace

START: Brevoort Lake National Forest Campground

END: Mackinac Bridge

APPROXIMATE HIKING TIME: 10–15 hours

LENGTH OF SECTION: 22.7 miles

Your nearly 500-mile trek across the Upper Peninsula is coming to an end as you leave the Hiawatha and enter St. Ignace. You'll notice that glaciers and the actions of both Lake Michigan and Lake Huron have heavily influenced the landscape. Old beaches, former sand dunes, marshes, sloughs, creeks, and several lakes have all been created and are still under the influence of the Great Lakes climate and fluctuating water levels.

Brevoort Lake is over 4,000 acres in size and at its deepest is only 25 feet. Making a dam on the Brevoort River created it. Hike the lakeshore and you'll have access to the two campgrounds on the west end of the lake, and then a rustic campground midway down. The trail will cross FR 3303, and you'll hike along several old dunes that were created thousands of years ago when lake levels were much higher. In between these dunes are swales, or lengthwise wetlands that protect many wetland plants from the pounding waves of Lake Michigan.

Cross Brevoort Lake Road and continue through the wooded dune and swales. As you approach Castle Rock Road, there is a former bluff (now forested) that you'll climb to the road, before going back downhill to negotiate around a swamp, then back to Castle Rock Road.

From this point, you'll take a multiuse trail south to St. Ignace, cross under I-75, travel into town on an abandoned rail grade, and then take surface streets until you reach Straits State Park and the Mackinac Bridge.

St. Ignace is the second-oldest European-founded settlement in Michigan. It is second only to Sault Ste. Marie, having been established by Father Jacques Marquette in 1671 (Sault Ste. Marie was also founded by Marquette in 1668). LaSalle's ship *The Griffon* landed

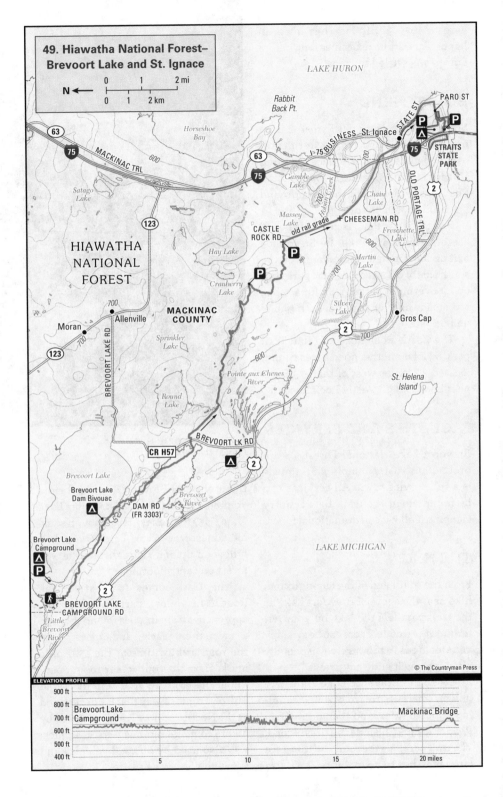

49. Hiawatha National Forest– Brevoort Lake and St. Ignace

N ←

0   1   2 mi
0   1   2 km

LAKE HURON

Rabbit Back Pt.

PARO ST

63

75   MACKINAC TRL

Horseshoe Bay

63

I-75 BUSINESS   St. Ignace

STATE ST

75

STRAITS STATE PARK

600

75

Gamble Lake

Satago Lake

HIAWATHA NATIONAL FOREST

123

700

Chain Lake

OLD PORTAGE TRL

2

Massey Lake   old rail grade

CHEESEMAN RD

CASTLE ROCK RD

Freschette Lake

Hay Lake

Martin Lake

600

Cranberry Lake

Silver Lake

700

MACKINAC COUNTY

Moran   Allenville

700

BREVOORT LAKE RD

Sprinkler Lake

2

700

Gros Cap

123

700

600

Round Lake

Pointe aux Chenes River

St. Helena Island

BREVOORT LK RD

CR H57

2

Brevoort Lake

Brevoort Lake Dam Bivouac

DAM RD (FR 3303)

Brevoort River

LAKE MICHIGAN

© The Countryman Press

Brevoort Lake Campground

2

BREVOORT LAKE CAMPGROUND RD

Little Brevoort River

ELEVATION PROFILE

900 ft
800 ft   Brevoort Lake
700 ft   Campground   Mackinac Bridge
600 ft
500 ft
400 ft

5   10   15   20 miles

here in 1679. St. Ignace has been an important trading post since long before Europeans settled the area.

HOW TO FIND

Brevoort Lake National Forest Campground is the northern/western trailhead, located west of St. Ignace by taking US 2 for 17.0 miles west to Brevoort Camp Road and turning north; the campground is 1.0 mile north on the right.

Straits State Park is the southern/eastern trailhead. Take the St. Ignace exit off I-75 and it is immediately on the south side of US 2. Inquire with park staff about overnight parking. St. Ignace has street-side and lot parking, both public and private.

The Castle Rock Road and Rail Trail parking lot is another good access point, located 2.4 miles west of the I-75 Business Loop exit on Castle Rock Road.

FACILITIES AND SERVICES

Brevoort Lake National Forest Campground has rustic camping. St. Ignace is a full-service town. All services can be found along the trail. Backcountry camping is allowed in the national forest.

THE HIKE

From the south end of the campground, hike near the shore of Brevoort Lake as the trail parallels the lake on your left through the woods. There can be swampy and wet areas in this stretch, especially after snowmelt and heavy rain.

Cross the Brevoort Lake Dam (2.9 miles), where there are bivouac camping opportunities, and then cross Dam Road/FR 3303 (3.8 miles), a gravel road. The trail parallels the road and there are large marshes to your south. You'll use

Dove Day

VIEW OF THE MACKINAC BRIDGE
FROM STRAITS STATE PARK

this to cross the Brevoort River just before your next road, the paved Brevoort Lake Road/H57 (6.6 miles). Hike though some old dunes, cross a small creek, and then follow an upland ridge through mixed forest on sandy footing.

The trail comes to Castle Rock Road (11.6 miles), parallels the road, approaches it again, goes inland through a few marshy places, and comes out to the road a third time at the 15.0-mile mark. Here the trail comes to an opening at the road. To your right is an old railroad right-of-way that is not certified as the North Country Trail but is used by hikers to make their way to St. Ignace; it is also used by off-road vehicles and snowmobiles, so be aware.

Cross Cheeseman Road (16.6 miles) and the railroad bed will parallel Cheeseman Road. Swamps, marshes, and Chain Lake are on your south. At 18.6 miles, pass under I-75 and enter St. Ignace on an abandoned rail grade and then sidewalks. The trail is on the west side of the Little Bear East Arena and extends out to the boardwalk across from the Museum of Ojibwa Culture. The trail goes through downtown on the boardwalk. It is the only place it is on Lake Huron!

Follow State Street through the park and marina district to Paro Street (21.2 miles), turning right (west) onto Paro Street, then left (south) into Straits State Park (21.7 miles). The trail winds through this very popular and highly used state park. Inquire with park staff if you plan on long-term parking. There is an overlook (22.0 miles) to the south before the trail descends downhill to the rest area (22.7 miles), where a trail kiosk welcomes you to the end of the Upper Peninsula.

50

Mackinac Bridge

START: Straits State Park

END: Mackinaw City

APPROXIMATE HIKING TIME: 1–2 hours

LENGTH OF SECTION: 4.6 miles

The long-distance hiker has three options to cross the bridge: they can participate in the annual Labor Day Bridge Walk, take a shuttle provided by the Mackinac Bridge Authority, or they can hopscotch across the Straits of Mackinac using one of the three ferries offering service between the peninsulas and Mackinac Island (for more information, see the Mackinac Bridge Authority website: www.mackinacbridge.org).

LABOR DAY

Every Labor Day, Michigan's governor leads tens of thousands of its citizens in walking south from St. Ignace to Mackinaw City. The walk starts at 7 AM with the governor in the lead. The strategy is to arrive in either Mackinaw City or St. Ignace before sunrise, score a parking spot, and either hike first (southward from St. Ignace) or take the shuttle bus (five dollars per person) to St. Ignace and hike back to your car.

Parking opportunities are better in Mackinaw City. Business owners are very forgiving of parking in their lots; remember to patronize them for using one of their spaces. In St. Ignace a special parking lot and shuttle have been established at the Little Bear East Arena on the north side of town on the I-75 Business Loop.

Hikers utilize the northbound two lanes, walking southbound, until 9:30 AM when only one lane is dedicated to them. Hikers are allowed to bring strollers and wheelchairs, but pretty much every other wheeled vehicle is prohibited—including wagons, skateboards, and in-line skates. Advertisements of all kinds are prohibited, including banners and signs. Animals are not allowed on the bridge (except for service animals). There are no bathrooms, either.

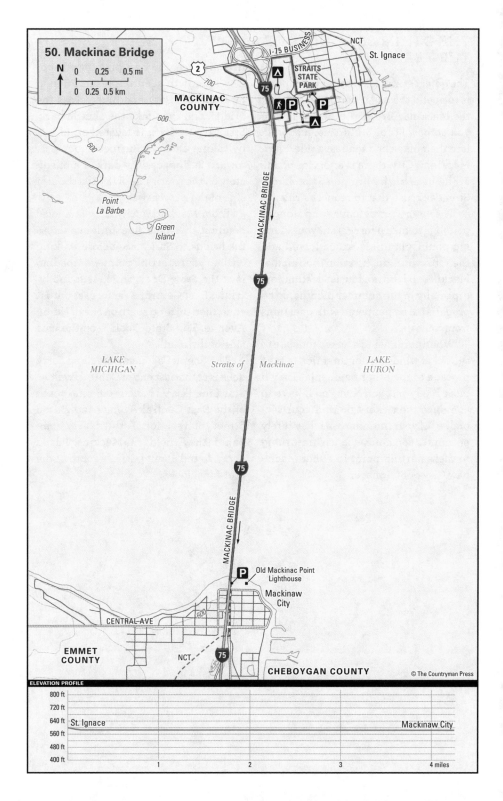

THE OTHER 364.5 DAYS OF THE YEAR

The quickest and least expensive option is to spend the $3.50 per person and let the Mackinac Bridge Authority shuttle you across. From St. Ignace, just walk into their office and request a ride. From Mackinaw City, there is a service phone at the base of the bridge at the Jamet Street exit; use that to request a ride.

The more expensive and longer option is to take a ferry from your starting peninsula to Mackinac Island and then to your destination peninsula. Mackinac Island is a tourist destination, especially in the summer months, so be prepared to be peppered with questions from tourists.

When purchasing a ticket, indicate to the ticket window your intention to take passage to the other peninsula. They'll most likely tell you that you'll have to convince the ticket taker on your second leg of your intentions, as they rarely encounter someone who isn't returning to their starting point in either Mackinaw City or St. Ignace.

HOW TO FIND

In St. Ignace, the best plan for a Labor Day hike is to secure a reservation at Straits State Park and hike across the bridge, and then take the shuttle back. Straits State Park is located off of I-75 by taking the I-75 Business Loop exit toward St. Ignace. The park is immediately on the south side of US 2 on the east side of the expressway.

From Mackinaw City, stay at a local hotel and then take the shuttle bus across the bridge to St. Ignace before walking back to your starting point. Bus loading is at the State Dock, which is found by taking East Central Avenue east until it ends, then turning south on North Huron Avenue. The State Dock is on the east side of the road.

The Shepler's Mackinac Island Ferry dock is at the east end of Central Avenue. Star Line Ferry is about 0.6 mile south of the East Central Avenue and Huron Street intersection. A third ferry company is the Arnold Line Mackinac Island Ferry, found about 0.2 mile south of the Star Line docks.

Index

Vans Lane, 73
Vasa Trail Network, 69
Victoria Dam, 195, 197, 198
Victoria Dam Road, 197–98
Victoria Mine, 195
Victory Park, 132, 134, 135
Vince Smith Bridge, 89, 91
Vogues Road, 171, 172, 174, 175

W

Wagner Falls, 231, 235
Waller Road, 39, 41
Walton Outlet, 78
Warner Creek Pathway, 52, 55, 56, 58
Warren Townsend Park, 112, 114
water, 18–19
weather, 13–14, 20
Weber Lake Road, 172, 175
Weidman Lake, 185
Welsh Road, 51, 52, 54
West Kalkaska Road, 66
West Mail Road Trailhead, 144, 148
West Trap Hills, 190–94; *191*
Wetmore Landing, 223
Wetmore Pond, 224
Wexford County East, 76–79; *77*
Whispering Pines Drive, 60
Whispering Waters Campground, 125
White Pine Trail, 108–11, 112; *109*
White River, 100, 103

Whitefish Bay Scenic Byway, 248, 250
Whitefish River, 226–30; *227*
Whitman Creek, 130
Wiggle Creek, 202
Wild Rivers State Trail, 148
Wildcat Canyon Creek, 219
Wilderness State Park, 34–38; *35*
wildlife, 15–16; safety, 21
Williamsburg Road, 64, 69
Wingleton Road, 92, 94–95
Winneboujou Bluff, 155
Wisconsin, 142–76. *See also specific hikes*
W. K. Kellogg Biological Station, 127, 129
Wolverine World Wide (Rockford), 114
wolves, 15, 19, 23
Woodland Park Campground, 236, 238
Wren Falls, 172, 175
Wycamp Lake, 38, 44

Y

Yankee Springs Recreation Area, 15, 121, 123, 125
Yankee Springs Road, 125

Z

Zmikly Road South, 44, 46